The Sarashina Diary

TRANSLATIONS FROM THE ASIAN CLASSICS

The Sarashina Diary

A WOMAN'S LIFE IN ELEVENTH-CENTURY JAPAN

SUGAWARA NO TAKASUE NO MUSUME

TRANSLATED, WITH AN INTRODUCTION, BY
SONJA ARNTZEN AND ITŌ MORIYUKI

Columbia University Press
New York

Columbia University Press
Publishers Since 1893
New York   Chichester, West Sussex
cup.columbia.edu

Library of Congress Cataloging-in-Publication Data
Sugawara no Takasue no Musume, 1008– author.
[Sarashina nikki. English]
The Sarashina Diary : a Woman's Life in Eleventh-Century Japan /
Sugawara no Takasue no Musume; translated, with an introduction,
by Sonja Arntzen and Itō Moriyuki.
pages cm. — (Translations from the Asian Classics)
Includes bibliographical references and index.
ISBN 978-0-231-16718-5 (cloth : acid-free paper)
ISBN 978-0-231-53745-2 (e-book)
1. Sugawara no Takasue no Musume, 1008—Diaries.
2. Authors, Japanese—Heian period, 794–1185—Diaries.
I. Arntzen, Sonja, 1945– translator. II. Moriyuki, Itō, translator·
III. Title.
PL789.S8Z4713 2014
741.5'973—dc23

Columbia University Press books are printed on permanent
and durable acid-free paper.
This book is printed on paper with recycled content.
Printed in the United States of America
c 10 9 8 7 6 5 4 3 2 1

 NEW YORK

Columbia University Press wishes to express
its appreciation for assistance given by the Japan Foundation
toward the cost of publishing this book.

Columbia University Press wishes to express
its appreciation for assistance given by the Pushkin Fund
toward the cost of publishing this book.

COVER IMAGE: Detail from "Azumaya I," in *The Tale of Genji* Scroll.
(© Tokugawa Art Museum Archive/ DNP Art Communications)

COVER AND BOOK DESIGN: Lisa Hamm

CONTENTS

Afterword 211
ITŌ MORIYUKI

PREFACE

A Collaborative Project

SONJA ARNTZEN

he *Sarashina Diary* (*Sarashina nikki*, ca. 1060) records the life of a Japanese woman from the age of thirteen to sometime in her mid-fifties. Rather than a daily account of events in the writer's life (as the term "diary" might suggest), it focuses on moments of personal meaning, often centered on the composition of a thirty-one-syllable *waka* poem. The author, Sugawara no Takasue no Musume, was a direct descendant of Sugawara no Michizane (845–903), one of the most distinguished literary figures in Japanese history. The *Sarashina Diary* has a long history of appreciation in Japan, with the first annotated text appearing in the thirteenth century. In the modern period, it was accorded the status of a "classic"—that is, one of the works representing the golden era of Japanese classical literature, the mid-Heian period (early tenth to eleventh century). During this period, women writers had the domain of prose writing almost to themselves, and they produced numerous works of sophisticated "self-writing" as well as fiction. Indeed, the surviving works by women in the mid-Heian period comprise the earliest substantial body of women's writing in the world. The *Sarashina Diary* was written after the other major autobiographical works by women, and it displays a subtle awareness of its predecessors.

The impetus for this translation and study of the *Sarashina Diary* was provided by my coauthor, Itō Moriyuki, who has dedicated most of his academic career to studying the *Sarashina Diary*.[1] Itō is unusual among native Japanese scholars of classical Japanese literature for the attention he has given to English-language scholarship on classical texts in general and the *Sarashina Diary* in particular. Moreover, he has made an effort to write papers in English on these texts and to present them at conferences in North America. We met at just such conference in 1998. Then, about nine years ago, Itō proposed that he and I do a new translation of the *Sarashina Diary*. He was keen to see a new translation of the work in English and to share his perception of the text with an English-reading public.

Just a few years earlier, I had completed the translation and study of another mid-Heian woman's autobiographical text, the *Kagerō Diary*, and thus felt prepared for the task. The animated conversations that Itō and I had had at conferences in the past indicated that we had compatible views of Heian women's literature, enough alike for easy understanding and enough different to be stimulating. Another inspiration for my participation in the project was my fresh view of the text from Edith Sarra's study of Heian diaries, *Fictions of Femininity: Literary Inventions of Gender in Japanese Court Women's Memoirs*. In this work, Sarra devotes a lot of attention to the *Sarashina Diary*, and her translations of excerpts for analysis reveal an utterly different text from the one I knew only from previous translations. Her work made me want to study the original for myself, so Itō and I began.

This project has been a mutual collaboration from start to finish. We did most of the work during brief periods every year when we could get together, either in Japan or on Gabriola Island, Canada, where I now live. My responsibility was creating the English rendering of the original text, and Itō's was explaining the problems of the text and guiding our interpretation. In our original plan, Itō was going to write the introduction, which I would translate. But because our understanding of the work evolved in conversation with each other, in the end it seemed appropriate to compose the introduction together. Although the foundation of the introduction rests on Itō's lifetime of research on the text, the articulation of our interpretation of the text has been significantly inflected by me.

Our approach focuses on the diary as a literary creation rather than an unmediated record of the author's life, yet at the same time we are deeply interested in the author herself. Most of all, we see her as an artist who creates different personae in this work to capture the full complexity of her life. Our translation and the accompanying introduction also pay close attention to the thirty-one-syllable poems (*waka*), which add depth and color to the text. In particular, we are interested in the role of poetry in the orchestration of the text's structure.

Itō has used the metaphor of a crystal for his overarching view of the diary as a complex and multifaceted work of art.[2] Although the diary's text may appear transparent superficially, it is not a simple transparency. Like the facets of a crystal that reveal different colors, each facet of the text offers different perspectives of meaning, depending on the angle from which it is viewed. Our analyses of specific passages show how they enable diverse readings and how opposite meanings are woven into the text by means of its structure. After years of reading the text together, Itō and I came up with a second metaphor, that of musical counterpoint, to convey how the patterning of contrasting motifs and intertextual references in the text brings its meta-meanings into play. We hope that together the introduction and the translation help readers, figuratively, see the color and hear the music in Takasue no Musume's remarkable work.

NOTES

1. Over a span of twenty years, Itō Moriyuki has published more than fifteen articles on the *Sarashina Diary*. His *Sarashina nikki kenkyū* (Tokyo: Shintensha, 1995) provides a synthesis of his findings and ideas.
2. Ibid., 9.

ACKNOWLEDGMENTS

*W*e are indebted to the following people, who read parts or the whole of our manuscript at various stages in its development and provided insights from a broad range of perspectives: Pamela Asquith, Beverly Maize, Wendy Strachan, Kit Szanto, and Naomi Wakan. Professor Janice Brown (University of Colorado at Boulder) and Professor Lynne Miyake (Pomona College) read the penultimate version of our manuscript and offered different but equally detailed critiques of the argumentation in the introduction, which had a significant impact on its final revision. Special acknowledgment also is due to Professors Stefania Burke, Christina Laffin, and Joshua Mostow of the University of British Columbia, who gave trial runs of successive versions of the translation in three different courses over five years. They not only provided critiques of the translation themselves but also gathered feedback from their students. We want to thank the students in all those courses for their thoughtful and useful comments. The introduction would have been much impoverished without the students' input. We are grateful as well to the two anonymous readers for Columbia University Press, whose constructive suggestions helped improve the final manuscript. Nick Halpin of Eyes Wide Open Studio artfully transformed the photo illustrations for this work and created the base maps. Richard Lynn provided valuable assistance in finding and downloading the Edo-period illustrations of famous places mentioned in the diary.

Sonja Arntzen wishes to express her appreciation for funding from Gakushūin Women's College that supported a two-month period of research at the college in 2008, as well as for accommodation in the Gakushūin guest house that she has received on numerous occasions. Moreover, Gakushūin Women's College's sponsorship of a symposium in 2008 on the *Sarashina Diary* provided the opportunity for valuable discussion with Carolina Negri, professor at the University of Lecce and translator of the *Sarashina Diary* into Italian, as well as for fruitful interactions with the distinguished professoriate of Gakushūin Women's College and other scholars in the Tokyo area.

Itō Moriyuki wishes to acknowledge the receipt of a Grant in Aid of Scientific Research from the Japan Society for the Promotion of Science from 2003 to 2006, which made possible six extended work sessions with Sonja Arntzen. During this time, the basic translation of the text was completed. In 2006 and 2007, Gakushūin Women's College provided special research funds that enabled him to travel three times to Canada to work with Sonja Arntzen on the annotations for the translation. He is particularly grateful that the sponsorship by Gakushūin Women's College of the 2008 symposium on the *Sarashina Diary* allowed the invitation of Professors Carolina Negri and Sonja Arntzen to Japan. That symposium attracted a large number of Heian literature specialists, and the lively discussion after the lecture sessions had a stimulating influence on the Japanese scholarly world.

At Columbia University Press, Jennifer Crewe's early interest in and constant encouragement for this project has been much appreciated. Kathryn Schell provided excellent editorial guidance through the first stages of preparing the manuscript. Margaret B. Yamashita's careful copyediting tightened the writing. Senior manuscript editor Irene Pavitt was our coach down the home stretch, answering every question about indexing promptly and with good humor. Lisa Hamm created an elegant design for the book and ingeniously managed the troublesome task of matching notes with text in the facing-page format. Publishing an academic book in this day and age involves so many skilled workers, many of whom we have corresponded with only once, and some with whom we have had no direct contact. Nonetheless, we want to thank them all, and we are simply grateful that academic publishing still thrives.

Last but certainly not least, we both would like to acknowledge the patience and support bestowed by our spouses, Richard Lynn and Itō Takako, over the ten years of our obsession with this project.

A NOTE ON THE TRANSLATION
AND TECHNICAL MATTERS

SONJA ARNTZEN

*T*he base text for our translation is the Shinchō Nihon koten shūsei edition of the *Sarashina nikki*, edited and annotated by Akiyama Ken (Tokyo: Shinchōsha, 1980). We also consulted a photo-facsimile edition of the thirteenth-century manuscript copy handwritten by Fujiwara no Teika, *Gyobutsubon: Sarashina nikki* (Tokyo: Musashino shoin, 1984), and have occasionally opted for readings from the original manuscript. Such deviations are signaled in the notes.

Notes to the translation contain not only the usual scholarly references to sources but also background information that would have been the natural possession of an "intended reader" for this text in the Heian period. Sugawara no Takasue no Musume wrote in an age when educated people had a lot of time to read, albeit a relatively small body of hand-copied works. Accordingly, readers knew the works available to them very well, and Heian authors could count on their contemporaries being able to recognize subtle allusions and read between the lines. Western nonspecialist readers of this text, however, need that background knowledge in order to understand the allusions, connotations, and social or literary connections underpinning the text. The notes are copious enough that providing them as footnotes would have significantly disturbed the flow of the text on the page. Consigning them to endnotes would have required readers to constantly flip to the back of the book. Instead, the notes have been placed on the facing page, which we feel offers a smoother reading experience. We are grateful to Columbia University Press for being willing to take on the extra trouble and expense to create this more "user-friendly" format.

We regard the poetry in the diary as key to both its structure and its meaning. Since the literary rendering of the poetry was my responsibility, one of the reviewers of the draft of this book recommended that I include an explanation of my approach to translating *waka*, to which the following remarks respond.

I developed certain principles of translating *waka* while working on the *Kagerō Diary*, although at that point I made no attempt to articulate these rules, even to myself. I felt that I was working intuitively. Once I fully understood the meaning of the poem, I would repeat it over and over to myself in Japanese, savoring its sound and how its meaning unfurled in the space of thirty-one syllables. Then it was as though the two linguistic sites in my brain came together, and I could feel the translation taking place. When I look at my translations objectively, however, I can see that two simple principles guide my translation. The first is trying to keep the five lines of the translation more or less within the 5-7-5-7-7 syllable pattern of the *waka* form. At least, I start with that intention, but most of the time I just try to keep to the "short, long, short, long, long" look of the lines. Nonetheless, for me, not padding the content of the poem takes precedence over keeping the lines within a certain length.

My second principle is to maintain as much as possible the original order of images and important semantic constructions. Although the fundamental differences between English and Japanese syntax does not permit this on a line-by-line basis, this principle can usually be observed with larger units of meaning within the *waka*. The following poem from the diary is an example:

nahashiro no	Until the paddies,
midzu kage bakari	where I saw only young shoots
mieshi ta no	mirrored in the water,
karihatsuru made	have ended up all harvested,
nagai shi ni keri	such a long stay have I had.

A more natural word order in English for the semantic content of that poem would be

> I have stayed here
> so long that all the young shoots
> I saw mirrored
> in the water of the paddy fields
> have ended up harvested.

It felt important to me, however, to keep the poet's reference to and realization of her own temporal and spatial position to the last line, even if it required slightly twisting the English syntax. Careful readers of the translations in this work will no doubt find places where I have violated both these principles. My only defense of such inconsistency is that translation sometimes requires freedom even from one's own principles.

Finally, I am attached to the five-line format for *waka* in English. Even though *waka* are not formatted into five lines when written in Japanese and some English translators opt for two- and three-line formats, all the prosodic rules for *waka* are based on its five-line structure, and no matter how quickly *waka* are recited in Japanese, the rhythm registers those line divisions. The only way to convey some impression of that structure in English is with visual line breaks.

Although we have used the standard Hepburn transcription system for Japanese terms, proper nouns, and place-names throughout the introduction and narrative sections of the translation, the romanization of poetry follows the modified historical style that Joshua Mostow developed in *Pictures of the Heart: The Hyakunin isshu in Word and Image* (Honolulu: University of Hawai'i Press, 1996): the hiragana characters of the original classical Japanese have been transliterated directly, thus maintaining the old distinctions between *he*, *we*, and *e*; between *wo* and *o*; and between *wi* and *i*; and also rendering づ as *dzu* and ぢ as *dji*. This romanization style makes the puns in classical verse more visible. The romanization of Chinese follows the *pinyin* system.

The references for poems in imperial and other important anthologies provide the poem number as given in the *Shinpen kokka taikan* (Tokyo: Kadokawa shoten, 1983–1992, CD-ROM version). The dates for the imperial anthologies follow those in Earl R. Miner, Hiroko Odagiri, and Robert E. Morrell, *The Princeton Companion to Classical Japanese Literature* (Princeton, N.J.: Princeton University Press, 1985). The titles of poetry anthologies are given by their common names—that is, omitting the *waka* that is part of their official title (for example, *Kokinshū* instead of *Kokin wakashū*). Unless otherwise noted, the translations of poems from imperial and other anthologies are ours.

The names of Japanese scholars working and writing in Japan are given in Japanese word order (surname first) in both the body of the text and the notes. For example, even the coauthor of this volume is referred to as Itō Moriyuki. Names for premodern Japanese people follow the traditional custom of adding *no* (of) after the surname, as in Fujiwara no Teika (Teika of the Fujiwara clan) and Sugawara no Takasue no Musume (Daughter of Takasue of the Sugawara clan).

The ages given for the author of the *Sarashina Diary* and other figures mentioned in the diary follow the traditional Japanese count; that is, at birth a person is considered to be one year old.

The Sarashina Diary

Introduction and Study

SONJA ARNTZEN AND ITŌ MORIYUKI

1

TEXT AND AUTHOR

THE *SARASHINA DIARY* IN THE CONTEXT OF *NIKKI BUNGAKU* (DIARY LITERATURE)

The *Sarashina Diary* (*Sarashina nikki*, ca. 1060) is one of six major literary diaries from the mid-Heian period, roughly 900 to 1100.[1] The other five are the *Tosa Diary* (*Tosa nikki*, ca. 935) by Ki no Tsurayuki,[2] the *Kagerō Diary* (*Kagerō nikki*, ca. 974) by Michitsuna's mother,[3] the *Pillow Book* (*Makura no sōshi*, ca. 1000) by Sei Shōnagon,[4] the *Izumi Shikibu Diary* (*Izumi Shikibu nikki*, ca. 1008) by Izumi Shikibu,[5] and the *Murasaki Shikibu Diary* (*Murasaki Shikibu nikki*, ca. 1010) by Murasaki Shikibu. We have chosen the term "diary" to translate *nikki* (literally, "daily record"), even though dated entries are rarely the norm in these texts and sometimes they appear closer to other forms of first-person writing in English such as memoirs and autobiographies. The term *nikki* is a Chinese loan word, and in a classical Chinese context, it refers to both public and private daily records. In the Heian Japanese context, the term *nikki* covers a wide range of official and personal court records and even documents like modern appointment diaries arranged as calendars with spaces by each date for recording activities. Writing these kinds of *nikki* in literary Chinese[6] was customary for the male members of the Heian court. In fact, the first *nikki* to be produced in the vernacular Japanese language, the *Tosa Diary* (ca. 935), calls attention to this fact in its opening lines: "They say that diaries [*nikki*] are kept by men, but I will see if a woman can also keep one."[7] This statement is used to announce a female persona for the male author, a persona that, among other things, enabled the author to write in vernacular Japanese rather than literary Chinese.[8] Since this first work of "self-writing" in vernacular Japanese had the title *nikki*, the term was applied to most later texts too, even though their content and form do not conform to the expectations of a daily record. After debating whether to translate the *nikki* in *Sarashina nikki* as "journal" or "memoir" in order to indicate its difference from a daily record, we finally opted for the simple literal translation of "diary." After all, the term "diary" in English, just like *nikki* in Japanese, is broad enough to encompass appointment diaries on one end of the scale and works of personal reflection such as *The Diary of Anne Frank* on the other. We have, accordingly, also used "diary" to refer to other Heian texts of the *nikki* genre.

Besides the six major literary diaries produced during the Heian period, several other, lesser-known texts that loosely fit the category of diary have survived as well.[9] This comparatively large body of literary diaries from so early in the history of Japanese writing has resulted in the canonization of the personal diary as a fully accepted genre in classical literature.[10] The early development of the personal diary form, and its modern canonization in Japan, is an anomaly in world literary history. Now when speaking of literature over that period, it has become a general practice to discuss this group of diaries collectively using the term *nikki bungaku* (diary literature).

Diaries in literary Chinese were only one source for the development of the diary in vernacular Japanese. The first and foremost source was the personal poetry collection (*shikashū*). The tenth century, during which the first diaries in vernacular Japanese were produced, also saw an efflorescence of the *waka* form of Japanese verse.[11] Almost all members of aristocratic society composed *waka* and kept collections of their verse for both their own personal record and posterity. The concern for posterity was connected with the importance of *chokusen wakashū*, imperially sponsored collections of *waka* poetry, twenty-one of which were produced between 905 and 1439. Immense prestige was attached to having one's poems included in an imperial anthology. It was the equivalent of having one's work published by a major press and being reviewed favorably in the *Times Literary Supplement* and the *New Yorker*, a way of feeling that one had achieved lasting literary immortality. Even if one were not fortunate enough to have a poem included in an imperial anthology during one's lifetime, one's descendants might still have a chance to submit a copy of one's personal poetry collection for consideration by the compiling committees of future anthologies. Furthermore, since one family member's fame as a poet shed glory on the whole family, personal poetry collections came to be considered family assets.

A collection of one's own poems with prose headnotes recording the occasions of their composition became almost a kind of diary. Since *waka* were often exchanged with others, others' poems also became part of one's personal record. In addition, short narratives resulted from sequences of exchanged poems: "On such and so occasion, I sent X this poem. He replied with that poem. I replied in turn . . ." and thus a story line would emerge. It might be one of a developing love affair, the disillusionment of professional hopes, the deepening of friendship, or the process of coping with grief and disappointment. Thus, just as the personal poetry collection overlapped with the diary form, both the personal poetry collection and the diary had much in common with the genre of prose fiction. We pointed out that Ki no Tsurayuki, the author of the *Tosa Diary*, adopted a female persona when writing his diary, something more readily associated with prose fiction than with diaries.

Monogatari, "tale" literature written in vernacular Japanese, also flourished in the Heian period. This, after all, was when the great *Tale of Genji* (*Genji monogatari*) was composed. Although tale literature was officially denigrated as reading fit only for the amusement of women and children, this did not hinder its popularity. Since Heian prose fiction tended to focus on human relationships, it naturally included exchanges of poetry. Thus both diaries and tales contained exchanges of *waka* poetry. This promiscuous mingling of diary, fiction, and poetry has blurred genre distinctions in the writing of this period, which is evident in the slippage of titles for some works that are known alternately as *nikki* or *monogatari*. Of course, genre categories were devised much later by literary scholars in an attempt to create order out of chaos, a situation further complicated by the genre definitions, which themselves originated in very different literary traditions. Suffice it to say that a creative blending of genres is what characterizes the literary production of the Heian period.

This situation helps explain why, from the beginning, the vernacular Japanese diaries of the Heian period display a more literary character than one would expect, judging solely from the development of the diary form in Western literature. Our simple definition of "literary" is the conscious aesthetic shaping of the text for the eyes of others, which might seem surprising in an era well before any form of print culture. In the Heian period, even though works were circulated only in handwritten copies, they nonetheless were circulated, and there is clear evidence that the authors of Heian diaries wanted their work to be read by others.[12] The fact that all Heian diaries contain greater or lesser amounts of poetry also contributes to their literary quality. In sum, the evolution of the diary form side by side with fiction led to a cross-fertilization between the two forms, which also tended to push the diary in a literary direction.

The Heian diary thus represents an exception in world literary history, in which at least until the modern period, the general trend has been for diaries to be kept distinct from fiction and poetry. A further anomaly is that five of these six canonized texts were written by women. Japanese literature stands alone on the world stage of literature for having so many female authors in the critical stages of its early development.

Although diaries continued to be written in the following Kamakura period (1185–1333), it is the texts of the Heian period that have received the most constant interest and high evaluation. Since the writers of three of these Heian-period diaries—Ki no Tsurayuki, Murasaki Shikibu, and Izumi Shikibu—also are famous writers in the genre of *waka* poetry (and, in Murasaki Shikibu's case, fiction too), the fact that they left behind diaries of high literary worth as well as historical interest is another reason that they have continued to attract readers.

The *Sarashina Diary* is the last of the six major diaries of the Heian period, coming nearly ninety years after the *Tosa Diary*, fifty years after the *Kagerō Diary*, and about one generation after the other three texts. Given the internal textual evidence in the *Sarashina Diary* and the fact that Takasue no Musume was linked through family connections to at least three of the other authors, it is reasonable to assume that she was aware of and had read all these earlier texts.[13] The *Sarashina Diary* covers the longest span of all the diaries, forty years, and its content displays a mixture of the elements of all the other five texts. Takasue no Musume records the experiences of both being locked in a household, as the author of *Kagerō Diary* was, and serving at court, as the memoirs of Sei Shōnagon and Murasaki Shikibu describe. The *Sarashina Diary* also contains extensive accounts of travel, as do the *Tosa Diary* and the *Kagerō Diary*. In one significant episode, the *Sarashina Diary* records a romantic encounter and poetry exchange worthy of the *Izumi Shikibu Diary*. At the same time, three defining features of the *Sarashina Diary* set it apart from its cohorts.

First is its portrait of the writer as a reader. Takasue no Musume gives us a firsthand glimpse into what it was like to be in the second generation of readers of the *Tale of Genji*, the first generation being Murasaki Shikibu's contemporaries at court. Her work bears witness to the mesmerizing quality of that epic tale and, on a personal level, its influence on her relation to language and reality (always so closely entwined), for both good and ill. The *Sarashina Diary* is a compelling account of the powerful effect of reading fiction, something that is found in all literate cultures.

Second, the *Sarashina Diary* stands out as the work of Heian self-writing most concerned with the role of religious belief and practice in a person's life. The author recounts dreams of spiritual significance, reflects on her youthful resistance to religious practice, and describes her constant sense of inadequacy with respect to religious devotion. In fact, the most obvious narrative line in her life story is the trajectory from youthful infatuation with romantic illusions fueled by her reading of fiction to the disillusionment of age and a concern for salvation. Conversely, her life story contains many passages deflecting that narrative line and even appearing to erase the dichotomy between literary illusion and religious truth.

Third, Takasue no Musume's work is noted for the long description at the beginning of the text of a trip she took at the age of thirteen from Kazusa (now roughly within the area of greater Tokyo) to the capital in Kyoto, a trip that took three months and marked her coming of age as a self-conscious individual. She records the journey with the fresh eyes of a child, and indeed, part of the appreciation for this text in Japan has been closely connected with the transparent innocence of the narrator's viewpoint in this opening travel account. At the same time, the account is constructed in a self-consciously literary way and sets up important motifs that recur throughout the work. Moreover, by starting with the eyes of a child and ending with the eyes of an old woman, the work as a whole demonstrates how the child shapes the adult and remains part of the self to the very end. Even the descriptions of pilgrimages from much later in her life, taken ostensibly for religious aims, are animated by a seemingly youthful curiosity, as though she felt most herself when she was on a journey and that self was the same one she began to record as a child.

To these three generally acknowledged defining characteristics, we would add a fourth. Of all the diaries of the Heian period, the *Sarashina Diary* reveals the most sophisticated orchestration of seemingly random fragments into a structure that, we contend, actually conveys the deeper meaning of the text. The structure is the result of the author's careful choice of the components of her life story. Life stories are constructed from memories, and although memories have a relationship to facts, they are not the same. That is, the reconstruction of the past inevitably entails the participation of our imagination. Although this also is true in our day-to-day exercise of memory, our imagination is even more involved in an autobiographical narrative. While any telling of a life story inevitably entails selection, Takasue no Musume's choices have a great impact on both the work's aesthetic quality and its ultimate meaning.

Before discussing in detail the special characteristics of the *Sarashina Diary* and expanding our argument about the role of the structure of the work, we provide some general information about the author and the background of the text itself, including its transmission.

FAMILY BACKGROUND OF
SUGAWARA NO TAKASUE NO MUSUME

The author's name literally means "Sugawara no Takasue's daughter." We do not know her personal name. While women would have had personal names for use by family members, particularly during childhood, women's names were generally not recorded in genealogical records (except in the case of imperial consorts). This is why we do not know the personal names of any of the other women diary authors of the mid-Heian period. The absence of most women's personal names from public records may be taken to reflect the lower status of women in that patriarchal society. Nonetheless, there also seems to have been a cultural practice of avoiding personal names. In their own texts, women did not use personal names when referring to either themselves or other women. Instead, they used nicknames, usually derived from the court offices held by their male relatives. It is interesting that even in works of fiction, women characters are never referred to by their personal names but by nicknames based on the name of their living quarters, or, often in the *Tale of Genji*, from the title of the chapter in which they first appear. What we want to stress here, however, is that the name Sugawara no Takasue no Musume does not make the author "anonymous" in any sense. On the contrary, Sugawara was a distinguished surname that identified her as a direct descendant of Sugawara no Michizane (845–903), a famous statesman, scholar, and poet of Chinese verse. The fact that allusions to Michizane's Chinese verse figure prominently in the *Tale of Genji* attests to the longevity and widespread knowledge of his poetry into the author's time. Heads of the Sugawara family had served as rectors of the court university for generations. Even though the author's father, Takasue, was not one of the most illustrious members of the family and did not assume that position, her elder brother, Sadayoshi, reclaimed that family honor and was noted in literary circles as well. In any case, the author's membership in the Sugawara family would have been noted by her contemporaries, but the full name of Sugawara no Takasue no Musume was for official records and not what her intimates would have called her. What that name was, we simply cannot know. Her name during her court service might have had the province name of Hitachi in it, because her father's last major post was as provincial governor of Hitachi.[14] In this book from now, we will on refer to her by the name that links her to her father, Takasue no Musume.

The author's father, Takasue, had a decent career as a provincial governor. Thus, like all the other women diarists of the Heian period, Takasue no Musume came from the *zuryō* (provincial governor) class, which occupied the middle rank of Heian aristocracy. Properly speaking, these men served as assistant governors for high-ranking nobles who held the governorship of the province as a sinecure. Although there was no prestige in leaving the capital to actually do the practical work of overseeing distant provinces, such posts usually were financially rewarding. Accordingly, Takasue appears to have profited very well from his governor's post in Kazusa[15] because when the family returned to the capital, they moved into a residence on a large property situated between the mansions of two imperial family members.[16]

The author's mother was a younger sister of Michitsuna's mother, author of the *Kagerō Diary*. The siblings' relationship would not have been close, however, since in addition to not having the same mother, Takasue no Musume's mother was thirty-six years younger. In fact, the two sisters may never have actually met in person.[17] Nonetheless, the family connection would have provided a conduit for the passage of a copy of the *Kagerō Diary* into the hands of Takasue no Musume.

Takasue no Musume also had a stepmother from the age of ten to thirteen when her father took her and her elder sister to Kazusa for the duration of his service there as the provincial governor. Takasue no Musume's mother stayed at home in the capital, presumably to oversee the family assets, so the father invited a young woman at court, with whom he was on intimate terms, to accompany him to the provinces and to assume the role of stepmother to his two daughters. She is identified in a marginal note by Teika as the daughter of Takashina no Nariyuki, a middle-ranking courtier from a family of some scholarly renown. Although the "wicked stepmother" scenario was stock material for fiction in the Heian period, the relationship between Takasue no Musume and her stepmother did not fit that stereotype at all. Although only briefly sketched, their relationship appears to have been exceedingly warm and was sealed with the exchange of poems on key occasions. Moreover, the opening of the diary credits the stepmother's oral renditions of episodes from the *Tale of Genji* and other tales with initiating the author into the enchanting realm of prose fiction. The fact that the stepmother had served at court explains her familiarity with the literature of the day, and her own literary skills are attested to by the inclusion of one of her poems in the imperial anthology *Goshūishū* (*Later Collection of Gleanings*, 1086).[18] In the first exchange of poems between the author and her stepmother, the stepmother alludes to a poem in the *Shūishū* (*Collection of Gleanings*, 1005–1011), an imperial anthology produced under the sponsorship of Emperor Ichijō, in whose court Murasaki Shikibu, Izumi Shikibu, and Sei Shōnagon all were employed. Her ability to allude to a poem in that comparatively recent anthology shows how up-to-date she was with contemporary poetry. Also of significance is the fact that the stepmother's uncle was married to Murasaki Shikibu's daughter. Thus it is possible that Takasue no Musume gained access to a copy of the *Murasaki Shikibu Diary* through her stepmother.

Another female relative, Lady Emon no Myobu, is mentioned in the diary as a source of reading material. Lady Emon served Princess Shūshi, daughter of Empress Teishi, in whose employ Sei Shōnagon had produced the *Pillow Book*. The author mentions that Lady Emon gave her a set of *sōshi* (booklets) that the princess had "deigned to pass down." Sei Shōnagon's *Pillow Book* was probably in that set. Furthermore, it was a nameless aunt "from the country" who is credited with finally obtaining for the author a complete copy of the *Tale of Genji*. In this way, a picture emerges of a family and social network in which prestige and economic standing passed to the author through the male line and access to vernacular literary works came through the female line.

SYNOPSIS OF THE AUTHOR'S LIFE

Takasue no Musume was born in the capital in 1008, coincidentally the same year that the *Tale of Genji* began to circulate as a completed manuscript.[19] From the age of ten to thirteen, she lived in the province of Kazusa in the East Country, where her father was serving as provincial governor. Upon returning to the capital in 1020, she resided with her family at the large residence on Sanjō Avenue until 1023, when their house burned down. It is not clear where the family lived during the next few years; in her diary, the author mentions living in temporary places. Other misfortunes plagued the family after the fire. In 1024, her elder sister died in childbirth. In 1025, her father, Takasue, failed to obtain a provincial governorship. This must have been a period of financial difficulty for the family, and it might have been one of the reasons why the author, already eighteen years old in 1025, did not get married. Heian aristocratic women did not leave their family home when they married; rather, they were visited by their husbands in their own homes. Without a suitably grand residence, it would have been difficult for the father to arrange a good marriage for her. In any event, her father did not receive a provincial governor posting until 1032, when the author was twenty-five years old, and the posting was in Hitachi, again far away in the east. This time, the author stayed with her mother in the capital, with her future still more or less on hold. Four years later, her father returned. The family was reunited and lived briefly in the suburbs of the Western Hills.

When they moved back into the capital, her mother became a nun, but as was the common practice among aristocratic women, she remained in the household. Taking the tonsure meant cutting her hair short, retiring from wifely duties, and devoting herself to religious practice within the home. Nonetheless, at this point, the author likely assumed the duties of mistress of the household for her retired father. In 1039, the author received an invitation to serve as a lady-in-waiting in the entourage of the infant Princess Yūshi (1038–1105). Princess Yūshi's mother, the consort of the reigning Emperor Go-Suzaku (1009–1049), had died, and the princess was being raised in the Takakura Palace of her grandfather Fujiwara no Yorimichi (992–1074), who held the powerful post of regent. Service in this household would have brought the author in contact with the highest-ranking members of Heian society. She was thirty-two years old, a little old to start a career at court, and her diary records her lack of self-confidence. Only a year later, however, as the author puts it, her parents "ended up shutting me away at home." In other words, they arranged a marriage for her. Her husband was Tachibana no Toshimichi (1002–1058), a middle-ranking aristocrat. The year was 1040, and the author was thirty-three, a very late age for marrying when marriages were often arranged for both boys and girls in their early teens. Despite her age, she bore at least two, possibly three, children to Toshimichi, even though he was away serving as provincial governor in Shimotsuke for four years starting in 1041. Her marriage did not end her court career entirely, however. She continued to serve from time to time and even with some regularity when she was asked to present her niece at court. During one of these periods of service in 1042, Takasue no Musume had an encounter with the high-ranking and talented courtier Minamoto no Sukemichi (d. 1060). This was the high point of her court career in the sense that on that occasion, she was able to converse and exchange poetry with someone who fulfilled the ideal of the courtly gentleman as portrayed in tale literature. Although she could not have foreseen it, the poem she produced in that encounter secured her a place in the *Shinkokinshū* (*New Collection of Ancient and Modern Poems*, 1205), one of the two most prestigious imperial anthologies of all time.

Takasue no Musume's middle years appear to have been spent in relative comfort. She records numerous pilgrimages and one trip to the province of Izumi at a time when her brother would have been serving as provincial governor there. In 1057, the author's husband, Toshimichi, was appointed governor of Shinano Province, the present-day Nagano Prefecture. He fell ill shortly after arriving and was given leave to return home, where he died the following spring. The author lived on after her husband's death, but we do not know for how long. The last entry in her diary seems to have been about a year after her husband's death.

At this point, we should note that none of these proper names (including the author's own name) are noted in the diary itself. We have this solid historical information because of the existence of an annotated manuscript copy handwritten by Fujiwara no Teika (1162–1241).

Indeed, the survival of the text itself into the modern period is credited to Teika's manuscript copy. It is to the story of this manuscript that we now turn.

LIFE STORY OF A TEXT: FUJIWARA NO TEIKA'S *SARASHINA NIKKI* MANUSCRIPT

Fujiwara no Teika was one of the most famous poets of his day, and he has the distinction of being the only poet to have participated in the compilation of two imperial anthologies. He was a member of the committee that compiled the *Shinkokinshū* (1205) and was the sole complier of the *Shinchokusenshū* (*New Imperial Collection*, 1235). He wrote works of criticism on *waka*, and he was also, in a sense, the first scholar of "Heian literature." His life spanned the cusp between the Heian period (794–1185) and the Kamakura period (1185–1333), not that he himself would have been aware of such period designations, which, like genre distinctions in literature, were created long after the fact. Nonetheless, with the establishment of a warrior government in Kamakura in 1185— ostensibly to assist the civil government in the capital but actually to control the country in all important economic and military respects— aristocrats like Teika were aware that their world had shifted significantly. At that point, the world of the past in which the capital had been the only center was imbued with a sense of nostalgia. Teika was one of the first to realize the importance of preserving the literary past, and he spent a great deal of his life collecting, copying, and collating manuscripts of works he considered important. This was especially important for the *Tale of Genji*, which, as we know from an entry in Murasaki Shikibu's own diary, had begun to circulate as a draft copy rather than a final clean copy because her employer, Fujiwara no Michinaga, had been too impatient to wait for the clean copy and stole a draft from her room to give to his daughter.[20] From that point, the *Tale of Genji* itself began to circulate in pieces, and people made copies for themselves. By Teika's time, many variant versions of the *Tale of Genji* existed, and it was Teika who painstakingly compared all the versions he could obtain and decided on the best text. His version remains the foundation for all modern editions. He did the same for the *Kokinshū* (*Collection of*

Ancient and Modern Poems, ca. 905) and *Tales of Ise* (*Ise monogatari*). Indeed, Teika played a preeminent role in preserving and transmitting the Heian texts that have come to constitute the canon of Japanese classical literature.

The *Sarashina Diary* is one of those texts. Teika not only copied the manuscript but also provided it with appendices and marginal notes. The appendices contain a short biography of the author and longer career résumés for her father, her husband, and the courtier Minamoto no Sukemichi, with whom the author had a brief encounter. Marginal notes on the manuscript itself identify the author's stepmother and the household in which the author served as a lady-in-waiting. Without these fruits of Teika's scholarly research, our knowledge of the objective facts about the author and her family would be very sparse indeed.

For example, Teika's colophon to the manuscript attests to the vagaries of manuscript transmission during this period:

> Some years ago, I was able to acquire this book. That copy was borrowed by someone and lost. That is why I have now made this copy from a copy made by someone else from that earlier one. In the process of this transmission, many errors have occurred. I have marked in red various places that seem doubtful. If I ever am able to get a reliable copy of the work, I would like to compare it and make corrections. In order to collate the historical dates, I have appended some excerpts of old records.[21]

Tamai Kōsuke, who produced the first modern edition of the *Sarashina Diary*, advanced the hypothesis that the phrase "some years ago" may refer to the time around 1210 to 1215 when Teika was assembling material for the *Shinkokinshū*.[22] Teika was known to be a good friend of Sugawara no Tamenaga, a direct descendant (sixth generation) of the author's father, Takasue.[23] It is possible that Tamenaga lent Teika the author's original manuscript, or a copy made from the original manuscript. Teika was avidly searching for new material for this ambitious anthology, and all his friends must have been happy to lend him material from their household libraries in the hope that a relative's poem might be included in the new compendium. This hypothesis is supported to some extent by the fact that the first appearance of a poem by Takasue no Musume in an imperial anthology occurs in the *Shinkokinshū*.

Teika may have read the *Sarashina Diary* even earlier. He notes in his biographical note about Takasue no Musume that she was also the author of the *Tale of the Hamamatsu Chūnagon* (*Hamamatsu Chūnagon monogatari*)[24] and three other works of fiction. The full list includes the *Tale of Nezame* (*Yowa no Nezame*), *Mizukara kuyuru* (Self-reproach), and *Asakura* (Tale of Asakura).[25] Teika himself was particularly drawn to the Hamamatsu tale and used it as a model for his own work of fiction, the *Tale of Matsura* (*Matsura monogatari*). Given that he was so impressed by the *Tale of the Hamamatsu Chūnagon*, he would have been interested in other works by the same author as well. Since he wrote the *Tale of Matsura* while he still held the title "Lesser Captain Teika" (1189–1202), he might have read the *Tale of the Hamamatsu Chūnagon* and the *Sarashina Diary* around the same time.

Regardless of exactly when Teika first read the *Sarashina Diary*, the loss of the first copy of the work to come into his hands was an unfortunate accident of history. Teika's surviving manuscript for the *Sarashina Diary* remains the best text available, but even he was aware that copyists' errors had already marred it. This was not the only misadventure, however, to befall the text.

In the seventeenth century, Teika's manuscript ended up in the library of the imperial household. Sometime before the manuscript had arrived at the library, the threads holding it together had disintegrated, and it had been rebound with its pages out of order. Consequently, early modern scholars and readers had difficulty appreciating the text as a whole. In 1924, the scholar Tamai Kōsuke discovered the physical reason for the seemingly chaotic order of the text,[26] reconstructed the page order, and accordingly laid the foundation for all modern scholarship on the text.[27] Even though Tamai used the metaphor of a broken pot to describe the text before its reconstruction, the beauty of the individual pieces had been appreciated for two hundred to three hundred years even without the benefit of their placement within a unifying design. One of the reasons that readers could not easily divine the diary's overarching structure was that it was so complex. Had the design painted on the shards been simple, it would have been easy to fit the pot back together. But the patterns created by the individual episodes are finely delineated and independent of the work's main narrative line, and the pieces could fit together in different ways. The appreciation of individual sections is thus linked paradoxically to the subtle structure of the whole.

CHOICES MADE ABOUT CONTENT

One of the ways to begin understanding the structure of the *Sarashina Diary* is to focus on what the author chose to include in her narrative and, even more important, what she chose to leave out. First, Takasue no Musume does not refer to being a direct descendant of Sugawara no Michizane or to her family's connection with literary scholarship. Because she devotes much space and attention to detailing her attachment to poetry and fiction, the fact that the Sugawara family could boast such literary fame and the fact that Chinese poems by Sugawara no Michizane are alluded to in important scenes in the *Tale of Genji* could not have been meaningless pieces of information to her, yet she makes no allusion to any of this. In this respect, the *Sarashina Diary* differs markedly from the *Murasaki Shikibu Diary*, which gives a comparatively detailed account of the education that Murasaki Shikibu received at home from her scholarly father.

Moreover, Takasue no Musume hardly mentions her marriage or the birth of her children and their upbringing. Particularly because marital relations and children are important themes in the other diaries of the same period, such as the *Kagerō Diary*, these omissions stand out.

One of the most striking omissions in the *Sarashina Diary* is the author's silence on her own writing of fiction. In his biographical note on the author, Teika credits Takasue no Musume with writing the *Tale of the Hamamatsu Chūnagon* and three other works. Although literary scholars have debated over the years the reliability of these attributions,[28] today, comparative research on the *Sarashina Diary*, *Tale of Nezame*, and *Tale of the Hamamatsu Chūnagon* tends to confirm Teika's attribution.[29] Indeed, we wonder why twentieth-century scholars even bothered to question the veracity of Teika's assertion at all, given that he was born only about one hundred years after the completion of the *Sarashina Diary* and had personal contact with direct descendants of the Sugawara family. Ironically, it is the particular nature of the *Sarashina Diary* itself that likely gave rise to these doubts.

The *Sarashina Diary* spans more than fifty years of Takasue no Musume's life. Except for the first ten years of her childhood, she describes the greater part of her life from youth to old age, but not once does she write a single word about her own composition of tales. In fact, we can even surmise that Teika's very deliberate addition of a note about her authorship of works of fiction is directly related to this omission. He had to mention it precisely because she did not. Given that the author conscientiously portrays herself as a dedicated reader of tales and that the relationship between literature and a person's life is an important theme throughout the *Sarashina Diary*, some readers find it odd that she does not mention her own creative efforts with fiction. This silence with respect to a clearly important aspect of her life is perhaps one of the most troublesome riddles connected with interpreting the *Sarashina Diary*. It is related to the difficulty of discussing what she "tells" on the basis of what she "did not tell." We assert that these "purposeful omissions" in the *Sarashina Diary* are closely connected with the distinctive character of the work.

Although a number of intentional omissions appear to be built into the structure of the *Sarashina Diary*, unless one has a specific interest in the chronology of the author's life, one will not necessarily be bothered by these omissions. Since the text is an assemblage of numerous, discrete fragments, the richness of the information about the human experience from so many different angles ends up obscuring these gaps in the narration. At the same time, this particular character of the text also gives rise to conflicting perceptions of the author and the meaning of the work. Japanese scholars of the *Sarashina Diary* are divided regarding the author's development as a character in her own text. On one side, such scholars as Ikeda Kikan and Ienaga Saburō view the work as an account of the author's progress from the delusion caused by her infatuation with fiction toward a religious awakening.[30] On the other side, Yasuda Yojūrō sees in it a "pure voice"[31] that does not change throughout the text. From his point of view, the diary displays no development or change in religious consciousness; rather, it is "a poem of one person's life."[32] How can such contradictory views of the same text be explained? From our point of view, the text supports both these readings. The main narrative line undeniably describes a process of disillusionment. Yet many passages of the work appear to work at cross-purposes to the main story line. These passages tend to focus on poetry and so probably gave rise to Yasuda's impression of the poetic character of the text as a whole. We believe, however, that it is in the interplay between these two types of passage that the deeper meaning of the text is revealed.

NOTES

1. For other translations, see Ivan Morris, trans., *As I Crossed a Bridge of Dreams: Recollections of a Woman in Eleventh-Century Japan* (New York: Dial Press, 1971); and Annie Shepley Omori and Kochi Doi, trans., *Diaries of Court Ladies of Old Japan* (Boston: Houghton Mifflin, 1920).

2. For translations, see Gustav Heldt, trans., "Tosa Diary" (partial), in *Traditional Japanese Literature: An Anthology, Beginnings to 1600*, ed. Haruo Shirane (New York: Columbia University Press, 2007), 204–13; Helen McCullough, trans., "Tosa Journal," in *Classical Japanese Prose: An Anthology* (Stanford, Calif.: Stanford University Press, 1990), 73–102; Earl R. Miner, trans., "Tosa Diary," in *Japanese Poetic Diaries* (Berkeley: University of California Press, 1969), 59–91; and G. W. Sargent, trans., "Tosa Diary" (partial), in *Anthology of Japanese Literature: From the Earliest Era to the Mid-Nineteenth century*, ed. Donald Keene (New York: Grove Press, 1955), 82–91.

3. For translations, see Sonja Arntzen, trans., *The Kagerō Diary: A Woman's Autobiographical Text from Tenth-Century Japan* (Ann Arbor: Center for Japanese Studies, University of Michigan, 1997); and Edward Seidensticker, trans., *The Gossamer Years: The Diary of a Noblewoman of Heian Japan* (Rutland, Vt.: Tuttle, 1964).

4. The *Pillow Book* of Sei Shōnagon is a unique work that does not fit under any one genre label, but a substantial portion of the work contains anecdotal records of the author's personal life that do have the character of a diary. Allusions to the *Pillow Book* in the *Sarashina Diary* confirm that it was certainly one of the texts that influenced Takasue no Musume's writing. For translations, see Meredith McKinney, trans., *Sei Shōnagon: The Pillow Book* (London: Penguin, 2006); and Ivan Morris, trans., *The Pillow Book of Sei Shōnagon*, 2 vols. (New York: Columbia University Press, 1967).

5. For translations, see Edwin A. Cranston, trans., *The Izumi Shikibu Diary: A Romance of the Heian Court* (Cambridge, Mass.: Harvard University Press, 1969);

and Earl R. Miner, trans., "Diary of Izumi Shikibu," in *Japanese Poetic Diaries*, 98–153.

6. It is important to note that this form of Chinese was not a transcription of any spoken Chinese dialect, but a specialized language for writing that had been honed by hundreds of years of development in China before its exportation to Japan. The existence of this universal written language for governmental and cultural purposes is what enabled China to communicate across a diversity of mutually unintelligible dialects within the Chinese language group and, for most of the premodern period, provided the foundation for the vast Chinese cultural sphere that extended from Vietnam to Japan.

7. Miner, trans., "Tosa Diary," 59.

8. For a detailed inquiry into the functioning of the female persona in the *Tosa Diary*, see Lynne K. Miyake, "*The Tosa Diary*: In the Interstices of Gender and Criticism," in *Women's Hand: Gender and Theory in Japanese Women's Writing*, ed. Paul Shalow and Janet Walker (Stanford, Calif.: Stanford University Press, 1996), 41–73.

9. Joshua Mostow, trans., *At the House of Gathered Leaves: Shorter Biographical and Autobiographical Narratives from Japanese Court Literature* (Honolulu: University of Hawai'i Press, 2004), 1.

10. For an overview of the process of canon formation for classical Japanese literature in the modern period, see Haruo Shirane, "Introduction: Issues in Canon Formation," in *Inventing the Classics: Modernity, National Identity, and Japanese Literature*, ed. Haruo Shirane and Tomi Suzuki (Stanford, Calif.: Stanford University Press, 2000), 1–27; and, particularly with respect to women's diaries, Tomi Suzuki, "Gender and Genre: Modern Literary Histories and Women's Diary Literature," in ibid., 71–95.

11. *Waka* 和歌, a verse form consisting of thirty-one syllables in Japanese divided into syllable line lengths of 5, 7, 5, 7, and 7. *Waka* can be translated alternatively as "Japanese verse" (as opposed to Chinese verse) or "harmonizing verse." For a full explanation of this latter option and a detailed study of the rise of the *waka* form, including its social and political context, see Gustav Heldt, *The Pursuit of Harmony: Poetry and Power in Early Heian Japan* (Ithaca, N.Y.: East Asia Program, Cornell University, 2008), 10.

12. For example, *Ōkagami* (*Great Mirror*), a fictionalized but generally reliable history of the mid-Heian period composed around 1119, mentions that Michitsuna's mother, the author of the *Kagerō Diary*, "allowed it [the diary] to be made public" (Helen Craig McCullough, trans., *Ōkagami, The Great Mirror: Fujiwara Michinaga [966–1027] and His Times* [Princeton, N.J.: Princeton University Press, 1980], 166).

13. The possible exception is the *Izumi Shikibu Diary* because there is no direct or indirect textual reference to it in the *Sarashina Diary*, nor does there appear to

have been a family channel by which Takasue no Musume may have obtained a manuscript of the text. This negative evidence alone, however, is not conclusive.

14. Fukuya Toshiyuki, "*Sarashina nikki* bōtō hyōgen to jōraku no ki no seiritsu-saburaina to dokusha no mondai," *Waseda daigaku kyōiku sōgōkagaku gakujutsu kenkyū*, no. 60 (2012): 37–50.

15. The province of Kazusa in the Heian period covered most of the Chiba Peninsula.

16. For a detailed discussion of the evidence for the location of the Sugawara residence, see Itō Moriyuki, *Sarashina nikki kenkyū* (Tokyo: Shintensha, 1995), 294–302. See also appendix 2, map 3.

17. The *Kagerō Diary* does, however, contain a poem of congratulations for the birth of the new sibling. See Arntzen, trans., *Kagerō Diary*, 331.

18. In the anthology, her name is given as Kazusa no Taifu, wife of the Kazusa governor, the nickname she would have acquired after accompanying Takasue to Kazusa. See the *Goshūishū*, poem 959.

19. For a discussion of Takasue no Musume's probable awareness that she was born in the same year that the *Tale of Genji* began to circulate as a complete manuscript, see Itō Moriyuki, "*Sarashina nikki* to *Genji monogatari* no sennenki," *Gakushūin joshi daigaku kiyō*, no. 11 (2009): 1–8.

20. Richard Bowring, *Murasaki Shikibu: Her Diary and Poetic Memoirs* (Princeton, N.J.: Princeton University Press, 1982), 95.

21. Akiyama Ken, ed., *Sarashina nikki*, Shinchōsha Nihon koten shūsei (Tokyo: Shinchōsha, 1980), 172.

22. Tamai Kōsuke, *Sarashina nikki*, Nihon koten zensho (Tokyo: Asahi shinbunsha, 1950), 57.

23. Itō Moriyuki, "*Hamamatsu Chūnagon monogatari* to *Sarashina nikki* no kōsaku suru tabiji," in *Heian kōki monogatari*, ed. Inoue Mayumi et al. (Tokyo: Kanrin shobō, 2012), 81.

24. Teika actually gives "Mitsu no Hamamatsu" as the title, which was an alternative for the work.

25. None of these works can be dated accurately, and of the four, only the *Tale of Nezame* and the *Tale of the Hamamatsu Chūnagon* survive, though sections of both are missing. Carol Hochstedler has done a partial translation of *Yowa no Nezame* in *The Tale of Nezame: Part Three of Yowa no Nezame Monogatari* (Ithaca, N.Y.: China-Japan Program, Cornell University, 1979). A complete translation of what remains of *Yowa no Nezame* is available in Kenneth L. Richard, "Developments in Late Heian Prose Fiction: 'The Tale of Nezame'" (Ph.D. diss., University of Washington, 1979). For a translation of the *Hamamatsu Chūnagon monogatari*, see Thomas H. Rohlich, trans., *A Tale of Eleventh-Century Japan: Hamamatsu Chūnagon Monogatari* (Princeton, N.J.: Princeton University Press, 1983).

26. For a translation of Tamai's exciting account of his discovery, see Morris, trans., *As I Crossed a Bridge of Dreams*, 33–34.

27. Tamai Kōsuke, *Sarashina nikki sakkan kō* (Tokyo: Ikuei shoin, 1925).

28. For example, in the introduction to his translation of *Hamamatsu Chūnagon monogatari*, Rohlich cites Inaga Keiji's argument that the postscript in question was merely part of the manuscript that Teika was copying and therefore reported hearsay, but in his later scholarship Inaga himself repudiated this position. See Rohlich, trans., *Tale of Eleventh-Century Japan*, 9.

29. For a selection of recent essays treating this issue, see Wada Ritsuko and Kuge Hirotoshi, eds., *Sarashina nikki no shinkenkyū—Takasue no Musume no sekai o kangaeru* (Tokyo: Shintensha, 2004).

30. Ikeda Kikan, "Seikatsu maka no geijutsu toshite no *Sarashina nikki*," in *Kyūtei joryū bungaku*, ed. Tokyo teikoku daigaku kokubungaku kenkyūshitsu (Tokyo: Shibundō, 1927), 133–50; Ienaga Saburō, *Jōdai bukkyō shisōshi* (Tokyo: Unebi shobō, 1942), 384–405.

31. Yasuda Yojūrō, "*Sarashina nikki*," *Kokugo to kokubungaku*, no. 8 (1935): 61.

32. Ibid., 82.

2

THE RELATIONSHIP OF THEME
AND STRUCTURE

*T*he ordering of passages in the *Sarashina Diary* has a close relationship to the two themes that run through the diary. One, overt, is the deluding force of an infatuation with literature, and the other, covert, is the saving, or at least consoling, powers of literature. The first theme is expressed in narrative passages of retrospective reflection; the second theme emerges implicitly from lyrical passages centered on poetry. The distinct qualities of these two types of passage provide a key to understanding how their alteration facilitates the unfolding of the covert theme and, more important, the development of a dynamic tension between the two themes.

NARRATIVE PASSAGES AND LYRICAL PASSAGES

Modern scholarship in Japan on the *Sarashina Diary* has recognized that the diary comprises two types of passage, one designated a "narrative type" and the other a "poetry collection type."[1] The first type focuses on the prose narration of events, scenery, or retrospective reflection, and the second type resembles selections from a personal poetry collection. That is, a poem or sequence of poems is the main point of entry, and the prose plays a secondary role.[2] For the sake of our discussion, we designate the first type as a "narrative passage" and the second type as a "lyrical passage." The mere presence or absence of poetry is not what distinguishes these two types of passages, because many of the passages we would classify as narrative also contain poems. Instead, our chief criterion is whether the main interest in a passage is on the prose or the poetry. For example, even though the long account of the trip from Kazusa to the capital at the beginning of the diary contains some poems, the overwhelming emphasis is on the prose narration of the movement through the landscape and the events along the way. Nonetheless, in the narrative passages of most interest to us here, those that carry the explicit theme of the diary contain no poems. The opening of the diary is a good example of this type of passage, as it sets up the major theme of the diary, the young girl's attachment to tales, and how this obsession was intertwined with her sense of religious devotion. It has a retrospective quality, and even though it is a first-person narration,[3] it produces an external view of the young girl almost as though she were a character in a tale. These narrative passages throughout the text build the story line for the diary as a whole: the fairly straightforward story of a woman's gradual disillusionment with the romantic fantasies of her youth. Yet time and time again, that simple story is undercut by the lyrical passages.

One effect of the lyrical passages is stopping the forward motion of the text, and in a sense, they also forestall any backward movement by means of retrospection. The moment of the poem—and therefore of the passages in which a poem or poems are the focal point—always seems to be the present. The lyrical passages were likely based on notes made at the moment of the poem's composition, and thus they preserve the immediacy of those experiences. When the author sets out in the narrative passages to write retrospectively and discursively, her consciousness at that particular time of writing shapes the narration. Contradictions arise between the content in the narrative passages, especially those consisting of retrospective reminiscences, and the content in the lyrical passages because of the gaps between the author's actual consciousness at given moments in her life and her consciousness of the past when she attempts to summarize stages in her life.

Sometimes the stopped moments of time in the lyrical passages have something akin to a musical effect. Take, for example, the following passage, which comes at the end of a long lyrical section recording a number of poems by people mourning the death of the author's sister. The poems of grief build to a crescendo of pain and loss, followed by

At a time when the snow had been falling for days, I imagined how it must be for the nun living in the Yoshino Mountains:

yuki furite	With the snow falling,
mare no hitome mo	even the rare visits of others
taenuramu	must have ceased—
yoshino no yama no	it is a steep path up to the
mine no kakemichi	peaks of the Yoshino Mountains.

Whereas the poems of grief preceding this passage end on an unresolved, wrenching chord, this passage sounds a quiet return to a sense of peace. This is accomplished by the shift to imagining another person's situation and what it must be like to be cut off from others, not by death, but by physical isolation, weather, and, significantly, the choice of a religious life.

Four lyrical passages contain poems addressed to nuns, all of which function to shift the diary's mood or tone. In these passages, as in the one just cited, we also see a veiled revelation of the author's empathy for a life of religious renunciation. In contrast, many of the retrospective narrative passages express a worldly view of religion that may be paraphrased as follows: "If only I had read sutras and performed pilgrimages seriously in my youth, perhaps I would have had a more successful life." Therefore, the lyrical passages containing poems addressed to nuns not only provide moments of quiet reflection but also undercut the socially dominant view of religious practice that preoccupies the retrospective narrative passages. The author makes no explicit claims for having a deeper and more spiritual understanding of Buddhism than the ordinary worldly view; rather, she lets that understanding show in these lyrical passages. We consider it important that the author chooses to end the diary itself with the fourth of such lyrical passages involving poetry exchanges with a nun, but we defer a detailed discussion of this point until the final chapter of this study. For now, note that in these lyrical passages, she has the poetry carry a spiritual meaning while declaring in the narrative passages that the frivolous pursuit of poetry and fiction led her astray.

THE HIGASHIYAMA RECORD CASE STUDY

The long sequence of lyrical passages known as the "Higashiyama record" can similarly be seen to undercut the diary's overt theme, but in an even more complex and paradoxical way. This section describes a six-month period in the author's eighteenth year when she took up temporary residence in the Higashiyama "Eastern Hills" District of the capital. This area in the foothills of Mount Hiei was more countryside than suburb, but still within easy reach of the capital. The Higashiyama record comes just after a series of misfortunes in the author's life that included the destruction of the family residence by fire, her elder sister's sudden and early death, and her father's career disappointment. The diary gives no reason for her move. She introduces the section casually by saying that "for a certain reason, I moved to a place in Higashiyama."

This sequence of lyrical passages occupies a significant portion of the diary as a whole, and no one has advanced a convincing explanation for its presence. Although we cannot know the author's intention, if we look into the meaning of this particular section from the point of view of the diary's internal structure, we can offer a reason for its existence. This reason is the section's relationship to what has come to be known as the "what I wished for" (*aramashigoto*) narrative passage, which follows shortly after the Higashiyama record. In it, the author summarizes her life as a young girl. Here is the entire passage:

> In this way, life went on, and airy musings continued to be my preoccupation. When on the rare occasion I went on a pilgrimage, even then I could not concentrate my prayers on becoming somebody in the world. Nowadays it seems that people read the sutras and devote themselves to religious practice even from the age of seventeen or eighteen, but I was

unable to put my mind to that sort of thing. Instead, I daydreamed about being hidden away in a mountain village like Lady Ukifune, happy to be visited even only once a year by a high-ranking man, handsome of face and form, like the Shining Genji in the tale. There I would gaze out in melancholy languor at the blossoms, the crimson leaves, the moon, and the snow, awaiting his splendid letters, which would come from time to time. This was all I mused about, and it was even what I wished for.

The passage comes just before her father finally succeeds in securing a provincial governorship, in Hitachi, and gives a retrospective assessment of the deluded state of her mind as a young girl. Her love of literature, particularly of romantic fiction, is held up to her own mind for scorn. She exaggerates the naïveté of her fantasies. What normal woman could stand to be visited only once a year by her lover, even if he were as charming as the "Shining Genji"? The author—who by this time has virtually memorized the *Tale of Genji*—knows that Ukifune is a tragic heroine, a character who is torn apart by her triangular relationship with Prince Niou and Captain Kaoru to the point that she contemplates suicide and finally ends up taking the tonsure.

This summation of her fantasies presents one of the most superficial readings possible of the *Tale of Genji*. Even the description of taking aesthetic joy in the seasons—"the blossoms, the crimson leaves, the moon, and the snow"—seems clichéd. But here in this passage clearly is the central narrative of Takasue no Musume's life story. To paraphrase once more: "If only I had not wasted so much of my life on my infatuation with fiction and poetry, I might have been able to devote myself properly to religious observances, and these would surely have resulted in a better life." This view of her life fits perfectly with the dominating religious worldview of the day. Moreover, she might honestly have felt this way at this point in her life, when she was still unmarried at the age of twenty-five and had no other prospects in sight. If, however, that was the sum total of what she considered to be the meaning of fiction and poetry in her life, then why did she allot so many precious pages to the record of her stay in Higashiyama, during which, to all intents and purposes, she was actually able to fulfill the desire expressed in her "airy musings" of living in a mountain village and savoring the passage of the seasons? During this period, she is even able to enjoy the visits of an intimate companion. If the experiences related in these passages were finally judged as trivial, then why include them? Moreover, far from depicting a frivolous and banal state of mind, the passages in the Higashiyama record contain some of the most evocative writing in the diary; they are not clichéd at all, but fresh and perceptive. The content and quality of the Higashiyama record completely undermines the author's easy dismissal of such preoccupations in the narrative section just cited. Although we do not have room here for a complete analysis of the subtle construction of the sequence and all its individual passages,[4] we later examine how the Higashiyama record achieves a unity of its own and then focus on one interlude that subtly reveals how precious the life of the imagination and literary play were for the author.

The Higashiyama record has a pleasing completeness that does not come from a story line with a beginning, climax, and end but from the natural movement of the seasons. The sequence begins in the Fourth Month with a description of the rice paddies:

> Toward the end of the Fourth Month, for a certain reason, I moved to a place in Higashiyama. Along the way, the paddies had been flooded and the rice shoots planted. I gazed out at the surrounding scene, somehow charmed by its green hue. The place where I was to stay was deep in the shade of the mountain, and right in front of me was the touching and forlorn sight of the evening twilight. Water rails cried out loudly.

tatakutomo	Knocking at the door,
tare ka kuhina no	"Who comes?" Only water rails
kurenuru ni	in the falling dusk
yamadji wo fukaku	must have come to visit
tadzunete ha komu	this path deep in the mountains.

After several passages covering experiences of the summer and early autumn, her stay ends with the following passage:

Upon starting my return to the capital, I noticed that all the rice paddies, which had been full of water when I came, had now been completely harvested.

nahashiro no	Until the paddies,
midzu kage bakari	where I saw only young shoots
mieshi ta no	mirrored in the water,
karihatsuru made	have ended up all harvested,
nagai shi ni keri	such a long stay have I had.

The sequence does not end here with her return to the capital, however, but with a passage that acts like a kind of coda. It records a second short visit to the Higashiyama residence in the winter:

Toward the end of the Tenth Month when I had the occasion to come back and view that place just briefly, every single leaf of that dark lush forest had scattered and lay in disorder on the ground. Looking around feeling terribly moved, I noticed that the stream that had burbled along so cheerfully was now buried in fallen leaves; all one could see was where it had been.

midzu sae zo	Even the water
sumitaenikeru	has clearly ceased to dwell here
ko no ha chiru	in the desolation
arashi no yama no	of this stormy mountain where
kokorobososa ni	all the tree leaves have fallen.

Thus the sequence encompasses a full cycle of the seasons: late spring, summer, autumn, and winter. The winter scene provides a strong closure. She cannot ever return to what had been one of the freest and most cheerful interludes of her life, but she tells us this only through the metaphor of a stream smothered in fallen leaves. In this final passage of the sequence, the prose introduction also assumes a poetic quality in which scene and emotion are fused together. This blurring of the distinction between prose and poetry is very typical of the writing in the *Tale of Genji*.

The next set of two passages we examine follows the author's arrival at the residence in Higashiyama. Although she makes a pilgrimage to a nearby temple, the focus of the passage shifts away from worship to literary dalliance:

> Since Ryōzen Temple was nearby, I went to worship there. Even though the path was steep, I made it all the way to the spring welling up between the boulders at this mountain temple. There was a person with me who, drinking the water from cupped hands, said, "One feels as though one could drink this water forever without tiring of it." I replied,

okuyama no	Cupping and lifting
ishi ma no midzu wo	to your lips this water from boulders
musubi agete	deep in the mountains,
akanu mono to ha	did you just realize now
ima nomi ya shiru	you would never tire of it?

> When I said this, the person who was drinking answered,

yama no wi no	More even than of
shidzuku ni nigoru	the "water clouded by drops" falling
midzu yori mo	into the mountain spring,
ko ha naho akanu	I feel as though I would
kokochi koso sure	never tire of this one.

> On the way back, with the evening sun glowing, the capital area lay spread out clearly before us. The person who had spoken of the "water clouded by drops" had to return to the capital but seemed very sorry to leave. The next morning, this came:

yama no ha ni	As the rays
irihi no kage ha	of the setting sun disappeared
iri hatete	on the mountain's rim,
kokoro bosoku zo	I could not help gazing out,
nagame yarareshi	lost in forlorn thoughts.

The mention of a companion in these passages has occasioned much speculation among Japanese scholars. Not only is the companion introduced suddenly and without explanation, but nothing in the original grammar identifies the companion as male or female. Inaga Keiji hypothesized that these passages (and a passage that follows a bit later and also mentions a companion) record the author's first love affair.

He posits that the visitor may have been Takasue no Musume's widowed brother-in-law, who may have become attracted to the younger sister during the year after the elder sister's death.[5] Takasue no Musume may have developed feelings for him, too. Despite this, as a young unmarried girl, she would likely have resisted simply becoming a substitute for her sister and therefore moved temporarily to Higashiyama to gain emotional distance from this internal conflict. This hypothesis, however, rests only on conjecture.

The only thing certain about these exchanges is that they rest on the "foundation" of an old poem that both of the companions recognize and use to create a playful and pleasurable exchange. The poem is from the *Kokinshū*, the most revered of the imperial anthologies, and is by Ki no Tsurayuki, himself one of the compilers of the *Kokinshū*. The poem is in the "Parting" section of the anthology. Here it is, with its headnote:

Composed on parting from someone with whom he had chatted at Ishii Spring on Shiga Pass.

musubu te no	My thirst still unslaked,
shizuku ni nigoru	droplets from my cupped palms cloud
yama no i no	the pure mountain spring—
akade mo hito ni	still would I tarry with one
wakarenururu kana	from whom I must now take leave.[6]

Commentators have recognized a romantic and even erotic aura in this poem that issues from phrases such as "thirst still unslaked" and "droplets from my cupped palms cloud / the pure mountain spring." With such a poem interwoven into and underpinning this exchange, it is easy to imagine the companion as a male lover. Takasue no Musume, however, chose not to make this reading explicit. Some commentators have assumed that she did this to modestly cloak an intimate episode in her life. One could just as easily argue, though, that by taking advantage of the romantic overtones in Tsurayuki's poem, she transformed a merely playful exchange into a scene of intimate communication that invites the reader to imagine a lovers' encounter. All that was really necessary was that the companion be able to appreciate the allusion to Tsurayuki's poem and participate in the play on it. This is not to deny that this could be a record of her first love affair; we simply want to emphasize that the way the author has composed the account focuses on the play of language and the pleasure of communication with someone who can equally savor that play.

During her Higashiyama sojourn, Takasue no Musume was able to imaginatively transform this rural seclusion into the fulfillment of her dreams. Such imaginative play involves the fictionalization of the material of life, and the writing bears witness to a deep sense of freedom and joy. When we remember the events that preceded this period in her life—the loss of her home to fire, the death of her sister, and her father's career disappointment—it is easy to understand her need to shift her consciousness away from the despair and disappointments of reality by pursuing a life of the imagination in Higashiyama.

As we pointed out earlier, on the surface the *Sarashina Diary* describes a process of disillusionment. Within that framework, Takasue no Musume has no choice but to dismiss in a one-dimensional way her literary illusions as "frivolous tales and poetry." This may be the principal reason why she could not mention her own fiction writing: it would have been too blatant a contradiction of the life story that she had chosen. But as we also have made clear, many of the lyrical passages undercut that story line. We thus suggest that even while the author was writing words that dismiss tales and poetry as frivolous, it is likely that she was acutely aware of the great importance of her love of tales and poetry as a resource for coping with a trying reality. The way that she methodically employed lyrical passages enabled her to capture the paradoxical value of tales and poetry in her life.

NOTES

1. The Japanese terms for these types of passages are 散文的章段 and 家集的章段.

2. For a more detailed discussion of this issue, including an overview of Japanese scholarship and a quantitative analysis of the proportion of these two types of passages in the *Sarashina Diary*, see Itō Moriyuki, *Sarashina nikki kenkyū* (Tokyo: Shintensha, 1995), 44–65.

3. Note that the distinction between first- and third-person narration is not as clearly demarcated in classical Japanese as it is in Indo-European languages.

4. For a full analysis, see Itō, *Sarashina nikki kenkyū*, 44–102.

5. Inaga Keiji, "Takasue no Musume no hatsukoi no hito wa 'shizuku ni nigoru hito' ka," *Kokugo to kokubungaku*, December 1968, 9–19.

6. Laurel Rasplica Rodd, trans., *Kokinshū: A Collection of Poems Ancient and Modern* (Princeton, N.J.: Princeton University Press, 1984), 163.

3

DREAMS AND RELIGIOUS CONSCIOUSNESS

*T*he deep concern for religion in the *Sarashina Diary* makes it unique among the Heian diaries. From the very opening of the text, in which the author describes setting up her own votive image of the Healing Buddha, to the last poem, in which she evokes the "final renouncement" of a nun's vocation, aspects of Buddhist practice are threaded throughout the work. Nowhere, however, are the hopes and fears that Takasue no Musume entertained with respect to Buddhist devotion more concentrated than in her accounts of her dreams. All together, she records eleven dreams in the *Sarashina Diary*, more than in any of the other Heian diaries, and all but one have religious import. Therefore, the study of religious consciousness in the *Sarashina Diary* must be closely connected with the nature of the author's dreams. In this chapter, we examine some of her dreams and explain how they were shaped by the belief system of her time. We show how the dream accounts reveal her hopes and ambitions for success in the world and demonstrate how the subtle resonances between the opening of the diary and the final dream account complicate the overall meaning of her religious dreams.

"MEMORIZE . . . THE *LOTUS SUTRA*"

The first dream that Takasue no Musume recorded was one she had in her fourteenth year, not long after she had moved to the capital with her family and shortly after she had finally obtained a complete copy of the *Tale of Genji*. The dream was a response to her total absorption in the *Tale of Genji*:

> With my heart pounding with excitement, I was able to read, right from the first chapter, the *Tale of Genji*, this tale that had confused me and made me impatient when I had read only a piece of it. With no one bothering me, I just lay down inside my curtains, and the feeling I had as I unrolled scroll after scroll was such that I would not have cared even if I had had a chance to become empress! I did nothing but read, and I was amazed to find that passages I had somehow naturally learned by heart came floating unbidden into my head. Around the same time, in a dream, I saw a pure-looking monk wearing a surplice of yellow cloth who said to me, "Quickly, memorize roll 5 of the *Lotus Sutra*." But I told no one, nor did I feel particularly inclined to memorize the *Lotus Sutra*. . . . [N]ow it seems to me that my thoughts were frightfully frivolous.

The young girl's subconscious awareness of the contradiction between her desire for fiction and her pious duty surfaces in the dream. During the Heian period, the Buddhist position with respect to secular literature was decidedly pejorative. While poetry was regarded with slightly less disfavor, fiction was especially singled out for vilification. This view is set out clearly in the preface to *The Three Jewels* (*Sambōe*), written around 984 by Minamoto no Tamenori (941?–1011), a work of religious instruction for a young princess who had taken the tonsure in 982. Tamenori warns the young nun about sliding back into the amusements of secular life, chief among which was romantic fiction: "Then there are the so-called *monogatari*, which have such an effect upon ladies' hearts. . . . Do not let your heart get caught up even briefly in these tangled roots of evil, these forests of words."[1] By recording this dream at the moment that her wish to read the *Tale of Genji* was fulfilled, Takasue no Musume makes it clear that even as a young girl, she was not ignorant of the Buddhist condemnation of fiction. Nonetheless, she begins her diary with a disarming declaration of desire for these "forests of words" built on "tangled roots of evil." In fact, her first conscious devotional practice was directed toward obtaining tales:

I made a life-size image of the Healing Buddha, and performing purification rituals when no one else was around, I would secretly enter the room. Touching my forehead to the floor, I would pray with abandon: "Please grant that I should go to the capital as soon as possible where there are so many tales, and please let me get to read all of them."

Although these actions are fitting for the character of the young girl created at the beginning of the work, her praying to the Buddha to give her access to these sinful pleasures is indeed ironic.

The mention of roll 5 of the *Lotus Sutra* in her dream is significant because that roll begins with the Devadatta chapter, which was considered to have special meaning for women believers. This chapter recounts the enlightenment of the Dragon King's daughter. Despite the orthodox view that women could not achieve enlightenment owing to the unclean condition of a woman's body and the "five obstacles," the daughter of the Dragon King achieved full enlightenment in an instant.[2] Although it is true that within that "instant" she also turned into a man before miraculously crossing over into Buddhahood, the chapter was regarded by women of the Heian and medieval periods as holding open the hope of instant Buddhahood for women.[3] Takasue no Musume informs us, however, that she felt no inclination whatsoever to follow the advice of the dream. Rather than memorizing sutras, she would much rather read the *Tale of Genji* over and over to the point that she was unconsciously memorizing it. Her account of this dream already has crystallized the problem between literature and religious duty. Clearly, her realization that religion exerted a curbing influence on the arts was not suddenly grasped only later in life; she had spent her whole life caught in the dilemma between the two. We thus posit that writing the *Sarashina Diary* allowed her to face this conflict.

"WORSHIP AMATERASU," WORLDLY AMBITIONS

The second dream recorded in the *Sarashina Diary* also occurred in the author's fourteenth year. Again, the dream account is prefaced by an admission of her absorption in tales, and we are meant to infer a causal relationship between her addiction to fiction and the arrival of a cautionary dream:

> I thought about tales all day long, and even at night as long as I could stay awake, this was all I had on my mind. Then I had a dream in which a person said, "For the sake of the Princess of the First Rank, daughter of the Grand Empress, I am constructing an ornamental stream at the Hexagonal Hall." When I asked, "Why?" the response was, "Worship Amaterasu, the Great Heaven Shining God."

The "Princess of the First Rank" referred to here was Teishi (1013–1027), a granddaughter of Fujiwara no Michinaga. Her Sanjō Palace was located next to the Sugawara family residence, and the Hexagonal Hall (Rokkakudō) was within walking distance of both residences (see appendix 2, map 3). Although the official name of the temple was Chōhōji, the distinctive architecture of its main building, the Hexagonal Hall, became the popular name for the temple, which was one of the oldest in Kyoto and dedicated to the worship of the Bodhisattva Kannon (figure 1). The worship of Kannon was very common among Heian women, and their three most popular pilgrimage destinations were Kiyomizu Temple, Hatsuse Temple, and Ishiyama Temple—all centers of Kannon worship. While Takasue no Musume does not mention Kannon by name in her text, she made pilgrimages to all these temples, some of them more than once. Yet the message delivered by the dream was to worship Amaterasu, the Shintō Sun Goddess and tutelary deity of the imperial household.

This connection of a Buddhist deity's place of worship with the injunction to worship a Shintō god is not so strange as it might seem at first glance. Heian Buddhism had a highly syncretic character. For a long time, the loose collection of indigenous beliefs and practices now subsumed under the category of Shintoism had been fitted into the Buddhist paradigm principally through the promotion of the doctrine of *honji suijaku* (Original Ground, Manifest Trace), by which Shintō deities were interpreted as manifestations of buddhas and bodhisattvas. Although this blurred the distinction between buddhas and gods, the most sacred sites of Shintō, such as the Ise and Kamo Shrines, did

FIGURE 1 The Hexagonal Hall (Rokkakudō) at Chōhō Temple.

maintain a separation between Shintō worship and Buddhism. Shrine officiates were forbidden to participate in Buddhist devotional practices and observed special taboos with respect to Buddhist vocabulary. Nonetheless, in Heian society, this was the exception rather than the rule.[4] In most people's minds, there was no clear distinction between Buddhist and Shintō deities. In fact, later in the diary, when Takasue no Musume talks about someone who is always advising her to worship Amaterasu, she admits to not knowing whether this was a god or a buddha. When she asks for clarification, she is informed that Amaterasu is the god that is worshipped in the imperial palace and at the Ise Shrine. This leaves her feeling at a loss because she cannot imagine ever having a chance to pay her respects to the god at either place. Rather poignantly, she says, "It seemed that all there was to do was to pray to the light of the sky." By default, she is thrown back on the most primitive form of sun worship.

The deeper meaning of the dream about the construction of a stream at a Kannon temple is that it links a member of the imperial family, a Buddhist offering to a Kannon temple, and an imperative to worship the tutelary god of the imperial family. This dream thus sowed a seed of the association of Amaterasu, Buddhist devotion, and service to the imperial family that grew in the author's mind throughout her life. Much later in her life, she had a dream on her way to Hatsuse Temple that also was connected with Amaterasu. A noble woman appears and predicts that one day she will live in the imperial palace and that she should discuss this with the custodian of the Mirror Room in the palace where Amaterasu is worshipped. These two dreams—and, indeed, all mentions of Amaterasu—are connected to Takasue no Musume's hope of serving the imperial household. These are dreams of success in this world.

Buddhist devotional practices in the Heian period were directed primarily toward gaining benefits and avoiding misfortune in this world, even though all the teachings of the various schools of Buddhism stress the vanity of worldly success and the need to escape the chain of karma and rebirth. Moreover, Buddhist philosophy denies the existence of any essential self. If no self exists in reality, then what is there to achieve success or be protected from harm? Although the philosophical foundation of Buddhism is shaped by these ideas, it is evident that the majority of believers, not only in the Heian period, but also down through the ages, have given no more thought to these concepts than we today pause to consider that the physical objects around us consist of more space than matter. Even though this is a fact proven by modern physics, it remains disconnected from our sensory experience of the world, and therefore we ignore it. Similarly, it is one thing to understand intellectually the tenet that the self is illusory and success in this world is in vain, but it is impossible to live without relying on a sense of a personal self, the most powerful of all illusions. It is so much easier to understand rewards in this life for this personal self than release from the chain of transmigration. Accordingly, most of the dreams in the *Sarashina Diary* that have religious meaning are connected with a concern for success in this world. In this respect, the author depicts herself as typical of her era.

THE MIRROR WITH TWO REFLECTIONS

A comparatively large amount of space in the diary is spent recounting a dream by a monk who made a pilgrimage to Hatsuse Temple on the author's behalf at the request of her mother. Even though this was someone else's dream, the detailed account of it underscores its importance to Takasue no Musume. Moreover, the passage stands out because the entries for her life between the ages of twenty and thirty are few. This dream took place when the author was in her mid-twenties and beginning to consider her future more seriously. Her father was away serving as the governor of Hitachi Province. She was living in the capital with her mother and starting to wonder why she had not gone on more pilgrimages. With her father away, there was no possibility of a marriage being arranged for her or any other step being taken to decide her future. Going on pilgrimages was therefore the only available means she had to influence the outcome of her future, yet her mother regarded pilgrimages as dangerous enterprises and was unwilling to undertake any outside the capital itself. Her mother then offered the compromise of sending a monk to Hatsuse Temple in her daughter's place. As mentioned earlier, Hatsuse Temple—now better known by its abbreviated name, Hase Temple (figure 2)—was a center of Kannon worship and figures prominently as a pilgrimage destination in most of the Heian women's texts as well as in the *Tale of Genji*. The following is the account of this event and the dream reported by the monk:

> Then Mother had a mirror cast, one foot in circumference, and declaring that it would take my place, she sent it with a monk on a pilgrimage to Hatsuse. She apparently told him, "Go perform devotions for three days. Please have a dream to divine what future is in store for my daughter." For that same period of time, she also had me perform purifying rituals.
>
> This monk returned and made the following report: "Were I to come back without having had at least one dream, it would be disappointing, and what would I have to say for myself? So I fervently made obeisances, and when I fell asleep, I saw a wonderfully noble and lovely looking woman garbed in lustrous robes emerge from behind a curtain-of-state; she was carrying the offering mirror in her hand. 'Was there a letter of

FIGURE 2 An overview of Hase (Hatsuse) Temple.

vows with this?' she asked. I respectfully replied, 'There was not. This mirror by itself is the offering.' 'How strange,' she said. 'This should be accompanied by a letter of vows.' Then she said, 'Look at what is reflected here in this mirror. What you see will make you very sad!' and she wept and sobbed softly. When I looked in the mirror, there was a reflection of someone collapsed on the floor crying and lamenting. 'When you look at this reflection, it is very sad, is it not? Now, look at this,' and she showed me the reflection on the other part of the mirror. Amid beautiful bamboo blinds and other hangings, various robes poured out from under curtains-of-state; plum and cherry blossoms were in bloom; and from the tips of tree branches, warblers were singing. 'Looking at this makes one very happy, does it not?' she said. That is what I saw in the dream." This, it seems, was his report. But I did not pay attention, not even to the extent of being surprised by how much he had seen and what it might mean.

The noblewoman who appears in the dream raises the issue of vows. That is, such offerings were usually accompanied by a written statement by the petitioner specifying the goal of his or her prayers. The fact that no such document was drafted might indicate that Takasue no Musume's mother had difficulty imagining a particular goal for the girl's future, given the current uncertainty of the family's position and her daughter's age, which was well past the prime time for either marriage or service at court. Nor does the author portray herself as having any clarity about what she wants for a future. Shortly after recounting the Higashiyama record, discussed in chapter 2, she asserts that she has given up the frivolous hopes to become someone like Ukifune, but the spell of those romantic notions still lingers in the background.

The content of the dream is ambiguous. It could augur either an unhappy or a happy future, since both possibilities are indicated. Indeed, it seems almost too convenient a dream for the monk to have had. Some scholars, like Saigō Nobutsuna, have suggested that the dream looks suspiciously like a fabrication by the monk and have therefore labeled the author as gullible for apparently accepting it at face value.[5] In the way we see the author, however, this dream was "convenient" for her, too. It sums up the dark and the light of life, which run through the text like a leitmotif. She had experienced enough death and loss in her life to know that happiness and sorrow were the two sides of the single coin of life. Although on the surface she portrays herself as motivated by the ordinary desire for happiness common to all humanity, she also alludes to darker desires in her heart that had been fueled by romantic illusion, such as wanting to become a tragic heroine like Yūgao or Ukifune. Both kinds of desire are integral parts of her, and both can be seen in the monk's dream. Moreover, the dream occurred at a time when her life was in limbo. She no longer was a young girl but had not quite crossed over into womanhood, which would entail marriage, the bearing of children, or perhaps the assumption of the responsibilities of a career at court. Thus it is appropriate that the dream be as vague and without resolution as her life was at that moment.

Immediately after this dream account, Takasue no Musume asks about the identity of Amaterasu. As discussed earlier, Amaterasu is connected with the possibility of serving at court, so making the inquiry at this point must indicate that a court career was a future she could imagine for herself. Periodic allusions to the *Murasaki Shikibu Diary* and the *Pillow Book* of Sei Shōnagon make it clear that she had read these accounts of court life as assiduously as the *Tale of Genji*. Therefore, it is not strange that she might imagine following in their footsteps, particularly since both Murasaki Shikibu and Sei Shōnagon entered court life at comparatively advanced ages, in their late twenties to early thirties. The happy scene in the monk's dream can be seen to foreshadow such a future, and indeed, upon her father's return, both service at court and marriage come to pass for Takasue no Musume. In so many ways, then, the monk's dream, whether fabricated or not, perfectly summed up her situation at that point in her life.

At the end of the account, Takasue no Musume states specifically that she paid no attention to the dream, though her recording it belies that assertion. Further proof that the dream was important to her and dwelled in the back of her consciousness throughout her life is revealed only much later in the diary when she faces the crisis of her husband's death. In the depths of her grief, she takes a retrospective look at many of the dreams she had had throughout her life and sums up her state of mind at that point by interpreting it in terms of the mirror dream. It is to that passage we turn next.

FROM DREAMS TO LIVING NIGHTMARE

Takasue no Musume's husband died in 1058 at the age of fifty-six. They had been married for seventeen years. Although she had barely touched on her relationship with her husband in the diary, she records experiencing profound grief at his death:

> On the twenty-fifth day of the Ninth Month, my husband fell ill; on the fifth day of the Tenth Month, he died. I felt as though it were a bad dream; I could not imagine something like this happening. The image seen in the mirror offered to Hatsuse Temple of a figure collapsed on the ground weeping; this now was me. The image of the joyous figure

had not come to pass. Now it seemed hardly likely that it could ever be in the future. . . .

Long ago, rather than being infatuated with all those frivolous tales and poems, if I had only devoted myself to religious practice day and night, I wonder, would I have been spared this nightmarish fate? The time that I went to Hatsuse Temple when someone in a dream threw me something, saying, "This is a cedar of good omen bestowed by the Inari Shrine," if I had just gone right then and there on a pilgrimage to Inari, maybe this would not have happened. The dreams that I had had over the years in which I had been told to "worship the god Amaterasu" had been divined as meaning that I should become a nurse to an imperial child, serving in the palace and receiving the protection of the imperial consort. But nothing like that had ever came to pass. Only the sad image in the mirror has been fulfilled. Pitifully, I grieved. Since I had ended up as one without one thing going as I had wished, I had drifted along without doing anything to accumulate merit.

This is a painfully accurate account of the psychological state of grief in which all previous experiences of happiness become meaningless. Her account up this point has included happy experiences at court and descriptions of periods of well-being, both economic and spiritual, but in the face of this loss, she is aware only of how deeply unhappy she is, and she reflects on the past, wondering whether there was any way she could have avoided this pain. Twice she reflects back on the mirror dream to find that now she can identify with only the image of the figure collapsed on the floor in tears. She discloses here for the first time that she had had her dreams divined, as well as the specific nature of the prediction, which was that she would become a wet nurse for an imperial offspring and receive the patronage of an imperial consort. This was one of the posts of highest respect and influence in the imperial court to which a woman of Takasue no Musume's station could aspire. Although Takasue no Musume does not reveal this prediction until the end of her diary, when it had been proved false, this disclosure indicates the power of the prediction lingering in the back of her mind all those years. Given her age and circumstances after her husband's death, there is no way this future could be realized. Yet immediately after this passage, she relates a dream that does give her hope for a kind of happiness in the future.

THE AMIDA DREAM AND A RETURN
TO THE BEGINNING

The Amida dream is singled out with a specific date, the only place in the entire diary where the author does this. This date indicates that she had the dream in the autumn of 1055, three years before her husband's death, yet she places it in her diary after that event. It is the first mention in the text of Amida Buddha. Amida worship increased in popularity during the Heian period and became the most widely practiced form of Buddhist devotion in the succeeding medieval period. It is based on the belief in Amida's vow to welcome into the Pure Land in the Western Heaven all those who call his name upon their death. A relatively large number of votive paintings from the Heian period, called *raigō-zu*, depict Amida arriving at the moment of a person's death, and this was the context for her dream:

> Yet somehow it seemed that even though life was sad, it would continue. I worried that perhaps even my hopes for the afterlife might not be granted. There was only one thing I could put my faith in. It was a dream that I had had on the thirteenth day of the Tenth Month in the third year of Tengi. Amida Buddha appeared in the front garden of the house where I lived. He was not clearly visible but appeared through what seemed like a curtain of mist. When I strained to look through gaps in the mist, I could see a lotus dais about three to four feet above the ground; the holy Buddha was about six feet in height. He glowed with a golden light, and one of his hands was spread open; with the other he was forming a *mudra*. Other people could not see him; only I could. Inexplicably, I experienced a great sense of fear and was unable to move closer to the bamboo blinds to see. The Buddha deigned to speak: "If this is how it is, I will go back this time, but later I will return to welcome you." Only my ears could hear his voice; the others could not. This was

the dream I had, and when I woke up with a start, it was the fourteenth. My only hope for my afterlife is this dream.

When her dream accounts are lined up in this fashion, the hypothesis that the story she tells in her diary essentially documents a simple trajectory from illusion to religious awakening seems reasonable. To paraphrase that story line once more: "I was infatuated with fiction and poetry as a girl and young woman to the point that I neglected religious devotions; neither did I memorize sutras nor make enough pilgrimages, so my life ended up unsuccessful and unhappy." It is a self-denigrating account that conforms to the ruling paradigm of her era. Yet there is so much more to the diary than this. In the previous chapter, we examined how the lyrical passages built around the poems contribute to the work and undermine this story line. Moreover, if her object had been to tell a story of faith in which she finally achieved a believing heart through the divine intervention of a dream, it would have made sense not only to excise all the lyrical sections but also to end the narrative with this dream of Amida, but she did not do this. We are saving for chapter 6 a detailed discussion of the significance of the ending to her diary, but here we want to show how the Amida dream passage subtly evokes the opening to her diary, in which she prays for access to tales and thereby also weaves a countertheme to the story line just summarized.

First, she sees Amida Buddha "through gaps in the mist" in much the same way she saw her Healing Buddha through "a heavy, unsettling fog" when departing from her home in Kazusa. The way in which Amida Buddha appears in her dream also accords more closely with the iconographic representations of the Healing Buddha than those of Amida. The height of approximately six feet for the image is appropriate for a life-size standing image, like that of her personal Healing Buddha image. In Heian representations, Amida is often shown seated and at least five times life size. The hand positions of one hand open and the other making a sacred *mudra* also is associated more often with the Healing Buddha than with Amida. In the dream, the author seems to be with "other people" who cannot see Amida, who has come alone to her garden. Again, in *raigō* representations, Amida is never shown alone but always with a retinue of heavenly beings. In sum, the Amida image in Takasue no Musume's dream recalls the Healing Buddha of her early devotions.[6]

What are we to make of this? As an account of the author's dream, we might surmise that the shadow of the first Buddha she worshipped lingered in her subconscious throughout her life and influenced the form that Amida took in her dream. At the same time, the parallels between the passage describing the first Buddha to whom she prayed for access to tales and this passage depicting the Buddha who appears to promise her entrance to the Pure Land operate in a literary way to bring the two together. This conflation of the Healing Buddha and Amida in this final dream helps unify the diary and creates the paradox that she began her life as a reader and writer infatuated with fiction and poetry and—although this entangled her in illusion and therefore could be viewed as the source of her troubles—that her lifelong engagement with literature also gave her the ability to appreciate the precious moments in this ephemeral existence, those moments when perhaps she was closest to a state of enlightenment.

Fiction and poetry themselves have a multifaceted effect on our thinking and imagination. On the one hand, they can be the source of simple delusion; on the other, they can lead to a greater awareness of the truths of life. For example, if the core truth of Buddhism is to recognize the suffering in human existence, then perhaps Takasue no Musume gained her sensitivity to the inherent sadness of life, the very seed from which Buddhist enlightenment grows, not only from her own experiences of loss and the loneliness, but also from her reading about the suffering of others in texts like the *Tale of Genji* or the poems of the imperial anthologies. Birth, sickness, old age, and death bring suffering, but to be able to write, to bring the magic of imaginative language to bear on this natural suffering, may be as much a consolation as religious faith itself. Furthermore, illusion and reality may not be diametrically opposed after all but instead are a dynamically intertwined pair, a view that accords with some of the more sophisticated formulations in Buddhist metaphysics. Since Takasue no Musume was not a scholar of Buddhism, such an abstract summation of this paradox was not available to her. Rather, this is something that she appears to have understood intuitively from a lifelong engagement with fiction and poetry.

Like the fictional characters of Murasaki and Genji in the *Tale of Genji*, Takasue no Musume was attracted to Buddhist renunciation, but she could not seem to take the final step to become a nun. She remained caught and oscillating between darkness and light, joy and sadness, this world and the next. Even the apparent blessing of the Amida dream was not enough to make life simple and one-sided for her. She continued to record her engagement with the multifaceted nature of human experience right to the end of her text. In the words of Emily Dickinson, whom Takasue no Musume might well have recognized as a kindred spirit, in order to tell "all the truth," she had to "tell it slant." That is what we see in the particular way the opening of the text and the account of this final dream mesh together as well as in the structuring of the work as a whole.

NOTES

1. Edward Kamens, *The Three Jewels: A Study and Translation of Minamoto Tamenori's Sanbōe* (Ann Arbor: Center for Japanese Studies, University of Michigan, 1988), 93.

2. Leon Hurvitz, trans., *Scripture of the Lotus Blossom of the Fine Dharma* (New York: Columbia University Press, 1976), 199–201.

3. For a number of poems by Heian women expressing the hope to achieve Buddhahood, as the Dragon King's daughter did, see Yoshida Kazuhiko, "The Enlightenment of the Dragon King's Daughter in *The Lotus Sutra*," in *Engendering Faith: Women and Buddhism in Premodern Japan*, ed. Barbara Ruch (Ann Arbor: Center for Japanese Studies, University of Michigan, 2002), 307–8.

4. For a discussion of the taboos and the general accommodation negotiated between Shintō ritual and Buddhist belief, see Edward Kamens, *The Buddhist Poetry of the Great Kamo Priestess: Daisaiin Senshi and Hosshin Wakashū* (Ann Arbor: Center for Japanese Studies, University of Michigan, 1990), 4–11.

5. Saigō Nobutsuna, *Kodaijin to yume* (Tokyo: Heibonsha, 1974), 77–79.

6. Kodama Rie was the first to note these four points of connection between the appearance of Amida in her dream and the image of Healing Buddha depicted in the opening of the diary. See Kodama Rie, "*Sarashina nikki*—Sakusha Sugawara no Takasue no Musume no shūkyō ishiki: Butsuzō no byōsha o megutte," *Kokubun*, no. 61 (1984): 55–65.

4

A CHILD'S VIEWPOINT
AND LAYERS OF NARRATION

OF AUTHOR, NARRATOR, AND PERSONAE

The *Sarashina Diary* has been appreciated by readers in Japan for the transparent innocence of a child's viewpoint that is so effectively conveyed in the long travel account that opens the work. Although this viewpoint appears to be the natural result of Takasue no Musume's having taken and recorded the journey as a child, it also is apparent that she reworked the account when she was older. Thus the story of the journey is not the spontaneous report of a child but one that has been shaped in a literary way to meet the needs of the text as a whole as well as to imaginatively re-create the experience of a child. We can clearly see the author's shaping hand in the opening phrase of the first sentence in the diary: "As a girl raised in the back of beyond, even farther than the end of the road to the East Country," which cites part of a poem from a late-tenth-century collection, the *Kokin rokujō* (*Six Quires of Ancient and Modern Poems*):

azumadji no	For even the length of time
michi no hate naru	given by the excuse of a sash of Hitachi,
hitachi obi no	that place even farther
kagoto bakari mo	than the end of the road to the East Country,
ahimiteshigana	I long to meet and see you.[1]

The poem refers to an ancient ceremony once held at the Kajima Shrine in Hitachi, in which various sashes were tied to a pole and young men and women were randomly paired by pulling the ends of the sashes. Although Takasue no Musume was raised in Kazusa rather than Hitachi,[2] the allusion to this poem allows her not only to subtly set up the longing for tales of romance expressed in the opening passage as a whole but also to overlay the account of her own upbringing with that of Ukifune in the *Tale of Genji*. Ukifune, the character with whom Takasue no Musume most closely identified, was raised in the province of Hitachi. At the opening of the diary, even though the child Takasue no Musume has not yet had the opportunity to read the *Tale of Genji*, she uses this allusion to prepare the way for the narrative that follows.

We identify three layers in the narration of this autobiographical text. First is Takasue no Musume the author, who is visible in the shaping of the text, such as in the preceding example in which an allusion foreshadows the content to come. Like a director behind the scene, the author selects the subject matter and structures the text to bring a variety of literary effects into play. Second is the persona of the child established at the beginning of the text, who appears to speak directly for the author and yet is a re-creation. Third is the narrative voice of an older self who views the young self from a distance and interjects critical comments from time to time. For example, in the account of the first dream, discussed in chapter 3, the breathless delight of the young girl finally in possession of the *Tale of Genji* is delivered with immediacy, but starting about the middle of the account, the narration shifts to evaluate the young girl's state of mind from the vantage of hindsight and ends with this direct criticism: "Now it seems to me that my thoughts were frightfully frivolous." Of course, an older self recognizing the actions of one's younger self as foolish is a common experience for most of us. It is at those moments that we become aware that our sense of self is actually multiple rather than unitary. But what we want to focus on here is that the alternation between a voice entirely absorbed in the experiences recounted and a voice judging them from a distance actually creates a multilayered effect in the text's narrative fabric. Moreover, although the voice of what we have termed "the child's viewpoint" is created at the beginning of the text, it remains a part of the self the author portrays in this diary right up to the end.

THE ASHIGARA MOUNTAINS EPISODE
AND WOMEN ENTERTAINERS

Let us examine the quality of the child's viewpoint in one of the most striking scenes in the record of the trip up to the capital, the account of the three women entertainers appearing out of the dark woods of the Ashigara Mountains:

> On a dark night with no moon, when anyone would lose his way in the darkness, out of nowhere appeared three women entertainers. One was about fifty, one about twenty, and the other about fourteen or fifteen. In front of our lodging they set up a large umbrella and sat down. When our servants brought torches so that we could see, one of them said, "We are the descendants of the famous Kohata of the old days." The women's hair was very long with lovely sidelocks hanging down; their skin was white and clean. Much impressed, people said, "They hardly seem suited to this sort of life. Why, they would not be out of place as maidservants for the nobility." The women's voices were incomparable as they sang wonderful songs that seemed to ring clear in the sky. We all were very moved and had the women move closer, so excited we were. When they overheard someone say, "There couldn't be entertainers as fine as these in the West Country," they sang in a splendid way: "When you compare us with those of Naniwa . . ." Their appearance was unsullied, and when they sang, their voices could not be matched. When they rose to go back into the mountains that were so menacing, everyone regretted their going and broke into tears. In my young heart, I regretted even that I would have to leave this temporary lodging.

This account conveys the magical quality of this experience. The women entertainers appear like apparitions out of the dark forest and perform with an almost supernatural beauty. The observed details, which include remarks by the audience, re-create the scene as though it were unfolding before us. The child records the evaluative comments of the adults only as part of the scene. Such comments as they "hardly seem suited to this sort of life" reveal the lowly status of these performers. Japan has a long tradition of women entertainers who make their living primarily by selling their artistic skills but whose profession is often associated with selling physical pleasures. Generally, such entertainers have occupied a liminal position in Japanese society, not quite respectable, though not denigrated. The social position of these three women who appear out of the forest does not concern the child, however. She hears the adults' comments and is aware that there is something unexpected about these performers' refined appearance and musical skills, but the overwhelming impression created by this account is one of sheer wonder.

The diary records a similar encounter with itinerant women entertainers much later in the author's life when she is on her way to Izumi Province (located now southwest of Osaka Prefecture), probably to see her elder brother, who was appointed governor of the province in 1049. The author would have been in her early forties. This time, she and her companions travel by boat down the Yodo River, and they stop for the night close to a port town:

> That night we anchored off a place called Takahama; it was very dark, and late at night, we heard the sound of boat oars. When someone asked what it was, it turned out to be the sound of women entertainers approaching. We all were interested and tossed a line to attach their boat to ours. In the light of lamps set at a distance, we could see these women wearing singlets with long sleeves, hiding their faces with fans and singing songs; it was very moving.

This account is much shorter and not as full of enchanted feeling as the earlier passage, but it still is notable for the fascination and empathy it expresses for the women entertainers. Once again, the author is on a journey where the unexpected could happen, and her perception is animated by her experiences as a child. In fact, most of her descriptions of her pilgrimages in her middle years portray this same feeling of fresh perception.

FEELING APART FROM OTHERS

There is more to be said about Takasue no Musume's empathy with female entertainers. When she had her first encounter with the female entertainers in the Ashigara Mountains, it was as though at that moment, she understood something fundamental about herself—that she was just as different from the others around her as these entertainers were. They had come out of the dark, and she, too, had come out of the "dark" East Country, something that would forever mark her in the world of the capital as someone who did not belong. She recognizes this in the very first sentence of the diary: "As a girl raised in the back of beyond, even farther than the end of the road to the East Country, how rustic and odd I must have been." Moreover, the comment at the very end of the passage describing the first encounter with the women entertainers in the mountains—"In my young heart, I regretted even that I would have to leave this temporary lodging"—draws attention to how she felt as a child apart from others. Along with the others, she regrets the departure of the entertainers and also that she herself would soon have to leave behind the place where this wonderful event occurred. This realization was not something she could share with others because it would not square with their expectations. It was one thing to regret the end of the performance, but once there is nothing more to see, why regret leaving an empty place? We suggest that for her, this place represented a psychological point of identification between the alien other within herself and the strange entertainers. In a sense, she never did leave that "lodging," in which darkness was a friend.

Her sense of being apart from others is apparent in the opening of the diary as well, when she talks about going to worship her Buddha "when no one else was around." She grew up in a kind of solitude that was increased by fate as she lost, one by one, the women to whom she felt close: her stepmother upon their return to the capital, her nurse who died the following spring, and finally her elder sister only three years after the return to the capital. Her sense of being apart from others also seems to have been nurtured by her habit of reading alone. It is noteworthy that when she finally obtains a complete copy of the *Tale of Genji*, she shuts herself away in her room and reads it all by herself. There is other evidence that reading in the Heian period could be a communal activity. In a scene from the twelfth-century illustrated scroll of the *Tale of Genji*, a group of women are depicted enjoying a tale together. One person is reading the tale aloud for the others, and one person is shown viewing illustrations of the tale in a separate book. That is not how Takasue no Musume describes her own reading, but it was not a lonely experience for her. Through reading, she was able to connect with the world. Along with reading, writing—and particularly sharing the writing of poetry—was her means of connecting to the world. Thus the way in which she viewed the world as a child, her sense of feeling apart from others, and her attachment to poetry and fiction all are related.

For example, most of the diary's accounts of communications with others are mediated by an exchange of poetry, such as her exchanges with her stepmother, with her elder sister, with the friend at Higashi-yama, with her father when he was away on his second appointment as governor in the East County, with her various co-workers at court, and with the courtier Minamoto no Sukemichi on the rainy night in winter. Indeed, the inclusion of many poems by others is one factor contributing to the text's many dimensions. In addition, many of the exchanges that involve poetry also weave the poetry and tales from past literature into the narrative by means of intertextual allusion. Again, the Higashiyama exchange based on the foundation poem by Ki no Tsurayuki is a good example. The entire account of the conversation and poetry exchange with Minamoto no Sukemichi, which is filled with references to the *Tale of Genji* (to which we turn in the next chapter), also exemplifies this. The same passages crystallize moments of heightened perception and sensibility, something for which the diary has been much appreciated.

THE OLDER WISER SELF, AN ORDINARY WOMAN

If the child's viewpoint and the poet's perspective offer extraordinary experiences, the self-critical voice is wrapped up with the mundane. We noted that in the retrospective narrative passages describing herself in her youth, the author disparages her frivolous turn of mind. After her marriage and the beginning of her service at court, two passages in particular give full rein to her self-critical voice, which is caught up in the business of day-to-day living. They coincidentally express a very pragmatic view of religious practice: pilgrimages are simply a means to an end. She presents herself as having become quite sensible (at least for the time being):

> Meanwhile, I became distracted by this and that and completely for-got even about the world of the tales. I actually ended up feeling quite down to earth. Over the years and months as I lay down and got up in meaningless activity, why had I not devoted myself to religious practices or pilgrimages? . . . Oh, how crazy I was and how foolish I came to feel. Such were the thoughts that had sunk in, and had I then carried on with my feet on the ground, maybe things would have been all right . . .

In the second passage, she speaks as a householder and, for the first time, as a mother. The "little sprout" she mentions is her first son. She now is more specific about what she wants to achieve in life:

> Now I had come to the point that I was deeply aware of regretting my absurd fancies of the past, and I also could not help recalling with vexa-tion that I had not been taken along on my parents' pilgrimages and such. So now, resolving to concentrate single-mindedly on achieving a state of wealth that would allow me to raise my "little sprout" with all the plentiful care I wished and to accumulate a status for myself that would exceed that of Mikura Mountain, and with aspirations extending to the world to come as well, just past the twentieth of the Eleventh Month, I set off on a pilgimage to Ishiyama Temple.

These passages give the sense of a bustling *mère de famille*. The posi-tive, optimistic tone of these entries is unusual in the diary. Life seems so simple. As long as one makes enough pilgrimages and performs other acts of devotion, one should be able to prosper, and even the life to come need not be a concern. In view of the dark note on which the diary ends, these passages seem naive and even ironic in retrospect.

Nonetheless, the period from her marriage to the death of her husband does seem to have been one of relative peace and security, and these passages reflect that. They also embody the author's existence as an ordinary woman motivated by all the same aspirations and concerns of every other woman. These passages are a very small part of the content of the diary, however. In the next chapter, we examine the first passage again and see that the passage actually sets up the record of her encounter with the courtier Minamoto no Sukemichi, which was anything but ordinary. Moreover, the accounts of her pilgrimages themselves are full of lyrical description and poems that have nothing to do with the pragmatic purposes of the trips.

PERSONA AND SELF-PORTRAYAL

When we look at what is missing from the account of the author's life, we find almost all the things normally considered important to human life: courtship, marriage, birth of children, deaths of parents—all the things that were part of her life and tied her to the fabric of society. Instead of these kinds of milestones in her personal and social life, Takasue no Musume gives priority to her experience of reading, her brief sojourn in Higashiyama, and her encounter with Minamoto no Sukemichi—all aspects of her life that display the strength of her attachment to herself as an individual, independent of life's usual obligations, and, most important, that connect her to a textual world embodied in poetry and tales. When these epsiodes of heightened awareness grounded in a literary sensibility are lined up against the older, wiser narrator's repeated statements that she has wasted her time on poetry and tales, we come back to the same contradiction or paradox noted in the previous chapters. From whichever angle one approaches this diary, a double meaning emerges. On the surface, the narrative voice repeatedly criticizes and denigrates Takasue no Musume's addiction to poetry and tales, but the fact remains that the content of the text as a whole gives priority to those passages intimately related to the enthrallment with poetry and tales. The voice associated with the child's viewpoint reveals not only a fascination for literature but also an individual who lived a rich life of unique experiences. The older narrator's voice speaks for the author as a member of her society, someone like everyone in her contemporary world concerned with their health, success, and salvation in a world to come. We began this chapter speaking of the child's viewpoint as a created "persona" for the author. The older, wiser narrative voice may also be regarded as a persona for the author, who ultimately may be unknowable but who has used these paired personae to give us insight into her life.

NOTES

1. Poem 3360 in the *Kokin rokujō*, a large collection of poetry attributed to Fujiwara no Kintō (966–1041). Although a private rather than an imperially sponsored collection, it circulated widely in the mid-Heian period.
2. Hitachi Province, the greater portion of modern Ibaraki Prefecture, was considered the actual end of the road to the East Country, which was the collective name for all the provinces east of Shiga Province. Strictly speaking, Kazusa is more to the side of that road than beyond the end of it, but the author was aiming more for poetic resonance than geographic accuracy.

5

TEXT AND INTERTEXT

The *Sarashina Diary* and the *Tale of Genji*

THE AUTHOR AS READER

The *Sarashina Diary* secured for its author a place in Japanese literary history as the first "reader" of the *Tale of Genji*, not merely because she recorded reading the tale, but because she communicated how this work affected her life. Takasue no Musume's reading of the *Tale of Genji* was closely intertwined with her reading of other texts as well, especially the *Kagerō Diary* and the *Murasaki Shikibu Diary*, which helped guide her to write the story of her own life. More than any other of the Heian period's autobiographical texts, the *Sarashina Diary* must be considered in relation to the texts that preceded it.

THE *KAGERŌ DIARY*, "OLD TALES," AND THE *TALE OF GENJI*

Takasue no Musume apparently wanted to write a text that was different from the other diaries, and the *Sarashina Diary* can be seen as resisting the *Kagerō Diary*, particularly its critique of fiction.

In the introduction to the *Kagerō Diary*, the oldest diary written in hiragana by a woman, the author, Fujiwara no Michitsuna's mother, states that the *furu monogatari* (old tales) circulating at that time were just "fantasy." To combat that, she declares her intention to compose a diary about her own personal life as a realistic corrective to the old tales.

Although Michitsuna's mother belonged to the middle-ranking aristocracy of the provincial governor class, she was courted by a scion of a much higher ranking branch of the Fujiwara family. Consequently, her life story followed one of the common story lines of the "old tales," the "Cinderella" plot, in which a lower-ranking woman is courted by a high-ranking man, marries him, and lives happily ever after. But unlike the old tales in which marriage to a young nobleman brings good fortune and happiness, the *Kagerō Diary* relates at length the reality of the author's marriage to a high-ranking man, a marriage full of anxiety and emotional suffering. In the light of the facts revealed in the *Kagerō Diary*, it thus becomes clear what Michitsuna's mother considered "fantasy" in the old tales.

It is not hard to imagine that a generation later when Murasaki Shikibu, a kinswoman of Michitsuna's mother, began to conceive of the *Tale of Genji*, it was impossible for her to ignore the criticism of the "old tales" in the introduction to the *Kagerō Diary*. In fact, just a glance at the plots and types of characters in the *Tale of Genji* shows that Murasaki Shikibu was very conscious of the *Kagerō Diary* when she was writing the *Tale of Genji*. For example, most of the marital relationships in *Genji* are followed into the unromantic stages of middle age. Even for characters that play out a scenario of young, pure love, such as Yūgiri and Kumoinokari, special attention is given to the unexpected turns in their later married life. Generally speaking, most of the marital relationships described in the *Tale of Genji* have a bitter aftertaste in common with the feeling generated by the *Kagerō Diary*. Moreover, Murasaki Shikibu took advantage of a new prose style pioneered by the author of the *Kagerō Diary* in which psychological states were described with great realism. It can be said that the *Tale of Genji* succeeded in raising tale literature to a new level because it responded to the critique of fiction in the *Kagerō Diary* as well as borrowing its new and subtle mode of psychological description.

Murasaki Shikibu set forth her own view of *monogatari* (tales) in the "Fireflies" chapter of the *Tale of Genji*. In the passage that became known as her *monogatari ron* (treatise on tales), she employs her protagonist, Genji, to make an argument for the truth of fiction. First, in keeping with his male identity, she has him express the dominant

Confucian view of fiction as a tissue of lies designed to dupe gullible women, but then he shifts to defend fiction:

> The Chronicles of Japan and so on give only a part of the story. It is tales that contain the truly rewarding particulars. . . . Not that tales accurately describe any particular person, rather, the telling begins when all those things the teller longs to have passed on to future generations—whatever there is about the way people live their lives, for better or for worse, that is a sight to see or a wonder to hear—overflow the teller's heart . . . but none of this, good or bad, is removed from life as we know it.[1]

When Murasaki Shikibu has Genji assert that the tales are better than the official histories of Japan for conveying all the particulars of lived reality, she is countering the *Kagerō Diary*'s simplistic criticism of tales as mere "fantasy." We also sense here her conviction and confidence in the success of her own tale in capturing "the way people live their lives, for better or for worse." Then, in the next generation, Takasue no Musume wrote the *Sarashina Diary* to describe her relationship with the *Tale of Genji* as an integral part of her own life.

THE *SARASHINA DIARY*, THE *KAGERŌ DIARY*, AND THE *TALE OF GENJI*

The opening passage of the *Sarashina Diary*—in which Sugawara no Takasue no Musume positions herself as a young girl in the country with a burning desire to read tales—is impressive on its own. But when it is compared with the opening passage of her aunt's *Kagerō Diary*, it makes a startling contrast and speaks volumes about the literary transformation with respect to the relationship between "reading" and "writing" that had taken place in the few decades from the end of the tenth century and the middle of the eleventh century. In one sense, Takasue no Musume can be seen as rejecting the *Kagerō Diary*'s critique of tales. The difference implied at the outset, however, is that Takasue no Musume is living in a very different world from that of Michitsuna's mother, simply because the *Tale of Genji* exists. Takasue no Musume also resists the example of the *Kagerō Diary* in her choice of subject matter for the story of her life. Whereas the *Kagerō Diary* focuses nearly exclusively on the author's relationships with her husband and her only son, Takasue no Musume—albeit a wife and mother herself—writes almost nothing about these relationships. Instead, she centers her story on her life as a reader and a person deeply concerned with the implications of reading for her spiritual development. The *Tale of Genji* is her touchstone for the entire genre of tales, as she finds her relationship to tale literature and specifically to the *Tale of Genji* a sufficient theme for her life's story. Nonetheless, as we noted earlier, the depth of her relationship to literature is a covert theme in the *Sarashina Diary*. On the surface, Takasue no Musume portrays herself in a self-deprecating way as a naive reader.

TAKASUE NO MUSUME'S SELF-DEPRECATION AND THE *MURASAKI SHIKIBU DIARY*

Takasue no Musume's portrayal of herself as a naive reader is, we believe, integral to her conscious construction of herself as an ordinary woman, which we discussed in chapter 4. Her penchant for this kind of self-image is itself related to the *Murasaki Shikibu Diary*, of which she also was an avid reader. In her diary, Murasaki Shikibu adopts a posture of reticence and speaks of hiding her learning and intelligence. For example, when a fellow lady-in-waiting spitefully spreads rumors about Murasaki Shikibu's flaunting her learning, Murasaki retorts: "How utterly ridiculous! Would I, who hesitate to reveal my learning in front of my women at home, ever think of doing so at court?"[2]

A little earlier in her diary, Murasaki referred to the scrutiny of her own serving women and then reconstructed critiques of herself that presumably she had overheard from her fellow ladies-in-waiting at court.

So aware am I of my women's prying eyes that I hesitate to do even those things a woman in my position should allow herself to do. How much more so at court, where I do have many things I wish to say but always think better of it. . . . So I seem to be misunderstood, and they think

that I am shy. . . . I am now known as somewhat of a dullard. "Well, we
never expected this!" they all say, "No one liked her. They all said that she
was pretentious, awkward, difficult to approach, prickly, too fond of her
tales, haughty, prone to versifying, disdainful, cantankerous, and scorn-
ful. But when you meet her, she is strangely meek, a completely different
person altogether!" How embarrassing! Do they really look upon me as
such a dull thing, I wonder.[3]

Sometimes Murasaki Shikibu warns about the dangers of a woman
making a show of herself: "Women who think too highly of themselves
and act in a pretentious and overbearing manner become the object of
attention, . . . and once this happens people are bound to find fault with
whatever they say or do."[4]

Behind all this is the hothouse atmosphere of court, in which criticism could be cruel and petty. Certainly, one's only security was avoiding the spotlight. Nonetheless, over the centuries most readers of the
Murasaki Shikibu Diary have seen in Murasaki's writing precisely the
opposite of what she says she is at pains to hide. For example, it is obvious that she knows she is not really a meek, dull person at all, and
she is amazed that people misinterpret her reserve. In fact, such sharp
critical opinions emanating from her discerning mind and her almost
unsettling powers of observation can be found throughout the diary.
Moreover, just after she says that she hid her learning from even her
own serving women, she reveals that the empress asked her to secretly
help her read Chinese poetry, particularly the "New Ballads" in the *Col-
lected Works of Bai Juyi*. Clearly, Murasaki's efforts to hide her learning
had not fooled the empress. In the same section, she explains how she
acquired such learning by simply listening to her father's lessons to her
younger brother and how much more quickly she understood the Chinese texts than her brother did, to the point that her father was moved
to exclaim, "What a pity she was not born a man!"[5] In this way, she
lets her readers see how much her learning was appreciated by others,
particularly by important others, like her father, the emperor, and the
empress. Key entries in the diary also reveal what a stir the *Tale of Genji*
made at court from its debut and, again, how people of superior status
and sensitivity quickly recognized its brilliance.

In other places in her diary, however, Murasaki appears to express genuine self-doubt about her abilities and accomplishments: "I criticize other women like this, but here is one who has managed to survive this far without having achieved anything of note and has nothing to rely on in the future that might afford her the slightest consolation."[6] Sometimes even her great creation fell short in her own eyes. Shortly after her employer took a copy of her manuscript, she writes, "I tried rereading the *Tale*, but it did not seem to be the same as before and I was disappointed."[7]

Although Murasaki Shikibu seems to advocate a pose of reticence and modesty principally as a survival strategy, hers was not a "false" modesty. It is possible to recognize that one is different from others and endowed with extraordinary gifts and still harbor self-doubt. That self-doubt, the foundation of true modesty, surely results in part from one's ability to appreciate great writing of the past. The writing that Murasaki Shikibu considered as her standard was Chinese poetry, the Chinese classics, and the more than four hundred years of Japanese *waka* poetry, as well as the more recent tale literature.

Takasue no Musume took the *Tale of Genji* and its author's diary as her foundation. From both these texts, she had learned that one must veil one's learning and intelligence in order to survive and also, paradoxically, to be true to them. When she looked at the *Tale of Genji* and the *Murasaki Shikibu Diary* as mirrors, she must have felt ordinary. Here, we admit, we are speculating, because nowhere in the *Sarashina Diary* does Takasue no Musume explicitly compare herself with Murasaki Shikibu or say that she modeled her own self-portrayal on her mentor's, but her reticence makes her conceal so much that she forces her readers to read between the lines.

ALLUSIONS TO THE *TALE OF GENJI* IN THE *SARASHINA DIARY*

Let us return now to textual analysis and what Takasue no Musume reveals in her direct allusions to the *Tale of Genji*. The topic of how she integrates references to the *Tale of Genji* into her own work has stimulated much critical inquiry and debate in Japan. As with other aspects of the work, critical opinion is divided into two camps. One camp sees Takasue no Musume as a superficial reader who did not pay attention to the context of references she makes to the *Tale of Genji*.[8] This position asserts that she extracted what she liked from the text and used it for her own, idiosyncratic purposes. The other camp, represented by Nishida Tomomi, sees a more subtle strategy at work in the author's references to *Genji*.[9]

One example that is cited to support the interpretation of Takasue no Musume as a shallow reader is the "what I wished for" passage, which we examined in some detail in chapter 2, in which she confesses that she desired to be someone like Ukifune and to be visited by someone like Genji. She appears to have intentionally paired her favorite heroine and hero, even though they are characters from completely different parts of the book. Genji dies long before Ukifune appears. Of course, a fan of a work of fiction is free to do such things in his or her daydreams. It is fiction after all, and a person's own imagination can claim the same liberty to invent, but some scholars have even suggested that here Takasue no Musume is exhibiting her ignorance of the structure of *Genji*.[10]

A closer look at this passage, however, reveals another layer of allusion to *Genji*. The phrase "happy to be visited even only once a year by a . . . man . . . like the Shining Genji" evokes the Tanabata myth about the Weaver Maid (Vega) and the Herd Boy (Altair), two stars separated by the Milky Way who are able to meet only once a year. Most important, this passage reminds us of the words spoken by Ukifune's mother on two occasions when she gets a glimpse first of Niou and then of Kaoru, the two high-ranking men who compete in the last five chapters of the *Tale of Genji* to possess Ukifune. While Ukifune's mother herself had had an unfortunate relationship with a man above her station, the Eighth Prince, she is nonetheless dazzled by the two men pursuing her daughter. In a curious reversal of the usual pattern in which a man gets a glimpse through a crack in a woman's blinds, Ukifune's mother gets a peek at both her daughter's suitors in just the same way. This is her reaction to seeing Prince Niou, the more reckless of the two lovers:

Ah, she said to herself, what a wonder he is to behold, and how fortunate she [Ukifune] is to be near him. From a distance one may entertain all sorts of dark thoughts about the terrible things he might do to her, however splendid a man like him may be, but that is foolishness! Just look at him! What an extraordinary privilege it would be to be with him that way just once a year, like Tanabata![11]

While recognizing the vulnerability of a daughter like hers, without a father's backing, she is swept away by Niou's good looks and breeding. A page or two later, she has an opportunity to spy on Kaoru, the more serious of the two men, and her reaction is the same:

"What an absolutely perfect gentleman he is!" The Governor's wife gave voice to her praise and went on again to ponder the idea first brought up and then often repeated by her daughter's nurse. I told her it was out of the question, but now that I have actually seen him, I would gladly have her await the light of that Herdboy Star, even if he has to cross the River of Heaven to reach her. She is just too pretty to give to anyone common.[12]

Ukifune's mother is a well-realized portrait of an "ordinary" woman in the *Tale of Genji*. In many respects, she is pragmatic and able to realistically assess her daughter's slim chances of achieving any lasting happiness in a liaison with either of these high-ranking men. The gap in social status is just too great, and her own experience has taught her that there is nothing to prevent either of them from abandoning Ukifune, just as she herself was cast out by the Eighth Prince. Nonetheless, she remains susceptible to the romantic fantasies encouraged by the idealization of court life in tale literature. One look at these two men, and she is utterly seduced by their outward appearance and refinement, so much so that she would agree to consign her daughter to either of them, even if it meant that her daughter might receive only rare visits.

The allusion to Ukifune's mother's words in Takasue no Musume's phrase "happy to be visited even only once a year by a . . . man . . . like the Shining Genji" is much more subtle than the girlish fan response of imagining her favorite female and male characters together. By injecting Ukifune's mother's foolish reactions into the passage, Takasue no

Musume is reaffirming the foolishness of her own youthful self. But her reaffirmation is based on the point of view of someone who has thoroughly absorbed the *Tale of Genji*. This allusion therefore suggests that the *Tale of Genji* itself is critiquing the romantic illusions it so beguilingly spins. Characters like Ukifune's mother demonstrate the shallowness of the ideal of courtly romance and, at the same time, its tenacious hold on the imagination. Ukifune's mother is a character created to make readers wince and want to admonish, "She should know better." As John Middleton Murry wrote, "A truly great novel is a tale to the simple, a parable to the wise, and a direct revelation of reality to a man who has made it part of his being."[13] Takasue no Musume's reading of the *Tale of Genji* comprehended all three of these dimensions. As a young girl, she read it naively as a seductive tale, the superficial story of her life as a reader. From time to time, she hints that she also recognizes the parables hidden in the *Tale of Genji*, as she does with the allusion to the words of Ukifune's mother. Most of all, however, the great tale had become a part of her being and enabled her to understand herself. But she does not reveal this on the surface of her narrative. Like Murasaki Shikibu, she knew enough to hide her deepest insights.

As evidence to support this assertion, we present an argument based on the structure of the *Sarashina Diary*, one of our book's main themes. A few entries before the "what I wished for" passage, the author devotes much space to the Higashiyama record, which represents her temporary achievement of the desires expressed in the "what I wished for" passage, desires that tantalizingly mix the literary and the erotic. About thirteen or fourteen years later in her narrative, she reprises the gist of the "what I wished for" passage after she has had an opportunity both to serve at court and to marry and, we assume, also bear a child, although she does not record the latter two experiences.

We cited part of this passage in chapter 4, the part in which she declares that she had finally come "down to earth" and regretted having been so distracted by romantic reveries. In the part of that passage not quoted earlier, she says, "After all, was a man like the Shining Genji ever likely to exist in this world? No, this is a world in which being hidden away at Uji by Captain Kaoru could never happen." Once again, Genji is held up as the paragon, and Ukifune's situation of being hidden away in the countryside still stands as a kind of idyll. The similar wording of the two retrospective passages links them together. As we pointed out in chapter 2, the first passage is preceded by a description of a peak experience that actually matched her desires. Interestingly, the second passage is followed by the account of an experience at court that produced one of the golden moments of her life—and also her first poem to be included in an imperial anthology. Her description of that experience contains several significant references to the *Tale of Genji*.

The experience at court is her encounter with the distinguished courtier Minamoto no Sukemichi. Takasue no Musume has been invited back into court service to act as a mentor for her niece, who has just begun court service. She writes how much more relaxed she feels during this second entry into court service. One rainy night in winter, she and a fellow serving woman go up to a gallery where monks "with particularly lovely voices" are chanting a service. Quite by chance, they bump into Minamoto no Sukemichi, although he is not identified by name in the diary account itself. Although the complete account of their interchange is too long to reproduce here, we quote an excerpt containing some of the interplay of allusions to the *Tale of Genji*. This literary interplay helped make this evening a special one for all three of the participants. Shortly after they have made one another's acquaintance, the gentleman launches into a lyrical speech on the beauties of the seasons, and at the end he inquires:

"If I may ask, ladies, with which season would your hearts be lodged?" In response, my companion answered that her heart was drawn to the autumn night, and since I did not want to say the same thing, I replied with this poem:

asa midori	Lucent green—
hana mo hitotsu ni	misting over, becoming one
kasumitsutsu	with the blossoms too;
oboro ni miyuru	dimly it may be seen,
haru no yo no tsuki	the moon on a night in spring.

Repeating this over and over softly to himself, he said, "Well, well, this consigns the autumn night to oblivion, doesn't it?"

koyohi yori	From this night on,
nochi no inochi no	if it should be that my life
moshimo araba	continues on,
sa ha haru no yo wo	I shall always consider the spring night
katami to omohamu	a souvenir of you and this occasion.

Then the person whose heart was drawn to autumn said,

hito ha mina	It would seem that
haru ni kokoro wo	all people's hearts are drawn
yosetsumeri	to spring.
ware nomi ya mimu	Shall I be left to gaze alone
aki no yo no tsuki	at the moon on an autumn night?

It seems that his interest was piqued by this, and yet having the air of finding himself in a difficult situation, he said, "I have heard that even in far Cathay, from ancient times when it came to choosing between spring and autumn, people were unable to decide.

Sukemichi's recitation of the beauties of the seasons in general recalls many such discussions in the *Tale of Genji*, but the first direct allusion to the *Tale of Genji* is made by the woman companion. Despite being first to name her favorite season, autumn, she finds herself left on the sidelines as Takasue no Musume's poem about the spring moon appears to completely capture their visitor's attention. But then the companion brilliantly reinserts herself into the conversation by reworking the following poem from "Bamboo River," chapter 44 of the *Tale of Genji*:

hito ha mina	It would seem that
hana ni kokoro wo	people's hearts have all gone over
utsusuramu	to the blossoms.

> *hitori zo madofu*   All alone I wander
> *haru no yo no yami*   through the spring night's
>   darkness.[14]

The companion adroitly twists this poem about the spring night to defend her championing of the autumn moonlit night. By doing so, she indicates that she is well aware that their shared conversation is like something out of the *Tale of Genji*. Sukemichi then responds in kind by alluding to the iconic conversation about the competing virtues of the four seasons that Genji has with his ward Akikonomu (literally, "Loving Autumn") in chapter 19, "Wisps of Cloud." Genji says:

> People have long weighed the flowering woods of spring against the lovely hues of the autumn moors, and no one seems ever to have shown which one clearly deserves to be preferred. I hear that in China they say nothing equals the brocade of spring flowers, while in Yamato speech we prefer the poignancy of autumn, but my eyes are seduced by each in turn, and I cannot distinguish favorites among the colors of their blossoms or the songs of their birds.[15]

These shared allusions weave the three companions into a harmony of shared sentiment and aesthetic appreciation. After this passage, Minamoto no Sukemichi recalls an episode from his life that etched onto his heart a fondness for clear moonlit winter nights, actually outdoing Genji for his sensitivity in this passage. For Takasue no Musume, who has lived her whole life measuring it against the *Tale of Genji*, this was one time when reality matched fiction. No wonder she devoted so many pages to preserving the experience. In the retrospective passage, she wondered, "Was a man like the Shining Genji ever likely to exist in this world?" A few passages later, she describes an episode in which someone appears who is as good as Genji, maybe even better, at least in regard to his later discreet and moral conduct. In fact, it appears that his rectitude prevents this incident from blossoming into a love affair, as she remarks at the end of the three passages recording all of her contacts with Sukemichi: "Since he was a person of very upright character, he was not one to make prying inquiries as a more worldly

man might, and so time passed and that was it." Nonetheless, unfulfilled and uncomplicated by being tested by "reality" as this encounter
was, the length of its record gives it pride of place in the diary. Takasue
no Musume could not give up her attachment to this memory, which
encapsulated a life experience as engaging as anything she had read
in the *Tale of Genji*. Once again, she undermines the dismissive comments on literature in the retrospective passages, a case of point and
counterpoint.

TAKASUE NO MUSUME'S IDENTIFICATION WITH UKIFUNE

We conclude this chapter with some reflections on the deeper meaning of Takasue no Musume's identification with the character Ukifune
in the *Tale of Genji*. This identification is supported by explicit references to Ukifune, as in the retrospective narrative passages, and by the
numerous subtle allusions to Ukifune, such as the poetic allusion to
Ukifune's country home of Hitachi at the very start of the diary. Other
than confessing to regard Ukifune's situation of being hidden away at
Uji as a kind of idyll, Takasue no Musume never explains why she felt
so drawn to Ukifune. Even her romanticization of Ukifune's reclusion
at Uji contradicts the character Ukifune's own negative feelings about
being, in effect, held captive in the countryside. Ukifune did not choose
to live at Uji; rather, it was Kaoru's way of keeping her out of Niou's
reach. Again, Takasue no Musume places on open display only her
romantic "misreading" of the text.

The congruences between Takasue no Musume and Ukifune become
apparent only when we look at Ukifune's character in general terms.
First, Ukifune is a common girl raised in the East Country. Even though
she has a noble father, the fact that she is never recognized as such
confines her to an obscurity that being raised in the "wild east" only
compounds. Second, perhaps because of her intelligence and sensitivity, she grows up feeling apart from others and withdrawn to the
point of introversion. Her main outlet for self-expression is poetry. Of
all the characters in the *Tale of Genji*, Ukifune writes the most poems

for herself alone rather than to communicate with others. (Most of these poems are in chapter 43, "At Writing Practice.") Ukifune writes to understand herself and her situation; writing is her only power. Third, in the "At Writing Practice" chapter, it is through her own writing that Ukifune also discovers in herself a genuine religious vocation. Several female characters in the *Tale of Genji* take the tonsure to escape social and political pressures, but Ukifune renounces secular life because her tempestuous triangular relationship with Kaoru and Niou has revealed to her the emptiness of the romantic ideal. Once she has escaped that relationship, she has no desire to return to that illusion. Thus limned, it is easy to see how Takasue no Musume could identify with Ukifune.[16]

Takasue no Musume, however, did not need a tumultuous love affair to understand the essential emptiness of courtly romance; instead, she learned this, as well as the seductiveness of that ideal, from reading the *Tale of Genji*. As we have stressed, of all the Heian women diarists, Takasue no Musume evinces the deepest concern for spiritual matters. Her dream at the age of fourteen—at the height of her excitement at finally having the whole of the *Tale of Genji* to herself—in which she is told to memorize roll 5 of the *Lotus Sutra*, takes on extra meaning in this context. This dream stayed with her throughout her life, and perhaps its hidden message was that it was precisely her absorption in the *Tale of Genji* that enabled her to have that dream. In other words, that tale brought her to higher states of realization, both spiritual and aesthetic, realms that were never far apart for her.

NOTES

1. Royall Tyler, trans., *The Tale of Genji* (New York: Viking, 2001), 461.
2. Richard Bowring, trans., *Murasaki Shikibu: Her Diary and Poetic Memoirs* (Princeton, N.J.: Princeton University Press, 1982), 139.
3. Ibid., 135.
4. Ibid.,137.
5. Ibid., 139.
6. Ibid., 133.
7. Ibid., 95.
8. For example, Nomura Seiichi, "*Genji monogatari* to *Sarashina nikki*—Monogatari riarizumu no kaitai," *Kokugo to kokubungaku*, August 1956, 18–28.

9. Nishida Tomomi, "*Sarashina nikki* no hyōgen to hōhō—*Genji monogatari* o megutte," *Kokugo to kokubungaku*, October 1994, 34–46.

10. Noguchi Motohiro, "*Sarashina nikki* to *Genji monogatari*—Sugawara no Takasue no Musume no sakkateki shishitsu," *Jōchi daigaku kokubun gakka kiyō*, January 1985, 10.

11. Tyler, trans., *Tale of Genji*, 984.

12. Ibid., 988.

13. Quoted in Robertson Davies, *Reading and Writing* (Salt Lake City: University of Utah Press, 1992), 27.

14. Abe Akio et al., eds., *Genji monogatari*, Shinpen Nihon koten bungaku zenshū 24 (Tokyo: Shōgakukan, 1997), 73.

15. Tyler, trans., *Tale of Genji*, 359.

16. Edith Sarra, *Fictions in Femininity: Literary Inventions of Gender in Japanese Court Women's Memoirs* (Stanford, Calif.: Stanford University Press, 1999), 132–41.

6

A LIFE COMPOSED IN COUNTERPOINT

MUSICAL METAPHOR

In this last chapter, we return to the issue of structure in the diary and the metaphor of musical counterpoint. As we observed earlier, we believe that the structure of the *Sarashina Diary* was the result of conscious and sophisticated choices by the author. Although the individual units of the autobiographical narrative are engaging on their own, their ordering enables a meta-layer of meaning. Through the repetitions of motifs and the juxtaposition of contrasting elements, Takasue no Musume constructs a complex, multidimensional network of signification. In turn, this pattern of contrasting elements allows her to capture the multiplicity of life experiences in a way that both challenges and complements the linear coherence of the story line sustained by the prose narrative sections. A loosely applied musical metaphor seemed appropriate to us because the alternating structure of the work unfolds in time and makes it seem as though the author has "scored" her piece to provide contrasting tones and leitmotifs. We next examine two of the recurring, oppositional pairs.

East Country and Capital

One contrast is between the East Country (Azuma) and the capital (*miyako*), which is established by the travel section that begins the diary.

Even though Takasue no Musume identifies with the benighted "wild east," she longs for the bright capital in the west portrayed in the tale literature. The first fifth of the *Sarashina Diary* is the account of the author's journey up to the capital, which reiterates the contrast between the East Country and the capital. Upon crossing the Sumida River, the author mentions Ariwara no Narihira's famous poem about the "capital bird," which evokes the feelings of forlornness that noble travelers felt as they crossed barriers that took them farther and farther away from the capital. For example, in the middle of the Ashigara Mountains, the party notices stalks of the *aoi* shrub, associated with the Kamo festival in the capital, and they find it poignant to see this plant growing in the wilderness.

These passages conform to the conventional perception, that the capital is the center of all that is desirable. One thus grows sadder the farther one moves away from it, and small reminders of the capital when one is far away have a nostalgic quality. Some passages, however, counter that conventional view. For example, when the three women entertainers come out of the dark woods in the Ashigara Mountains and members of their audience remark that they were refined enough to serve in noble households in the capital and that "there couldn't be entertainers as fine as these in the West Country," another name for the capital area, the contrast between the refined capital and the wild east is nicely reversed.

The most striking example of this kind of reversal is the retelling of the Takeshiba legend, which occupies a large section of the author's account of her journey to the capital and describes a trip in the reverse direction from the capital down to the East Country. In the story, the daughter of an emperor happens to hear a homesick man on corvée duty from the East Country singing a folk song from his home. Entranced by his song, she calls him close to the veranda and has him repeat it for her. Then on an apparent whim, she orders the man to carry her to the East Country so that she can see it herself. He complies and carries her away. The girl's imperial parents are distraught and send an expedition to bring the girl back. But by the time the delegation arrives, the princess has married the man and has no desire to return to the capital. She says that she finds her new home "very pleasant." Since the damage is irrevocable, the emperor makes the man the governor of the province and grants the offspring of their union the surname Musashi, the name of that province. Scholars have exhaustively examined this episode.[1] It reverses not only expectations with respect to desirable location but also the genders in the courtship romance, as it is the princess who initiates the affair. Moreover, the story has a happy ending, also a reversal in the conventions of court love poetry. In some ways, the princess is the mirror image of Takasue no Musume on her way to the capital. In the construction of this narrative by the author as a mature person, this mirror-image quality must have been pleasing, as it enables a double track of meaning. That is, the Takeshiba legend can be seen to covertly inscribe Takasue no Musume's fondness for her childhood home in the East.

Light and Dark

By far the most frequently recurring contrast in the *Sarashina Diary* is the counterpoint pattern of light and dark. Sometimes the descriptions focus on the simple visual contrast between light and dark—for example, the second poem in the diary composed on the journey up to the capital:

madoromaji	I will not sleep a wink!
ko yohi narade ha	If not for this evening, then when
itsuka mimu	could I ever see this—
kuroto no hama no	Kuroto's black beach beneath
aki no yo no tsuki	the moon of an autumn night.

This is a play on the ironic quality of the place-name Kuroto. As the introduction to the poem indicates, although the beach is named Kuroto (Black Beach), the "sand stretched white into the distance" under the bright moon. It is the vivid visual contrast between the blackness of the night and the bright moonlight that is the focus of the poet's attention and delight.

Images of the moon also are common in the diary, and contrasts of light and dark most often use the moon as the source of light. Often, as with the poem just cited, the moon is connected with feelings of joy and a lightness of mood, though sometimes the emotional mood is dark, and the moonlight serves only to amplify that darkness.

The first time the moon darkens the mood is on the journey up to the capital when Takasue no Musume's nurse, who is about to give birth, must be left behind in a temporary shelter while the traveling party proceeds ahead. When Takasue no Musume visits her to say farewell, the moonlight pours through the reed screens, and she describes the nurse as "bathed in moonlight, . . . lying there in some discomfort. For one in such a state, she was brightly lit and looked white and fair." The disjunction between the nurse's distressed state and the moonlight making her look beautiful increases the unsettling quality of the scene.

Even darker and more ominous is the night after Takasue no Musume's elder sister has died and she places her sister's orphaned infants to sleep on either side of herself. When "the moonlight leaked in and shone on the face of one of the little ones," she covered the child's face with a sleeve and had terrible thoughts. Just a few pages earlier, she described an episode from the year before, when a nearly full moon had shone brightly and she and her sister had sat up all night to admire it. It was a moment of close communion between the sisters as they enjoyed watching a small romantic encounter next door. Yet in the middle of this pleasant scene, her sister remarked, "How would you feel if I were to simply fly away and disappear right now?" Her question strikes fear in Takasue no Musume, and seeing this, her sister changes the subject, but a foreboding remains that is fulfilled by the sister's death a year later. All these scenes are bathed in moonlight but are not conducive to serene feelings.

Further precluding any simple identification of moonlight with joy and darkness with sadness is the fact that some of the most enjoyable and engaging experiences recorded in the diary occur in complete darkness. The three women entertainers emerging out of the dark in the Ashigara Mountains is one. In the dim light of the torches, the skin of the performers looks particularly "white and clean." Light is never so precious as when it is a small spot in the encompassing darkness. The other striking example of this kind of experience is Takasue no

Musume's meeting with the courtier Minamoto no Sukemichi, which takes place on a drizzly winter night. It is so dark that they cannot see one another, and Sukemichi even remarks that this is fortunate because they all would likely feel uncomfortable otherwise. In the darkness, the author and her companion compose poems that evoke, in succession, the spring moon and the autumn moon. Then Sukemichi adds a long account of his visit to the Ise Shrine on a moonlit winter night, which has given him a special affection for the winter moon. The moon shining in the imagination and memories of these three illuminates this scene in a way that the real moon could not.

Only one thing is certain: the symbolic value of the moon in the *Sarashina Diary* is not fixed, any more than that of the darkness itself is. In addition to its symbolic quality, the moon appears to signify something beyond itself, but as with the use of symbols in modern symbolist poetry, the meaning shifts and evades definition.

THE ENDING OF THE *SARASHINA DIARY*

Our survey of examples of the way that light and dark are both conjoined and contrasted in the *Sarashina Diary* prepares us to appreciate the way that Takasue no Musume ends her diary.

As we argued earlier in our discussion of dreams, if the author's only intention had been to narrate a simple story of spiritual progress from youthful romantic delusion to humble faith in old age, it would have made much more sense to end her story with the dream about Amida. But since she did not, we have to assume that she had something else in mind. Accordingly, we contend that the short prose episode and coda of poems that come at the end of her text reflect the complexity of the vision that informs her work. Here is the episode that immediately follows the Amida dream:

> My nephews, whom I had seen day and night when we lived in the same place, had gone off to different places after this regrettably sad event, so I seldom saw anyone. On a very dark night, the sixth youngest nephew came for a visit; I felt this was unusual. This poem came spontaneously:

tsuki mo idede	Not even the moon has
yami ni kuretaru	emerged in the darkness deepening over
wobasute ni	Old Forsaken Woman Peak.
nani tote koyohi	How is it, then, that you
tadzune kitsuramu	have come visiting this night?

"Old Forsaken Woman Peak" is a translation of Obasuteyama—literally, "the mountain where old women are abandoned," a poetic toponym with complex associations. Obasuteyama, in the Sarashina district of Nagano, is famous both for its connection with the folk belief about an ancient custom of abandoning old women and for being a beautiful place to view the moon. *Kokinshū*, poem 878, is the locus classicus for the place-name's association with the moon:

waga kokoro	My heart
nagusamekanetsu	is inconsolable—
sarashina ya	ah, Sarashina!
wobasuteyama ni	Over Old Forsaken Woman Peak
teru tsuki wo mite	I see the moon shining.[2]

This poem was given a narrative context by the *Tales of Yamato* (*Yamato monogatari*), episode 156, in which a man is goaded by his shrewish wife into abandoning his old aunt on the mountain. He carries her there on his back, and when he gets home, he looks out and sees the moon shining over the mountain. Moved by its beauty, his heart is softened; he composes the preceding poem and then goes back up the mountain to carry his old aunt home. The fact that Takasue no Musume took the title for her diary from this allusion to the place-name Sarashina as it appears in both the *Kokinshū* poem and the *Tales of Yamato* is a clear indication that she wanted her readers to be aware of it. To this we should add that the place-name Sarashina had another personal association for Takasue no Musume, of which her contemporary readers also would have been aware. Sarashina and Obasuteyama are in Shinano Province, which was the last posting of her husband and where he fell fatally ill. The place-name Sarashina thus evokes her widowhood.

In his introduction to his translation of the *Sarashina Diary*, Ivan Morris asserts that the title of the work was given by "subsequent copyists and scholars for purposes of identification," but he cites no evidence to support that assertion.[3] We find it very difficult to imagine anyone other than the author coming up with such a subtle and allusive title. Moreover, the implication of the title, "here is the diary of an old widowed woman who was consoled only by the moon," is too self-deprecating and dark to have been invented by a later redactor.

Coming just after the Amida dream in the ordering of the text, this passage and poem as a whole convey the essence of the author's last years. On the one hand, her poem evokes an ever-deepening darkness and solitude that makes the nephew's visit verge on the incomprehensible. Could she even be sarcastically criticizing him: "You come so seldom; why do you bother coming at all?" This poem can seem very bleak. On the other hand, the allusion to the Sarashina poem and story, which unites her beloved genres of fiction and poetry, summons an image of radiance from the memory and imagination of those readers who recognize it. From under a net of darkness, the brightness of the moon and the kindness of kin peek through. With this allusion, darkness and light are again conjoined in a symbolic way that does not permit simple conclusions. At this dark time in her life when she must face loneliness, sickness, old age, and death, the moon still shines, and the story from the *Tales of Yamato* ends with a compassion inspired by beauty. The message she intended her nephew to take away might therefore be reconstructed as "even without the light and inspiration of the moon, you have come visiting your old aunt—how kind."

Takasue no Musume follows this episode with a coda of four poems, each with a short introduction. Although the first two of the poems are separate entries, they form a pair:

And to a friend with whom I had corresponded warmly before but from whom I had not heard since I had come to this pass:

ima ha yo ni	Is it that you think
araji mono to ya	I am one no longer living
omofuramu	in this world of ours?

| *ahare naku naku* | Sadly I cry and cry, |
| *naho koso ha fure* | yet I do indeed live on. |

At the time of the Tenth Month, crying as I gazed out at the exceeding brightness of the full moon:

hima mo naki	Even to a heart
namida ni kumoru	clouded by tears that fall
kokoro ni mo	with no respite,
akashi to miyuru	the light pouring from the moon
tsuki no kage kana	can appear so radiant.

One poem is addressed to a friend; the other is for herself. One speaks of life that continues despite sadness, and the other speaks of the consoling radiance of the moon despite her sorrow. It seems particularly fitting that Takasue no Musume should bring the bright moon into her narrative one last time, since it has functioned as a kind of leitmotif throughout the work, brought in sometimes as a bright, major chord and at other times as a sad, minor chord, and sometimes to sound both at once.

One might be tempted to find a religious meaning in this poem because in the Heian period, the moon was associated with Buddhist teachings and the promise of salvation. An example is Izumi Shikibu's famous poem:

kuraki yori	From darkness
kuraki michi ni zo	onto an even darker path . . .
irinubeki	so must I go,
haruka ni terase	oh, shine on me from afar
yama no ha no tsuki[4]	moon on the mountain's rim.

This poem clearly uses the moon as a metaphor for the light of the Buddha, but Takasue no Musume's poem is not so easily interpreted in that way. The headnote, for instance, indicates that the poem is about the actual moon in the phenomenal world, and the phrase "even to a heart clouded by tears" does not fit well with assigning such a metaphorical meaning to the moon. From a Buddhist point of view, suffering and sorrow in this world are precisely what lead sentient beings to realize the vanity of all sensual pleasures. Accordingly, it would make more sense to say something like *"for the sake of* this heart clouded by tears, the moon shines with such radiance." Here again, as with so many other aspects of this diary, Takasue no Musume has left her meaning slightly obscure.

Having summoned the moon one more time, she closes her diary with two poems that are a conventional trope of darkness, a neglected garden overgrown with mugwort.[5] The prose introduction sums up the time that has passed since her husband's death and then provides the context for her final communication with a nun. As we pointed out earlier, passages containing poems either sent to or exchanged with nuns earlier punctuate the narrative at key points.[6]

The months and years change and pass by, but when I recall that dream-like time, my mind wanders, and it is as though my eyes grow so dark that I cannot recall clearly the events of that time.

Everyone has moved to live elsewhere; only I am left in the old house. One time when I stayed up all night in gloomy contemplation, feeling bereft and sad, I sent this to someone from whom I had not heard for a long time:

shigeri yuku	Mugwort growing
yomogi ga tsuyu ni	ever thicker, sodden
sobochitsutsu	with dew;
hito ni toharenu	a voice sought by no one
ne wo nomi zo naku	cries out all alone.

She was a nun,

yo no tsune no	In the mugwort of a
yado no yomogi wo	dwelling in the everyday world,
omohiyare	please imagine
somuki hatetaru	the dense grasses in the garden
niha no kusa mura	of final renunciation.

Although many Heian-period poems use the image of overgrown mugwort, it may be most famously associated with the character of Suetsumuhana in the *Tale of Genji*. In fact, chapter 15, the second chapter that features Suetsumuhana as the main character, is called simply "Yomogiu" (The Mugwort Patch). Suetsumuhana is a painfully shy and old-fashioned daughter of a deceased prince, who is stubbornly clinging to the shadow of her former life while her house and garden fall into ruin around her. Genji, hearing about her, hoped to find a beautiful flower bud fallen on hard times that he could cause to blossom with his attention. She turns out, however, to be disappointing, incapable of a passionate response to him and even ugly in appearance. Her nickname, Suetsumuhana (Safflower), refers to her long nose, which is red at the tip. The portrayal of Suetsumuhana in the *Tale of Genji* is both comic and poignant. She maintains a fusty dignity, and in the end, Genji does shelter her. In one short passage, Suetsumuhana is shown to be an enthusiastic reader of tales,[7] which fits with Takasue no Musume's self-deprecating identification with Suetsumuhana through the mugwort image, particularly at the end of her life. Most important, this connotation can be regarded as the last understated reference to the tale that has absorbed her throughout her life.

The dominant interpretation of this last set of two poems is that it is an exchange of poems between Takasue no Musume and a nun. Although we basically agree with that interpretation, we also find thought provoking Satō Kazuyoshi's challenge to this viewpoint.[8] Briefly, he contends that Takasue no Musume composed both poems. Note that the second poem of the pair is introduced with only "She was a nun" and not "She was a nun *and replied*." This leaves open the possibility that Takasue no Musume also wrote the second poem. However, Satō's case for Takasue no Musume as the author of this poem is based primarily on his interpretation of the grammar of the original. He argues against the traditional reading, which sees the particle *wo* at the end of the second line as a conjunctive particle. This reading makes "mugwort" a metaphorical and appositive reference by the nun to Takasue no Musume and results in a meaning that could be paraphrased "Oh, you mugwort still living in the vulgar world, please imagine what it is like to have cut off all connection with the world as I have done." In contrast, Satō sees the *wo* as marking "mugwort" as the direct object, which also has the effect of making the grammar flow more naturally into the third line.[9] This would result in the following paraphrased meaning, spoken in the voice of Takasue no Musume herself: "Please imagine my situation as mugwort in the everyday world, you who dwell in the dense grasses of the garden of final renouncement." We find this interpretation interesting because it points again to the open-ended meaning of poetry and the complexity of even the seemingly simple utterances of this text. From our point of view, however, it does not really make much difference whether the speakers in this poem are changed, because the function of these two poems in the text's structural pattern remains roughly the same.

We see Tsukahara Tetsuo's observation as key to appreciating that pattern: "The *Sarashina Diary* is ended for eternity with the juxtaposition of a subjective gush of emotion and an expression of objective restraint."[10] Certainly the first poem registers as a gush of self-pity: "a voice sought by no one cries out all alone." The meaning of the second poem is not so easily summarized, however, particularly because its full meaning can be discerned only in its juxtaposition to the preceding poem. On the one hand, the final poem can be seen as affirming the main narrative line of Takasue no Musume's life story, her progress from delusion to detachment. A voice from the outside, that of a nun, reminds the author of the true letting go that is required by religious commitment. In the original, the phrase "final renouncement" is a verbal expression, *somuki hatetaru* (reaching the ultimate position of going against). That is, to renounce the world, one turns one's back on the natural attachments to family and the ordinary desires for worldly happiness and success. The nun can be seen as chiding the author for her self-pity, which can come only from remaining attached to the world. Throughout the text, the author has placed on the surface of her narrative a display of her shallow understanding of both fiction and religion, but by placing these two last poems together at the end, she signals an affinity with a true religious vocation. In other words, she can be regarded as identifying with the nun's position. In the juxtaposition of "subjective gush and objective restraint," we can see something beyond both those states of mind. In our view, it does not matter whether the last poem is the author's own, asking a nun to imagine her capacity to let go even without taking the tonsure, or a poem from a nun that the author juxtaposes to her own poem to create the same mental space, or even whether the "novelist" author wrote the poem in the voice of the nun; the result is the same. Although the two poems comprise a somber ending, the distant view implied in the second one creates a sense of peace. Once again, seeming opposites (in this case, unendurable pain and calm acceptance) are conjoined and relativized by being positioned next to each other, a final oscillation before the unity of silence.

NOTES

1. Edith Sarra discusses this passage in *Fictions of Femininity: Literary Inventions of Gender in Japanese Court Women's Memoirs* (Stanford, Calif.: Stanford University Press, 1999), 101–8.

2. Okumura Tsuneya, ed., *Kokin waka shū*, Shinchō Nihon koten shūsei (Tokyo: Shinchōsha, 1978), 299. For another translation, see Laurel Rasplica Rodd, trans., *Kokinshū: A Collection of Poems Ancient and Modern* (Princeton, N.J.: Princeton University Press, 1984), 303.

3. Ivan Morris, trans., *As I Crossed a Bridge of Dreams: Recollections of a Woman in Eleventh-Century Japan* (New York: Dial Press, 1971), 23.

4. In the "Grief" section of the imperial anthology *Shūishū* (1005–1011), poem 1342.

5. Mugwort (*Artemisia vulgaris*), also known as common wormwood, has culinary and medicinal uses in many cultures, including Japan, but it is always associated with wild, uncultivated places because it needs no help from human beings to grow and it quickly takes over waste spaces.

6. The first one is after the poems grieving for her sister and was discussed in chapter 2. The second one is just after the Higashiyama record, and the third one comes shortly after the account of the dream of the two-sided mirror.

7. Royall Tyler, trans., *The Tale of Genji* (New York: Viking, 2001), 303.

8. Satō Kazuyoshi, "*Sarashina nikki* saishūka wa 'tasha' no uta ka," *Nihon bungaku*, December 1993, 60–64, and "*Sarashina nikki* uta no saikentō," *Kokugo to kokubungaku*, June 1994, 14–30.

9. Satō, "*Sarashina nikki* saishūka wa 'tasha' no uta ka."

10. Tsukahara Tetsuo, "*Sarashina nikki* sakuhin kōsei—Nigen shiten no kasetsu kenshō," *Kaishaku*, April 1978, 36.

Sarashina Diary

———— ⟡ ————

*A*s a girl raised in the back of beyond, even farther than the end of the road to the East Country,[1] how rustic and odd I must have been. But however it was that I first became enthralled with them, once I knew that such things as tales existed in the world, all I could think of over and over was how much I wanted to read them. At leisure times during the day and evening, when I heard my elder sister and stepmother[2] tell bits and pieces of this or that tale or talk about what the Shining Genji[3] was like, my desire to read these tales for myself only increased (for how could they recite the tales to my satisfaction from memory alone?). I became so impatient that I made a life-size image of the Healing Buddha,[4] and, performing purification rituals when no one else was around, I would secretly enter the room. Touching my forehead to the floor, I would pray with abandon: "Please grant that I should go to the capital as soon as possible where there are so many tales, and please let me get to read all of them." Then the year I was thirteen,[5] a transfer up to the capital did come about, and on the third day of the Ninth Month, we made a preliminary start by moving to a place called Imatachi [Departing Now].[6]

At sunset, a heavy, unsettling fog drifted in and covered the house where I had been so used to playing for years; it was turned inside out with the goods all dismantled and scattered about in preparation for our departure. Looking back, I was so sad to leave behind the Buddha standing there (where I used to go when no one else was looking and touch my forehead to the floor) that, without others knowing, I burst into tears.

The place to which we decamped had no protective enclosures; it was just a temporary thatched hut without even shutters and the like. Bamboo blinds and curtains had been hung. To the south, one could gaze out far in the direction of the moor. To the east and west, the sea was nearby, so fascinating. Since it was wonderfully charming, when the evening mists rose over the scene, I did not fall into even a shallow slumber, so busy was I looking now here, now there. I even found it sad that we were going to have to leave this place. On the fifteenth day of that same month as rain poured out of a dark sky, we crossed the provincial border and stopped at a place in Shimōsa Province[7] called Ikada [Raft].[8] Indeed, the rain fell so hard it seemed as though our

1. Takasue no Musume has been residing in Kazusa Province, which, in the Heian period, occupied the central part of present-day Chiba Prefecture, directly east of Tokyo. See the beginning of chapter 4 for a discussion of how the poetic allusion in the phrase "even farther than the end of the road to the East Country" not only evokes Takasue no Musume's longing for the world of romance but also indicates her lifelong attachment to the *Tale of Genji* as well as her identification with Ukifune, the main character in the last chapters of the *Tale of Genji*.

2. This stepmother, a member of the Takashina family that was noted for its literary accomplishments, was herself a recognized poet and had served at court, where she would have picked up her knowledge of all the popular tales, including the *Tale of Genji*.

3. The Shining Genji is the main hero of the *Tale of Genji*, which was completed slightly more than ten years before the time recorded here. It is clear from this entry that stories from the tale were being transmitted orally years before most people could obtain a copy of the massive work for themselves.

4. The Healing Buddha, Yakushi nyorai. Since the author says literally that she made it herself, she may have made a drawing of the Healing Buddha on a large piece of paper to place on the wall. A statue seems out of the question, but her father may have had one made for her.

5. She is closer to twelve by the Western count, but from here on, we refer to her age by the traditional Eastern count. The year is 1020 in the Western calendar. Thanks to the mention of her age here, Takasue no Musume is the only Heian woman author for whom we have a firm year of birth.

6. It was the custom in the Heian period to start journeys on astrologically auspicious days or from auspicious directions, which usually necessitated removal to a nearby temporary lodging from which the actual trip could begin. The author is playing with the place-name Imatachi (literally, "Departing Now"). Making wordplays on place-names is a feature of Ki no Tsurayuki's *Tosa Diary*, and it is likely that Takasue no Musume is emulating his practice.

7. In the Heian period, Shimōsa Province occupied the northern end of Chiba Prefecture.

8. This is another instance of the author's making puns on place-names. Although there is no record of a place in the area they are passing through called Ikada (Raft), today there is a place-name Ikeda in the same area. If that place-name has a longer currency than records show, either its original pronunciation was Ikada or the author altered the place-name to create the pun. Or she may have invented the place-name for the wordplay. No matter which, the context indicates that she wanted her readers to understand the pun here.

little hut might float away. I was so frightened that I could not sleep a wink. In the middle of the moor was a place with a small hill on which only three trees were standing. We stayed the day there, drying out the things that had been soaked in the rain and waiting for the others in our party who had got off to a later start.[9]

We left early on the morning of the seventeenth. Long ago, a man named Manoshitera[10] lived in Shimōsa Province. We crossed by boat a deep river where it is said there are the remains of the house where he had tens of thousands of bolts of cloth woven and bleached. The four large pillars standing in the river's flow apparently were the remnants of his old gate pillars. Listening to the others recite poems, I composed to myself,

kuchi mo senu	Not rotted away,
kono kaha bashira	if these pillars in the river
nokorazu ha	did not remain,
mukashi no ato wo	how could we ever know
ikade shiramashi	the traces of long ago?

That night we stayed at a place called Kuroto [Black Beach].[11] On one side was a wide band of hills, and where the sand stretched white into the distance, groves of pine grew thickly; the moon was shining brightly; the sound of the wind was thrilling and unsettling. Moved by the scene, people composed poems. I composed this:

madoromaji	I will not sleep a wink!
ko yohi narade ha	If not for this evening, then when
itsuka mimu	could I ever see this—
kuroto no hama no	Kuroto's black beach beneath
aki no yo no tsuki	the moon of an autumn night.

We left there early the next morning and stopped at a ferry landing called Matsusato[12] on the upper reaches of a river on the border of Shimōsa and Musashi called Futoigawa [Broad River];[13] the whole night through, our goods were ferried across by boat. My nurse, whose husband had died, was about to give birth here at this border, so we

9. The move of a provincial governor would not have been a small affair. The entire party likely contained forty or fifty people, including armed guards and servants. Part of the party would bring up the rear with extra provisions.

10. This transcription is based on what appears in Fujiwara no Teika's copy of the manuscript. Manoshitera is an unlikely personal name, and modern commentators, such as Akiyama Ken in the Nihon koten shūsei (NKS) version, have revised this to Mano no Chō (a wealthy man named Mano). See Akiyama Ken, ed., *Sarashina nikki*, Shinchō Nihon koten shūsei (Tokyo: Shinchōsha, 1980), 15.

11. This place-name does not correspond to any present-day place. There is some conjecture that it might be Kurosuna (Black Sand) in Chiba Prefecture. Geographically, it would make more sense if it were the Tsudanuma Makuhari area in the present-day prefecture. There also is a disjunction between the name that contains the color black and the fact that she describes the sand as white. For the author, it was likely the contrast itself between the black in the name and the actual moonlit white sand that created an interesting irony.

12. Matsusato likely corresponds to present-day Matsudo City.

13. This would be the lower reaches of the river now known as the Edo River. It is not this river, however, that marked the boundary between Shimōsa and Musashi Provinces but the Sumida River, which is mentioned later. The author either is mistaken about the geography or had a literary reason for wanting to place the Sumida River later in her narrative.

were to leave her behind and go on up to the capital.[14] Since I loved
her so much, I wanted to visit her, so my elder brother[15] carried me on
horseback to her side. It could be said that our whole party was staying
in temporary huts with only curtains hung up to try to keep the wind
out, but because she had no husband accompanying her, this shelter
for my nurse was ineptly constructed and rude. It had only one layer
of reed screens that had been woven together; the moonlight poured
in. She was covered with a scarlet robe and, bathed in moonlight, was
lying there in some discomfort. For one in such a state, she was brightly
lit[16] and looked white and fair. Moved by the rarity of the moment, she
stroked my hair and cried. Although I found it painful to abandon her,
I could not help feeling pressed to return; my regrets were hard to bear.
I was so sad when I recalled her face that, not even feeling anything for
the beauty of the moon, I lay down in a gloomy frame of mind.

The next morning, the carts were lashed to boats and ferried across
and then pulled up onto the other bank; those who had sent us off to
this point all turned back.[17] We who were going up to the capital halted
until those returning were no longer in sight; those going and those
staying behind all were in tears. Even my young heart felt this very
poignantly.

So now we were in Musashi Province.[18] There was nothing especially charming to be seen. There was no white sand on the beaches.
It seemed very muddy, and although there was a moor on which I had
heard the purple-rooted gromwell[19] grew, there were only tall rushes
and reeds growing so thickly and so high that one could not even see the
tips of the bows of those mounted on horses. Parting our way through
its midst, we went along and came to a temple called Takeshiba. In
the distance there were the remains of buildings in Hahasō.[20] When I
asked, "What kind of a place is this?" someone told this story:

"Long ago there was a place here called Takeshiba Slope. A man
from this area was sent to be a fire keeper for the palace's fire huts.[21]
Once when he was sweeping the imperial garden, he murmured to
himself this complaint: 'Why, oh why, have I met such a cruel fate?

On the seven, on the three,
saké vats of my home country

14. The nurse must be left behind not only because her confinement prevents her from traveling but also because the taboo associated with blood in the birthing process would result in defilement and require a ritual seclusion for the entire travel party. Of course, the nurse will not be left all alone but will have some attendants.

15. It is assumed that she is referring to her eldest brother, Sugawara no Sadayoshi (1002?–1064).

16. Our translation follows a different interpretation from that in Akiyama, ed., *Sarashina nikki*, 17. Akiyama is following a tradition of reading the text as "for a person such as this, it seemed excessive"; in other words, the beauty of the moonlit scene seemed somehow inappropriate for someone of the nurse's status. This reading interprets the verb in the utterance as *sugite*, although it is written in the original manuscript as *sukite*. Voiced sounds were normally not marked in medieval manuscripts. We would prefer to leave it as *sukite* (being brightly lit) and taking the *sa yau no hito ni ha* literally (for a person in that state), referring not to the nurse's social status but to her current state of dishabille and physical discomfort. An absence of concern about the social status of people in the account is a notable characteristic of the *Sarashina Diary*.

17. The Kazusa provincial office staff would have accompanied the returning governor's party this far and then would have returned to the provincial seat to serve the new governor.

18. In the Heian period, Musashi Province covered most of the area now occupied by the city of Tokyo.

19. Musashino (Musashi Moor) was an *utamakura* (poem pillow), a place-name with associations created by famous poems of the past. Poem 867 in the *Kokinshū* fixed the connection between the place-name Musashino and the gromwell (*murasaki*), a wild perennial from which a purple dye was obtained: *murasaki no hitomoto yuwe ni/musashi no no/kusa ha minagara/ahare to zo miru* (Because of this single/purple root of the gromwell,/all the wild grasses/across Musashi Moor/arouse a sigh as I gaze). A knowledge of these poetic place-names and their associations was essential for poets of the Heian period. See Edward Kamens, *Utamakura, Allusion, and Intertextuality in Traditional Japanese Poetry* (New Haven, Conn.: Yale University Press, 1997). Although this is the first of several poetic place-names that Takasue no Musume mentions on her journey up to the capital, she rarely composes a poem on them. Often, as here, she signals her knowledge of the famous place but remarks on the discrepancy between the scene before her eyes and the expectations aroused by the place-name's associations. From here on, notes on *utamakura* place-names and their principal associations follow Yōichi Katagiri's dictionary, *Utamakura, utakotoba jiten* (Tokyo: Kasama shoin, 1999).

20. Over the centuries, the place-name here, Hahasō, has puzzled commentators. The *sō* part of the name is usually taken to mean *shōen*, or estate, an extensive parcel of tax-free land. In the ninth century, many such grants were made to the imperial household or individual members of the imperial family. See Dana Morris, "Land and Society," in *The Cambridge History of Japan*, vol. 2, *Heian Japan*, ed. Donald H. Shively and William H. McCullough (New York: Cambridge University Press, 1999), 224–26. The Takeshiba legend related after this involves a case in which estate land held by the imperial house is transferred to a princess.

21. Fires were maintained in special huts on the grounds of the imperial palace to make live coals available for small braziers and cooking tasks. The estate would have provided rotating manpower for this task, among others, at the imperial palace.

lie straight handles
of gourd ladles.
South blows the wind,
they drift to the north;
north blows the wind,
they drift to the south;
west blows the wind,
they drift to the east;
east blows the wind,
they drift to the west.[22]

None of which I see, just stuck here like this.' At that moment, the emperor's daughter (a much treasured person) was standing by herself at the edge of the bamboo blinds. Leaning against a pillar, she gazed out and was much moved by the serving man's solitary complaint. What kind of gourd ladles were they? How did they drift one way and another? Becoming curious about this, she raised the bamboo blinds and summoned him, 'You over there, come here.'[23] When, full of trepidation, he came over beside the balustrade, she ordered him, 'That which you just spoke, repeat it one more time for me.' And so he repeated the words about the saké vats one more time. At this point, she ordered him, 'Take me there and show me these things; I have a reason for saying so.' Although he felt terribly afraid (was this not something fated to happen?),[24] he carried her on his back down to his home country. Now, thinking that surely they would be followed, that night he set down the princess at the foot of the Seta Bridge[25] and destroyed a whole section of it. Leaping back over it, he hoisted the princess on his back, and seven days and seven nights later,[26] they arrived in the province of Musashi.

"The emperor and empress were distraught when they realized the princess had disappeared. When they searched for her, someone said, 'There is a man servant, a fire keeper from the province of Musashi, who flew away with a very fragrant bundle around his neck.' When they inquired after this man servant, he was gone. Surely he must have returned to his home province, they thought. But when the members of the court's envoy expedition who were chasing after him found the

22. This appears to be a folk song from his home region. It speaks of ladles for scooping saké that were made from splitting a dried bottle gourd so that the narrow part of the gourd formed a straight handle. These ladles are light and float on the surface of the vats. Their moving to and fro freely in response to the wind arouses a happy feeling that is also associated, of course, with the pleasurable anticipation of drinking the saké.

23. The preceding section describes behavior that was unthinkable for a princess or any noblewoman of the author's time.

24. The phrase in parentheses functions as the storyteller's interjection explaining why such an unusual thing should happen despite the impropriety of the situation and the man's own fearful reservations. Karmic predestination explains everything.

25. The Seta Bridge crossed the narrow eastern neck of the Lake Biwa part of the main road to the East Country.

26. Even at the fastest possible pace on foot, this journey would take more than two weeks.

Seta Bridge broken, they could not continue. Three months later, when they arrived in Musashi and found this man servant, the princess summoned the imperial envoy into her presence and made the following pronouncement: 'I, for it seems to have been meant to be, became very curious about this man's home, and when I said, "Take me there," he brought me here. I find it very pleasant here. If this man is punished for having committed a crime, then what about me? For me to have sought out this country must be a fate determined in a former existence. Quickly return to the court and report what has happened.' There was nothing he could say, so the envoy went back up to the capital and reported to the emperor, 'It is such and so.' It was useless to say anything; even if this man had committed a crime, it was not as though the princess could be removed now and brought back to the capital. So, the emperor issued a proclamation putting the Takeshiba man in charge of Musashi Province for as long as he lived and exempted the province from public taxes and corvée duties, in effect making the princess the patron of the province. At that time, the man's house was converted to a palace. Now, this house where the princess lived was turned into a temple after she passed away, and that is why it is called Takeshiba Temple. All the children born to the princess were given the surname Musashi, just like that. From that time forward, it is said that the imperial palace fires were attended by women."[27]

There was nothing in particular to note as we passed through rushes and reeds, over moors and hills. Between the provinces of Musashi and Sagami is a river called Asuda (this is the river called Sumida in the *Ariwara Middle Captain Collection*),[28] and where as he crossed it, he composed the poem "Then I would ask you something . . ."[29] When we crossed over it by boat, we were in Sagami Province.[30]

The mountains of a place called Nishitomi[31] look like beautifully painted screens standing in a line.[32] On one side was the sea, and the lay of the beach, as well as the waves rolling in, was terribly lovely. At a place called the "Chinese Plains,"[33] the sand was amazingly white, and it took two or three days to pass by. Someone remarked, "In summer, Japanese pinks bloom all over here; it looks like lengths of brocade in deep and pale colors. But since it is the end of autumn, we can't see them." Nonetheless, still here and there were specks of color where

27. For a discussion of the Takeshiba legend, see chapter 6.

28. This is a reference to the personal poetry collection of Ariwara no Narihira (825–880).

29. The episode and the poem are included in the *Tales of Ise*, episode 9, and in the *Kokinshū*, poem 411. The poem's headnote records that it was written when Narihira was crossing the Sumida River and was told that the birds he saw were called "capital birds": *na ni shi ohaba / iza koto tohamu / miyakodori / waga omofu hito ha / ariya nashiya to* (If your name be true, / then I would ask you something. / Say, Capital birds, / of the one who has my heart: / does she live or has she died?) (Joshua Mostow and Royall Tyler, trans., *The Ise Stories: Ise Monogatari* [Honolulu: University of Hawai'i Press, 2010], 36). This poem created the poetic associations regarding the Sumida River.

30. The geographical information in this passage is incorrect. As mentioned earlier, the Sumida River actually marked the border between Shimōsa and Musashi Provinces, not between Musashi and Sagami. This passage either reveals the author's geographical ignorance or is a case of poetic license. The citation of the *Tales of Ise* episode can be interpreted as working better here than it would have in the previous section about the Futoigawa. By invoking Narihira's "capital bird" poem here, Takasue no Musume conveys the meaning that just at this point of crossing the river, she feels as though she is leaving her East Country home behind in the same way that crossing the Sumida River made Narihira aware that his home in the capital was now far behind him.

31. The exact location of this place-name is uncertain. There are two places with the name Nishitomi in the general area, one closer to the mountains and one closer to the sea. From the description, it seems that the Nishitomi closer to the sea is more probable, which would place it near present-day Fujisawa City.

32. The mention of screen painting is significant. In this era, *waka* poems often were composed to be placed onto screen paintings. The screen paintings themselves became interpretive filters for the landscape.

33. The place-name Chinese Plains must roughly correspond to the whole Ōiso region in present-day Kanagawa Prefecture, since it was a large area that took two or three days to cross.

they bloomed charmingly. "How about that, on the Chinese Plains, Japanese pinks are blooming all around." People found this amusing.[34]

The mountains called Ashigara loomed menacingly on the horizon for four or five days.[35] Once we entered the foothills, we could not even see the complexion of the sky clearly, and the trees were indescribably thick; how frightening it was! On a dark night with no moon, when anyone would lose his way in the darkness, out of nowhere appeared three women entertainers.[36] One was about fifty, one about twenty, and the other about fourteen or fifteen. In front of our lodging they set up a large umbrella and sat down. When our servants brought torches so that we could see, one of them said, "We are the descendants of the famous Kohata of the old days." The women's hair was very long with lovely sidelocks hanging down; their skin was white and clean. Much impressed, people said, "They hardly seem suited to this sort of life. Why, they would not be out of place as maidservants for the nobility." The women's voices were incomparable as they sang wonderful songs that seemed to ring clear in the sky. We all were very moved and had the women move closer, so excited we were. When they overheard someone say, "There couldn't be entertainers as fine as these in the West Country," they sang in a splendid way: "When you compare us with those of Naniwa . . ."[37] Their appearance was unsullied, and when they sang, their voices could not be matched. When they rose to go back into the mountains that were so menacing, everyone regretted their going and broke into tears. In my young heart, I regretted even that I would have to leave this temporary lodging.

At the first light of dawn, we crossed the Ashigara Mountains. There is no way to describe how even more frightening it was to be in the middle of them. Why, the clouds—we walked upon them. Right in the middle of the mountains in a small space under the trees were just three stalks of the *aoi* shrub.[38] When someone said, "Here in a place like this isolated from the world, I wonder how it has managed to grow," people found it very poignant. The river of that mountain flows in three branches.

Finally we crossed those mountains and stopped at the mountain barrier station. From here on, we were in the province of Suruga.[39] Beside the Yokohashiri Barrier[40] was a place called Iwatsubo [Rock Basin].

34. The play on the names containing Japanese and Chinese is amusing because the intertwining of Chinese and Japanese cultural elements was so much a part of Heian literary culture.

35. This range of mountains extends north from the Hakone range and, in the Heian period, was the border between Sagami and Suruga Provinces. The main route to the East Country passed through this mountain range. Again, however, the geographical information conveyed by the text appears to be inaccurate. It seems unlikely that, even at a snail's pace, the profile of that mountain range would be visible for that long; perhaps it only seemed that long. Ashigara was an *utamakura* associated with travel and barriers.

36. The women are *asobi*, itinerant female entertainers who performed dance and *imayō* (modern-style) songs. This is the first of three descriptions of female entertainers. The *Sarashina Diary* is the only one of the women's diaries of the Heian period to devote so much attention to these women performers of lowly status.

37. The singers improvise a song about being compared with the entertainers of Naniwa, present-day Osaka, and therefore the West Country. Because the West Country was the region of the capital, it always connoted higher quality. The itinerant performers are flattered by this favorable comparison and make a quick-witted response.

38. Branches of the *aoi* plant are used as decorations for the Kamo Festival in Kyoto and therefore refer to the splendor and liveliness of the capital at festival time. The name *aoi* (or *afuhi* in the old spelling) is also understood as a pun for "meeting day" and evokes romantic affairs. To find just a few stalks of the plant in the isolated mountains strikes the party as incongruous and touching. It is the author's special touch to record that there were exactly three stalks, which gives a feeling of immediacy to her account.

39. In the Heian period, Suruga Province occupied the central part of present-day Shizuoka Prefecture.

40. The Yokohashiri Barrier is the name of the mountain barrier mentioned in a general way at the beginning of this entry. Although its exact location is no longer known, it was somewhere in the mountains on the upper reaches of the Sakawa River. Barriers like this one were established at the borders of provinces and other strategic points to check the identification of travelers and sometimes levy tolls. Some of the barrier names acquired poetic connotations from their use in poetry, but Yokohashiri was not one of them. It was included, however, in Sei Shōnagon's list of barrier names in Ivan Morris, trans., *The Pillow Book*, 2 vols. (New York: Columbia University Press, 1967), 1:123.

In the middle of an amazingly large, square rock was an opening from which flowed water that was extremely cold and clear.

Mount Fuji is in this province. It is the mountain we could see to the west of the province that I grew up in. It looks like nothing else in the world. Among its unusual features are that its flanks are as though painted a deep indigo blue; and since snow always covers its summit, it is as though someone is wearing a white short robe over an indigo gown; and from the mountain's slightly flat top, smoke rises. At dusk, one can even see flames shooting up.[41]

Because the sea and several buildings are on one side of the Kiyomi Barrier,[42] the station forms a crossbar up against the sea.[43] Might smoke be rising to meet smoke?[44] I thought; the waves at the Kiyomi Barrier seem to be high indeed. It is an endlessly fascinating sight.

At Tago Bay, the waves were high, and we rowed around in a boat.[45]

At the river called Ōi, there is a ford.[46] The water of that river is unusual; it is as though a lot of rice flour has been dissolved in it, and the white water flows very rapidly.

The Fuji River is so named because its water flows down from Mount Fuji. A person from that province came out and told us the following story:

"One year some time ago, when it was very hot, I sat down to rest by the edge of this river and saw a yellow object coming down in the river's current. It caught on something and when I looked at it, I discovered that it was discarded paper. I picked it up and noticed that there was formal writing in deep red ink on the yellow paper. Thinking this very strange, I read what was there and found that it contained the names of those to be promoted to provincial governor in the next year's round of appointments.[47] Our province's governorship was coming vacant that year, and on the spot noting the governor's name, two names were side by side. Thinking this strange and unsettling, I took the paper with me, dried it, and put it away. Then, sure enough, in the next year's appointments, the person who became governor of this province was indeed the same as the first name written on the paper. Within three months, that person died, and the one who replaced him was the man whose name was written beside the first. There are such things in the world. From this we know that each year, the many gods

41. Mount Fuji was an active volcano in the ninth century but subsided by the beginning of the tenth century. It became active again around 1020, the very year of Takasue no Musume's journey to the capital. Mount Fuji was one of the most famous *utamakura* on the journey between the East Country and the capital. Using the mountain as a metaphor for "smoldering love" was the preferred theme for poetry on Mount Fuji. Instead of writing a poem on that codified theme, Takasue no Musume provides an evocative description of the mountain in front of her.

42. The Kiyomi Barrier was not yet a well-established *utamakura* when Takasue no Musume passed through it, but it was a scenic spot with a view of the open sea, the mountains of the Izu Peninsula to the southwest, and Mount Fuji to the northwest. Seiken Temple in Shizuoka Prefecture apparently was constructed on the site of the Kiyomi Barrier.

43. The barrier buildings seem to have been built up against the sea, so when approaching them from the land, they appeared to have been etched against the background of the sea.

44. This poetic expression looks like the citation of a line from an old poem, but a source has not been identified. It expresses a situation in which the foam from the waves is seen to rise up to meet the smoke from Mount Fuji's summit.

45. Tago Bay had been an important *utamakura* since the Nara period. In the mid-Heian period, this place-name was closely associated with poem 489 in the *Kokinshū*: *suruga naru / tago no uranami / tatanu hi ha / aredomo kimi wo / kohinu hi ha nashi* (In Suruga / at Tago Bay, even though / there are days when / the waves do not rise, never is there / a day when I do not long for you). Contrary to the general statement in the old poem, on the day Takasue no Musume was there, the waves were high.

46. In the Heian period, the Ōi River marked the boundary between Suruga and Tōtōmi Provinces.

47. The assignment of provincial governorships was made twice a year, once in the spring and once in the autumn.

gather on Mount Fuji and decide the appointments for the next year. It is an amazing thing."

We had passed uneventfully through the place called Numajiri,[48] but after that I fell seriously ill as we entered Tōtōmi Province.[49] I was barely aware of crossing Saya no Nakayama[50] and other places. Since I was in such pain, a temporary shelter was prepared [for me] by the side of Tenchū River,[51] and after staying there for as long as several days, I gradually recovered. As winter was deepening, the wind off the river continuously blew fiercely; I found it difficult to bear.

Crossing over that river, we arrived at Hamana Bridge.[52] On our trip down to the provinces, the Hamana Bridge had been a rough hewn structure of logs, but now, since not a trace of it was to be seen, we had to cross by boat. The bridge had been built over a shallow inlet of the sea. This time, out beyond on the open ocean, it was very rough and the waves were high. The only things growing profusely on the barren sandbanks at the mouth of the inlet were pine trees; from between these pines, the waves surged and receded. Looking like iridescent jewels, it truly seemed as though the waves were sweeping over the tips of the pines—fascinating![53]

Farther along from this point on the route, we had an indescribable struggle climbing up the slope called Inohana,[54] and then we arrived in Mikawa Province[55] at a place called Takashi Beach.[56]

Only the place-name Yatsuhashi [Eight Bridges] remains; there is not the merest remnant of any bridges, and nothing else to see, either.[57]

We stayed one night in the middle of the Futamura Hills.[58] Our servants built us a shelter there under the branches of a large persimmon tree. All night long, persimmons fell down on the roof of the shelter and people gathered them up.[59]

When we crossed the mountain called Miyaji [Imperial Way],[60] even though it was the end of the Tenth Month, the crimson maple leaves were at their best; none of them had scattered.

arashi koso	It seems even storms
fukikozarikere	stay away and do not blow on

48. There is no surviving record of Numajiri.
49. In the Heian period, Tōtōmi Province occupied the western part of Shizuoka Prefecture.
50. Saya no Nakayama (Saya's Middle Mountain) was an *utamakura* associated with difficult travel.
51. The Tenchū River is the present-day Tenryū River.
52. Another *utamakura* in Tōtōmi Province, the Hamana Bridge was built over an outlet from Hamana Lake into the sea. Poems about the bridge usually focused on mist and fog, which were depicted as "crossing" the bridge.
53. Once again, Takasue no Musume ignores the codified connotations of the *utamakura*, which in this case were mist and fog. Instead, since she passed the place on a sparkling clear day, she uses the scene to deepen her appreciation of a famous poetic hyperbole, which had its source in poem 1093 in the *Kokinshū*: *kimi wo okite/adashi gokoro wo/waga motaba/sue no matsuyama/nami mo koenan* (If I had/a fickle heart and set you aside,/then the sea waves would/sweep over the pines/of Mount Sue). In this case, however, her attention is captivated not by the hyperbole as a means to describe something that could never happen but by the fact that thanks to the topography, she is actually seeing waves surging over the tips of pine trees.
54. Inohana was a barrier conjectured to have been in the Araichō area of the Hamana District of Shizuoka Prefecture.
55. In the Heian period, Mikawa Province occupied the eastern part of present-day Aichi Prefecture.
56. Takashi Beach is in the southeastern section of the present-day town of Toyohashi in Aichi Prefecture.
57. There is a memorial place marker for this place-name in present-day Chiryū City in Aichi Prefecture. Because of the poem in episode 9 of the *Tales of Ise*, this is one of the most famous of all *utamakura*. The poem was said to have been written by Ariwara no Narihira on his way to a self-imposed exile in the East Country. At this place, he recorded the existence of eight bridges over the spiderlike arms of a river. Irises were growing there in great profusion, so someone suggested that Narihira compose an acrostic poem in which each line would start with one of the syllables for the Japanese name for irises, *kakitsubata*. He wrote a touching poem about missing his wife, who was as familiar to him as his well-worn travel robe. See Mostow and Tyler, trans., *Ise Stories*, 32–33. Even though the bridges and irises apparently did not survive for later generations, it became de rigueur when passing this place to write a poem recalling Narihira's account, but here again, Takasue no Musume ignores that imperative.
58. The Futamura Hills are likely the hilly area in the Kutsukake District of present-day Toyoake City.
59. Persimmons are almost never mentioned in the aristocratic literature of the Heian period, so this reference stands out and gives a sense of the freshness of the author's outlook.
60. Imperial Way Mountain is in the Hoi District of Aichi Prefecture. The author's poem expresses the orthodox sentiment that even storms will respect the imperial connection in the name. This poem was selected for the "Winter" section of the imperial anthology *Gyokuyōshū* (1313), poem 891. Interestingly, this is another place where the geographical order of the place-names is out of order. Futamura actually comes after the Imperial Way rather than before, although this error in geography makes for a smoother literary account. That is, it sounds better to have a place-name like the Imperial Way occurring closer to the capital.

miyadjiyama	Imperial Way Mountain;
mada momidjiba no	the crimson maple leaves
chirade nokoreru	remain unscattered.

At the Shikasuga Ford between the provinces of Mikawa and Owari,[61] it was amusing to think that truly, one could be bewildered as to whether to go or return.[62]

In Owari Province, where we were to pass by Narumi Bay,[63] the evening tide kept coming in while we were wondering whether to try to stay there that night, but then we thought that if the tide were to continue rising, we might not be able to get by at all, so the whole company hurried by the place in some disarray.[64]

On the border of Mino Province,[65] we crossed at a ford called Sunomata[66] and finally arrived at the place called Nogami.[67] At that place, many female entertainers appeared and sang the whole night through. I could not help recalling our experience at Ashigara and was moved with the strongest longing.[68]

Beset by a heavy snowfall, with our sensibilities numbed, we crossed Atsumi Mountain and through the Fuwa Barrier.[69] In Ōmi Province,[70] we stayed for four or five days in the residence of a person called Okinaga.[71]

At the foot of Mitsusaka Hill,[72] winter drizzle mixed with hail fell for a day and a night; the sunlight was dim; and it was very gloomy.

After leaving there, we passed without incident through places called Inukami,[73] Kanzaki,[74] Yasu,[75] and Kurumoto.[76] The lake spread out before us into the distance, and we could see the islands called Nade[77] and Chikubu.[78] It was very fascinating. The Seta Bridge[79] had completely collapsed, so we had difficulty crossing there.

We stopped at Awazu,[80] and on the second day of the Twelfth Month,[81] we were to enter the capital. In order to arrive in the dark, we started out in the late afternoon.[82] Close to the barrier,[83] from above some temporary screening next to the mountain, we could see only the roughly carved face of the Buddha,[84] about one *jō*, six *shaku*, in height.[85] I gazed at it as we went by, thinking, "How touching, a Buddha here, not really anywhere and far away from people."

61. The border between Mikawa and Owari Provinces is now in the western part of Aichi Prefecture.
62. Shikasuga was a ford at the mouth of the Toyo River. The place-name Shikasuga is homophonous with the expression *shikasuga ni* (That's so, however), and it became an *utamakura* thanks to a poem written by a mid-Heian court woman, Nakatsukasa (920?–980), which makes a pun on the two meanings: *yukeba ari/yukaneba kurushi/shikasuga no/watari ni kite zo/omohi wadzurafu* (Whether I cross or not,/it will be painful,/here I have come indeed/to the "That's So, However" Ford,/and I am troubled). This was included as poem 29 in her personal poetry collection, the *Nakatsukasashū*. It was knowledge of this poem that gives rise to the author's comment on this place.
63. Narumi Bay was in the area of present-day Nagoya City, Narumi machi. The area is now reclaimed land, but apparently in the Heian period, the great differences between high and low tide here used to cause troubles for travelers.
64. This brings to an end the record of places in Mikawa Province. As noted, some of the places are not in the correct order. The geographically correct order for the place-names would be Inohana, Takashi Beach, Shikasuga Ford, Imperial Way Mountain, Eight Bridges, Futamura, and Narumi.
65. In the Heian period, Mino Province occupied the southern part of present-day Gifu Prefecture.
66. The ford was near the Anpachi District of Gifu Prefecture. The Sunomata River is the present-day Nagara River.
67. Nogami was in the present-day Sekigahara chō area of the Fuwa District of Gifu Prefecture.
68. As mentioned earlier in regard to the first episode involving the female entertainers appearing out of the darkness in the Ashigara Mountains, the affinity that this sheltered daughter of a noble family feels for itinerant entertainers is quite unusual in the context of the time.
69. The Fuwa Barrier was in the Seki ga Hara chō area of the Fuwa District, but the location of Atsumi Mountain is uncertain.
70. Ōmi Province is present-day Shiga Prefecture.
71. The Okinaga family was an ancient and powerful family in the Ōmi District. Their host was likely Okinaga Masanori, who, although not of particularly high rank, was a well-known local dignitary of the time.
72. The location of Mitsusaka Hill is unknown.
73. Inukami was in the present-day Inugami District of Shiga Prefecture.
74. Kanzaki was between present-day Hikone City and the Aichi District.
75. Yasu was in the area of present-day Yasu City in the Yasu District.
76. Now a district in Ōtsu City, the old name for this place was Kurimoto, which has changed to Kurita. Teika's manuscript, however, shows the reading as Kurumoto.
77. Nade is an uncertain place-name.
78. The island of Chikubu is visible on the northern horizon of Lake Biwa.
79. The Seta Bridge then, as now, crossed the narrow neck of Lake Biwa at its eastern end. From this entry, we can see that the bridge was not always kept in good repair.
80. Awazu was the general area from Ōtsu City along the lakeshore to the Seta Bridge.
81. They had started out on the third day of the Ninth Month, so the journey has taken close to ninety days, a very slow trip even for the Heian period. The normal traveling time between Musashi Province and the capital district was noted as thirty days in the *Engi shiki*, a fifty-volume compendium of laws and regulations completed in 927 and expanded in 967.
82. It was customary for such entourages to enter the city at night so as to avoid the attention of onlookers.

[Despite] having passed through many different provinces, of all the border crossings, only the Kiyomi Barrier in Suruga and the Ōsaka Barrier stand out. It became very dark, and finally we arrived at the place west of the Sanjō Palace[86] where we were to live.

It was a large wild place, almost as wild as the mountains we had passed through. There were huge frightening trees like those in the deep mountains; it was a place one could scarcely believe was in the capital.[87] We were not yet settled and extremely busy with one thing or another, but I felt that I just could not wait, so I pestered my mother,[88] "Please find me some tales to read, please!" She sent off a letter to a relative of ours known as Lady Emon no Myōbu, who served the Sanjō Princess.[89] She was delighted to hear from us after such a long while and sent us some reading material that "Her Highness has deigned to pass down to me."[90] These were particularly splendid booklets[91] packed in the lid of an inkstone box. I was beside myself with joy; day or night, the first thing I applied myself to was reading these booklets. I wanted to read more and more. In this city, where we were not really settled yet, where might there be a person who could seek out more tales for me?

Now, my stepmother was a person who had left court service to go down to the provinces, but things had not worked out as she wished, and she seemed to feel some resentment, so she went elsewhere, taking along her child of about five years.[92] She said, "There will never come a time when I will forget the kindness of your heart." Pointing to a big plum tree close to the eaves, she said, "I will come to visit when this tree blossoms again," and leaving these words behind, she went away. In my heart, I kept missing her and feeling sad; I could weep only in secret. The new year came around again.[93] "Whenever will you bloom so that she will come for a visit, as she said? I wonder if she really will." Such were my thoughts as I kept my eye on the tree and waited. Even when all the blossoms were out, there was not a word from her. Sick with longing, I broke off a blossoming branch and sent it to her:

tanomeshi wo	Must I wait longer
naho ya matsubeki	for that which was promised, see—
shimogareshi	spring has not forgotten

83. This is the famous Ōsaka Barrier (not to be confused with the contemporary city of Osaka), which was located in the gentle pass between the hills separating the capital from the Lake Biwa area. In the Heian period, it marked the border between the capital district and the provinces. Once a Heian aristocrat went through this pass, he sensed that he had left the capital behind. Conversely, traveling from the east toward the capital, once he was through the barrier and going down the pass, he felt as though he had arrived back home. Accordingly, the place was a famous *utamakura* for poems about leaving the beloved capital behind. Because its old spelling, *afusaka*, means "meeting slope," the place-name was used in love poetry as a metaphor for the meeting between lovers.

84. This refers to the construction of the statue of the Miroku Buddha at Sekidera (literally, "Barrier Temple"). The temple was located on the Lake Biwa side of the Ōsaka Pass and was destroyed during the large earthquake of 967. Reconstruction of the temple was delayed until 1017 and was not completed until 1022. Takasue no Musume passed through there in 1020. Sekidera was destroyed again in the warfare preceding the establishment of the Tokugawa shogunate. The present-day temple of Chōanji is in roughly the same location.

85. This measurement corresponds to roughly sixteen feet.

86. The Sanjō Palace was located at the intersection of Sanjō Avenue and Takakura Kōji Street. Beginning in 1013, it was the residence of Princess Shūshi (997–1050), the daughter of Emperor Ichijō (980–1011) and the short-lived Empress Teishi (976–1001), who was the patron of Sei Shōnagon, the author of the *Pillow Book*.

87. From this description, it is clear that the author is describing the residence not as a familiar home to which she is returning but as a completely new place to her. This was likely the case. Her father, Takasue, was returning from a tour of duty in a distant but wealth-producing province, so he could now afford to buy a large piece of property in the capital. Moreover, it was an excellent location on Sanjō Avenue, flanked by two imperial family residences. As mentioned earlier, Princess Shūshi lived on the east side, but it later becomes clear that Princess Teishi (1013–1094), the third daughter born to Consort Kenshi and Emperor Sanjō (and not to be confused with Empress Teishi), lived at the Sanjō In residence to the west. For a discussion of the location of the Sugawara residence, see Itō Moriyuki, *Sarashina nikki kenkyū* (Tokyo: Shintensha, 1995), 295–300; and appendix 2, map 3. Nonetheless, the author does not identify this new residence by its stylish address and what must have been comparatively luxurious appointments. Instead, she emphasizes its large grounds and forests, likening it to a wild place.

88. This is the first mention of the author's birth mother, who had not accompanied her father to the provinces. The author's mother was the youngest daughter of Fujiwara no Tomoyasu (d. 977), who was also the father (by an earlier wife) of Michitsuna's mother, the author of the *Kagerō Diary*.

89. The Emon part of this relative's name (literally, "gate guard") indicates that she had a father, brother, or husband serving as a member of the palace gate guard. Myōbu was the general title given to a middle-ranking court woman serving in the inner palace. This woman was a lady-in-waiting to Princess Shūshi, known formally as the Sanjō Princess, owing to her residence on Sanjō Avenue. The rekindling of this family relationship was also made very easy because Princess Shūshi's residence was just next door to the new Sugawara residence.

90. Copies of tales and other works in manuscript form would have been commissioned by people of means, such as the princess. Once the person who had originally commissioned the tales had tired of them, they would be passed down to others in their service. The ladies-in-waiting would also have had an opportunity to copy manuscripts of works they liked. As noted earlier, Princess Shūshi was the daughter of the short-lived Empress

| *ume wo mo haru ha* | even this plum tree |
| *wasurezarikeri* | that was withered by frost. |

Since I had sent this poem, she wrote back and shared many touching thoughts:

naho tanome	Still wait, steadfast.
mume no tachi e ha	As for the plum's young branch tips,
chigiri okanu	even with no pledge placed,
omohi no hoka no	I hear that unexpectedly
hito mo tofunari	someone will visit you.[94]

That spring, the world was in an uproar,[95] and also the nurse whom I had seen so poignantly in the moonlight at Matsusato Crossing died on the first day of the Third Month. I grieved for her helplessly, and I even lost all interest in reading tales. All day long, I spent crying, and when I glanced out, the setting sun shone brightly[96] on the cherry blossoms all fluttering down in confusion:

chiru hana mo	Scattering blossoms,
mata komu haru ha	when spring comes around again,
mimo ya semu	I may see them, but
yagate wakareshi	oh, how I long for the one
hito zo kohishiki	from whom I am parted forever.

There was more news. The daughter of the provisional major counselor[97] had passed away. Since I heard about how her husband, His Lordship the middle captain,[98] grieved for her just at the same time as my own bereavement, I was deeply saddened by the news. When we went back to the capital, Father gave me some calligraphy in this young lady's own hand and told me, "Make this a model for your own practice."[99] She had written such poems as "As night deepens, if I do not stay awake . . ."[100] and

Teishi, consort of Emperor Ichijo. Because Sei Shōnagon, author of the *Pillow Book*, had served Empress Teishi, it is highly likely that a copy of the *Pillow Book* would have been among the booklets that Emon no Myōbu passed on to Takasue no Musume. This entry documents how literary works circulated in the mid-Heian period.

91. The original here is *sōshi*, which referred to hand-copied material stitched in booklet form.

92. From this passage, we gain an understanding of why the author's stepmother was so familiar with the tales being circulated at court. Between the lines, the difficult situation of the stepmother also is revealed. The author's father had taken the presumably younger woman down to the provinces with him and had had a child with her, but back in the capital the stepmother must have found it difficult to live in the shadow of his first wife.

93. The year is 1021, and the author is fourteen years old.

94. The stepmother's poem alludes to Taira no Kanemori, *Shūishū* (1005–1011), poem 15: *waga yado no/ume no tachie ya mietsuran/omohi no hoka ni/kimi ga kimaseru* (Is it that/the young branch tips, of the plum tree in my garden/have come into view?/For unexpectedly my lord,/you have been moved to visit) (Akiyama, ed., *Sarashina nikki*, 32). The stepmother is gently trying to let Takasue no Musume know that she is not in a position to visit her anymore, the reasons for which she likely explained in the "shared thoughts" of her communication. But she hopes that Takasue no Musume will be visited by some fine man and even pretends that she has heard rumors to that effect. Her hinting at a future lover evokes the world of romantic tales. After all, the warm relationship between stepmother and stepdaughter was initiated by their mutual infatuation with the romantic tale literature.

95. The uproar concerns an epidemic of the plague, which was recorded in the histories of the time. Apparently, the epidemic raged from the beginning of the year 1021 to that autumn.

96. In "Wisps of Cloud" (Usugumo), chapter 19 of the *Tale of Genji*, the expression "the setting sun shone bright" is used when Genji is looking at blossoming cherry trees on the hills just after the death of Fujitsubo, the stepmother he loved to the point of excess. At this point in the objective chronology of the *Sarashina Diary*, however, the author has not yet had a chance to read the *Tale of Genji*. Of course, when she was revising this diary, the phrase may have crept in. Moreover, this coincidence of experience, suffering the loss of a loved one at the height of blossom time, may have been one of the things that contributed to making her reading of the *Tale of Genji* profound.

97. Fujiwara no Yukinari (972–1027), one of the three most famous calligraphers of the Heian period, assumed the post of provisional major counselor in 1020.

98. Yukinari's daughter had been married at the age of twelve to the youngest son of Fujiwara no Michinaga, Fujiwara no Nagaie (1005–1064), who was fifteen at the time of their marriage. The *Tale of Flowering Fortunes* (*Eiga monogatari*) says that when Yukinari proposed the marriage between the young people to Michinaga, Michinaga replied that they "would look like a pair of dolls," presumably because of their youth (William H. McCullough and Helen C. McCullough, trans., *A Tale of Flowering Fortunes: Annals of Japanese Aristocratic Life in the Heian Period*, 2 vols. [Stanford, Calif.: Stanford University Press, 1980], 2:482). Yukinari's daughter died at the age of fifteen (2:526–27).

99. Since she was the daughter of a well-known calligrapher, her own hand had an impeccable pedigree. The fact that the author's father was able to acquire samples of this young woman's calligraphy indicates the closeness of his relationship with the girl's father, Fujiwara no Yukinari.

100. Mibu no Tadami, *Shūishū*, poem 104: *sayo fukete/nezamezariseba/hototogisu/hitozute ni koso/kikubekarikere* (As night deepens,/if I do not stay awake,/the cuckoo's voice/will be something I can only expect/to hear in the accounts of others) (Akiyama, ed., *Sarashina nikki*, 33).

toribeyama	"If the smoke rises from
tani ni keburi no	the valley of Toribeyama,
moe tataba	I would have you
hakanaku mieshi	realize that it is me
ware to shiranamu	who looked so ephemeral."[101]

Seeing this written in such a charming and skillful way, my tears flowed forth all the more.

My mother worried about the depression into which I had sunk and thought to brighten my spirits by finding some more tales for me to read, and, indeed as a matter of course, this did lighten my spirits. After I read the part of the *Tale of Genji* about the *murasaki* affinity,[102] I desired even more to see what would happen next, but there was no one I could approach to obtain the rest of the tale, and everyone else in our household was still so new to the capital that they were unable to find it for me. Feeling terribly impatient and eager to read more, I prayed in my heart, "Please grant that I may get to read the *Tale of Genji* from the first chapter the whole way through." Even when I went along with my parents into religious retreat at Uzumasa (figure 3),[103] this was the only object of my prayers, and when we left the temple, I thought for certain I would get to see this tale, but it did not appear and I regretted this sorely. Then my parents had me go to meet an aunt who had come from the countryside.[104] "My, what a beautiful girl you have grown into," she said, among other things, and seemed to take a great liking to me. When I was about to return home, she said, "What shall I give you for a present? Certainly it should not be anything practical. I would like to give you something you really want." Then she gave me the fifty-odd chapters of the *Tale of Genji* in a large box,[105] as well as the *Ariwara Middle Captain*,[106] *Tōgimi, Serikawa, Shirara, Asōzu*,[107] and others in a bag. Carrying them home, the joy I felt was incredible.

With my heart pounding with excitement, I was able to read, right from the first chapter, the *Tale of Genji*, this tale that had confused me and made me impatient when I had read only a piece of it. With no one bothering me, I just lay down inside my curtains, and the feeling I had as I unrolled scroll after scroll[108] was such that I would not have cared even if I had had a chance to become empress! I did nothing but

101. Anonymous, *Shūishū*, poem 1324: *toribeyama / tani ni keburi no / moe tataba / hakanaku mieshi / ware to shiranamu* (Akiyama, ed., *Sarashina nikki*, 33). Toribeyama is a place for cremation, so in retrospect, the poem seems to foretell the young girl's own death.

102. Genji's mother, who died when he was only two years old, was referred to as the Kiritsubo (Paulownia Pavilion) Consort, and the paulownia tree has purple flowers. Genji's step-mother, with whom he had a secret affair, was called the Fujitsubo (Wisteria Pavilion) Consort, and wisteria also has purple flowers. Genji falls in love with young Murasaki, one of the principal heroines in the story, because of her resemblance to Fujitsubo. The roots of the *murasaki* plant (gromwell) are used to make a purple dye. The connection among these three characters is called the *murasaki no yukari* (purple affinity). The author is likely referring to the chapters of the *Tale of Genji* in which the character Murasaki first appears. From this entry, we also learn that individual chapters of the *Tale of Genji* were circulating at that time.

103. Uzumasa is in the western part of the city, and the family likely visited Kōryū Temple, which still exists.

104. Nothing is known about this aunt, but she probably was the wife of a provincial governor who had accompanied her husband to his provincial duties and had now returned to the capital for a visit.

105. This comment is key evidence that at this time, the full length of the *Tale of Genji* was "fifty-odd" chapters—in other words, perhaps the same length as the current extant version, fifty-four chapters. Scholars of the evolution of the *Genji* text are disappointed that Takasue no Musume was not more numerically specific here.

106. This was an alternative title for the *Tales of Ise* (*Ise Stories*).

107. None of these four tales survives. This brief reference indicates how much fictional literature of the Heian period has been lost.

108. It is known that women often read tales aloud to one another, but this comment is evidence that some people also read silently to themselves.

FIGURE 3 The lecture hall at Kōryū Temple in Uzumasa (1165).

read, and I was amazed to find that passages I had somehow naturally learned by heart came floating unbidden into my head. Around the same time, in a dream, I saw a pure-looking monk wearing a surplice of yellow cloth who said to me, "Quickly, memorize roll 5 of the *Lotus Sutra*."[109] But I told no one, nor did I feel particularly inclined to memorize the *Lotus Sutra*. I just was infatuated with tales. I was rather ugly in those days, you know, but I was sure that when I grew up, I would be extremely beautiful and my hair, too, would be splendidly long. I would be just like the Shining Genji's Yūgao[110] or the Uji captain's Ukifune[111]— now it seems to me that my thoughts were frightfully frivolous.[112]

Around the first of the Fifth Month, gazing at the scattered and ever so white petals of the nearby orange blossom tree, I composed this:

toki narazu	Gazing at this,
furu yuki ka to zo	I might think that snow had fallen
nagamemashi	out of season,
hanatachibana no	if it were not for the fragrance
kaworazariseba	of this orange blossom tree.

109. Roll 5 of the *Lotus Sutra* contains the Devadatta chapter (chapter 12), which describes the enlightenment of the Dragon King's daughter. For an overview of the meaning attributed to this chapter by women in the Heian period, see chapter 3.

110. Yūgao is the subject of "The Twilight Beauty" (Yūgao), chapter 4 of the *Tale of Genji*. The chapter is as tightly constructed as a short story and tells of the ill-fated love between Genji and Yūgao, who is the runaway lover of Genji's best friend and brother-in-law. The romance of the love affair is that despite being of inferior status, Yūgao is the first woman to arouse a powerful attachment in Genji, and she suffers an untimely death.

111. Ukifune is the principal heroine of the last five chapters of the *Tale of Genji*. She is a young woman of low status, despite her impeccable lineage on her father's side. Both heroes of the latter *Genji* chapters, the Uji captain (Kaoru) and Prince Niou, fall in love with her. For a discussion of Takasue no Musume's particular sense of identification with Ukifune, see chapter 5.

112. This is one of the places in which author makes it clear that she is writing retrospectively.

Since our place was as thick with trees as the dark woods on the flanks of the Ashigara Mountains, the crimson leaves of the Tenth Month were even more beautiful than those of the hills on all sides. When they were just like bolts of brocade spread over the forest, some visitors came who said, "There was a place on the way here that was simply beautiful with crimson leaves!" On the spot, it came to me:

idzuko nimo	It is not likely
otaraji mono wo	inferior to anywhere else
waga yado no	this lodging of ours,
yo wo aki hatsuru	scenery at the end of autumn
keshiki bakari ha	that brings weariness of the world.[113]

I thought about tales all day long, and even at night as long as I could stay awake, this was all I had on my mind. Then I had a dream in which a person said, "For the sake of the Princess of the First Rank, daughter of the Grand Empress,[114] I am constructing an ornamental stream[115] at the Hexagonal Hall" (figures 4 and 5).[116] When I asked, "Why?" the response was, "Worship Amaterasu, the Great Heaven Shining God."[117] Such was my dream, but I did not tell anyone and let it go without a thought; what a hopeless case I was.

Every spring I would gaze next door at the garden of the Princess of the First Rank with this sort of feeling:

saku to machi	About to bloom, I anticipate them,
chirinu to nageku	once fallen, I lament them:
haru ha tada	in spring, it is as though
waga yado gaho ni	I were seeing cherry blossoms
hana wo miru kana	on the face of my own garden.

Toward the end of the Third Month,[118] to avoid the taboo of the earth god,[119] we went to stay at someone else's house where the cherry trees were in full bloom, so lovely, not a one scattering even this late in the spring. Upon returning the next day, I sent this to them:

113. This poem puns on *yo wo aki* (weary of the world) and *aki hatsuru* (autumn ending). It was included in the "Miscellaneous" section of the imperial anthology *Shokusenzaishū* (1320), poem 1776. With its play on Buddhist terminology, the poem is unusual for a girl still in her teens to have written.

114. The Grand Empress is Michinaga's second eldest daughter, Kenshi (994–1027), who was the principal consort of Emperor Sanjō (976–1017). Kenshi had been granted the title of Grand Empress in 1018, the year after her husband's death. The Princess of the First Rank is Princess Teishi (1013–1094), who was the third daughter of Kenshi and Emperor Sanjō. This identification was made specifically by Teika in a marginal note on the manuscript. There appears to be a chronological error here, however, because Princess Teishi was actually granted Princess of the First Rank status in 1023, one year after this entry. Nonetheless, since the entry itself was likely written sometime after the event it records, it would be natural for the author to refer to Teishi by her later title. As mentioned earlier, this princess resided in the Sanjō In, just west of the Sugawara residence.

115. Ornamental streams were a common feature of both Heian-period aristocratic residences and gardens around temples. The phrase "for the sake of" implies that this person has received a commission from the Princess of the First Rank to construct this stream as an offering to the temple. Even though it has no connection to the *Sarashina Diary*, it is of coincidental interest that an elaborate ornamental stream graces the current Hexagonal Hall (Rokkakudō) complex.

116. The Hexagonal Hall was the main hall of Chōhō Temple, one of the oldest temples in central Kyoto. It is located in the heart of the city and was within walking distance of both the author's family home and Princess Teishi's residence. An illustration from the Edo period gives an idea of the temple complex when the capital had more space and greenery.

117. Amaterasu (literally, "Illuminating Heaven") is the Sun Goddess, the tutelary deity of the imperial family. Later on, the author reveals that she had only a vague idea of the identity of this deity, and it appears to be her gradual discovery of that identity that gives significance retrospectively to this dream.

118. Teika's note on the manuscript identifies the year as Chian 2 (1022).

119. The Heian aristocracy followed an astrological calendar based on Chinese cosmology, which, among other things, plotted the various gods' movements. Accordingly, from time to time people had to vacate their residences to avoid conflict with these gods.

FIGURE 4 The ornamental stream at the Hexagonal Hall (Rokkakudō).

akazarishi	Not sated at all
yado no sakura wo	with the blossoms of your house,
haru kurete	spring drew to a close—
chirigata ni shimo	I got a glimpse of them
hitome mishi kana	just before they started to fall.

Always at about the time the cherry blossoms fell, since that was the season when my nurse had died, I could not help feeling sad. Moreover, looking at the calligraphy of the provisional major counselor's daughter who had died around the same time also made me sad. Then, in the Fifth Month as night fell, when I was still up reading tales, I heard the soft meow of a cat coming from where I knew not. I was startled to see an incredibly charming cat.[120] When I was looking around to see where it had come from, my elder sister said, "Hush, don't let anyone know. It is such a lovely cat, let's keep it as a pet," and so we did. The cat got very used to us and would lie down right beside us. Since we wondered if someone might come looking for it, we hid it from the others and did

120. Keeping cats as pets was quite common in Heian society, at least judging from some key references in literature. The *Pillow Book* of Sei Shōnagon mentions a cat kept in Empress Teishi's residence that was even granted a court title. See Morris, trans., *Pillow Book*, 1:9–10. In "Spring Shoots I" (Wakana jō) and "Spring Shoots II" (Wakana ge), chapters 34 and 35 of the *Tale of Genji*, a pet cat sparks an illicit love affair and then serves as a surrogate love object.

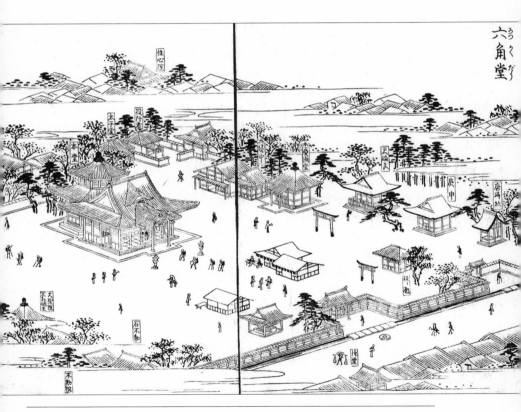

FIGURE 5   An Edo-period print of the Hexagonal Hall (Rokkakudō).

not let it go at all to the servants' quarters. It stayed right with us all the time, and if something unclean was put in front of it to eat, it would turn its head away and refuse to eat it.

It stuck to us two sisters. We were so happy and enchanted with it, but just around then, my sister fell ill. Since the house was in an uproar, I had the cat kept in the north wing[121] and did not call it to our side, at which point it raised a fuss, meowing noisily. Of course, this was understandable. Then my sister woke up from a painful slumber and said, "Where is the cat? Bring it here." "Why?" I asked, and she said, "In my dream, the cat came to my side and said, 'I, who was once the daughter of the provisional major counselor, have been reborn in this form. Since the younger daughter of this household felt so sad remembering me, it created a small karmic bond that brought me to be with you for a while.[122] But now I have been shut away with the servants; how awful it is!' and the appearance of the cat crying was just like a well-born beautiful woman. I woke up with a start, and hearing the cat meowing, I was struck with pity." I was very moved by her story and brought the cat out of the north wing, treating it very kindly after that. When I was all by myself, the cat would come to me, and I would stroke it saying, "So you are the beloved young daughter of the provisional major counselor. How I would like to let him know." When I spoke like this, the cat would stare into my eyes meowing softly. There was no doubt about it; from even one glance one could tell this was not an ordinary cat. The way its face looked when it seemed to listen and understand was touching.

I heard about someone who owned a copy of the "Song of Lasting Regret,"[123] which had been adapted into the form of a tale.[124] Although I was curious to see it, the person was not someone I could approach directly. Seeking out a suitable intermediary, I sent over this poem on the seventh day of the Seventh Month:[125]

chigirikemu　　　　　　Curious this day
mukashi no kefu no　　 on which long ago they must
yukashisa ni　　　　　 have pledged their troth;
ama no kaha nami　　　 like the River of Heaven's waves
uchiidetsuru kana　　　 rising—this is sent out.

121. That is, the servants' quarters.
122. Owning samples of the young woman's calligraphy caused Takasue no Musume to feel close to her and to grieve for her passing, even though they had never met.
123. A famous ballad by the Tang poet Bai Juyi about the ill-fated love between Emperor Xuan Zung and his concubine Yang Gueifei. See Paul W. Kroll, trans., "The Song of Lasting Regret," in *The Columbia Anthology of Traditional Chinese Literature*, ed. Victor Mair (New York: Columbia University Press, 1994), 478–85.
124. Presumably, this would be a vernacular Japanese translation of the poem with illustrations. It was a story made for romantic renderings. The emperor's excessive love for his concubine Yang Gueifei causes him to neglect official duties and spend all his time with her. A wily general, sensing weakness in the central government, foments a rebellion. The emperor is forced to flee, and the palace guard refuses to defend him unless Yang Gueifei, whom they hold responsible for the disaster, is put to death. The emperor reluctantly agrees, but once the rebellion is subdued, he spends the rest of his days sadly longing for his lost lover. This tale is mentioned at the beginning of the *Tale of Genji* as an analogy for the love between the emperor and Genji's mother.
125. Tanabata is the festival of the stars when the Weaver Maid (Vega) and the Herd Boy (Altair) are allowed to meet for one night by crossing a bridge created by the joined wings of magpies over the River of Heaven (Milky Way). Takasue no Musume chooses this day for the communication because one of the most touching moments in the "Song of Lasting Regret" is on the seventh day of the Seventh Month, when the emperor and Yang Gueifei promise to be born in their future lives as "birds of coupled wings" or "trees with intertwining limbs" (Kroll, trans., "Song of Lasting Regret," 485).

The reply:

tachi idzuru	This is sent out to
ama no kahabe no	the one so curious
yukashisa ni	about the River of Heaven;
tsune ha yuyushiki	one even forgets this is a story
koto mo wasurenu	that was unhappy in the end.[126]

On the night of the thirteenth of the same month, the moon shone brightly, lighting up every corner of the house.[127] When everyone was asleep, my elder sister and I went out onto the veranda, and my sister stared intently at the sky, "How would you feel if I were to simply fly away and disappear right now?"[128] Seeing the uncomfortable and fearful look on my face,[129] she changed the subject and laughed merrily. Just then, at the house next door, a carriage for which the way had been cleared[130] stopped, and someone called out, "Reed Leaf, sweet Reed Leaf," but there was no answer. Tired of calling out, whoever it was played beautifully on a flute and moved on. I said,

fue no ne no	Even though she heard
tada akikaze to	the flute's sound as no more
kikoyuru ni	than the autumn wind,
nado wogi no ha no	why would Reed Leaf not
soyo to kotahenu	at least rustle in response?

With an air of "Well done,"[131] my sister responded,

wogi no ha no	That he did not keep
kotafuru made mo	playing until Reed Leaf responded,
fuki yorade	but passed by
tada ni suginuru	just like that, how awful
fue no ne zo uki	the sound of that flute![132]

In this way, right until dawn, we contemplated the brightness of the moon, and when dawn finally broke, we both went to bed.

126. The warmth of this reply intimates that the owners of the scroll were happy to lend it to her.
127. In the lunar calendar, the full moon always occurs on the fifteenth of the month; thus a moon on the thirteenth night is nearly full.
128. The sister evokes the story of the *Tale of the Bamboo Cutter* (*Taketori monogatari*), in which an old bamboo cutter finds a magical girl and adopts her as his own daughter. She brings wealth to the family and grows into a beautiful woman who is pursued by many suitors until finally the emperor falls in love with her. But because she is actually a princess from the moon, even the emperor is powerless to restrain her return to the heavens when, on a bright moonlit night, her people come to fetch her away. See Donald Keene, trans., "The Tale of the Bamboo Cutter," *Monumenta Nipponica* 11, no. 4 (1956): 1–127. The end of the *Tale of the Bamboo Cutter* resembles the end of the "Song of Lasting Regret." After the moon princess's departure, the emperor is inconsolable, living on in the same kind of "lasting regret." By placing these two entries side by side, the author appears to create a sympathetic resonance between them.
129. The author's anxious reaction can also be related to her memory of parting with her nurse on the way up to the capital. Bathed eerily in the bright moonlight, her nurse was about to give birth.
130. The fact that the person has an entourage and has his way cleared for him indicates his high status. This, along with a visit under the bright moon, lends a romantic, tale-like atmosphere to the scene.
131. Reeds and the autumn wind were a standard set in the lexicon of classical poetry, but her sister is impressed because the author has spontaneously struck just the right note with the expected images.
132. The elder sister's riposte is a little stilted in comparison with her younger sister's wit but is humorous in the exaggerated exclamation at the end. This is the last entry in the diary that records the warm relationship between the author and her elder sister. The entry makes it obvious that the deep bond between them was nurtured by their mutual infatuation with tale literature. In fact, with this exchange of poems, we see the two sisters beginning to write a tale themselves.

That next year,[133] in the Fourth Month in the middle of the night, there was a fire and the cat on which we had lavished such care, thinking it to be the reincarnation of the major counselor's daughter,[134] was burned to death. Whenever we called "Young Miss of the Major Counselor," that cat would meow and come walking up, looking for all the world as though it understood what we were saying, and just before the fire, even Father had said, "This is strangely touching; I must tell the major counselor about it," so it seemed terribly sad and such a shame to lose her.

Since the spacious grounds of our house had been like the scenery in the deep mountains, I had got used to seeing the flowers and crimson leaves of the passing seasons, which were more splendid than those of the mountains on all sides. So now we had moved to an incomparably cramped place, with hardly a garden at all and no trees; how depressing I found it. Even when the white and red plums[135] of the house in front of this place were blooming in gay profusion and I was bathed in the fragrance brought by the wind, still how much I missed the old home I was used to and yearned for it:

nihohi kuru	Redolent with scent,
tonari no kaze wo	the wind from the neighbor's yard
mi ni shimete	soaks into me.
arishi nokiba no	Oh, how I yearn for the plum tree
mume zo kohishiki	by the eaves where I once dwelled.

On the first day of the Fifth Month of that year,[136] my elder sister died in childbirth. Ever since I was a child, even the news that someone I did not really know had died would plunge me into deep sorrow; I grieved now with a sorrow that was beyond description. Mother and the others observed the wake with the departed one, so I took her young children, the keepsakes she had left behind, and put one on my left side and one on my right side. Through the cracks in the rough boards of the roof, the moonlight leaked in and shone on the face of one of the little ones. Finding this inauspicious, I covered his face with a sleeve and pulled the other one closer;[137] how terrible were my thoughts!

133. The year is 1023, just three years after the family left the East Country, and the author is sixteen years old.

134. Their acquisition of the cat and the dream that associated it with the major counselor's daughter was described earlier. The young girl's father, Fujiwara no Yukinari, was earlier referred to by his full title, provisional major counselor.

135. From the mention of plum blossoms, we know that this single entry is from the following year. Their house burned down in the Fourth Month (May in the Western calendar) of the previous year.

136. The year is 1024, and the author is seventeen years old.

137. This passage recalls the entry of a little more than a year earlier when she and her sister sat up all night in the moonlight, and her sister seemed to foretell her own death.

After that period of time had passed,[138] a message came from a relative: "Since I had a note from your late sister saying, 'Please do everything in your power to find this tale and deliver it to me,' I tried to find it for her but was unsuccessful on that occasion. Someone has just given me a copy, how terribly sad." The message was accompanied by a copy of the tale entitled *The Prince Who Sought the Remains of His Beloved*.[139] Truly, it was heartbreaking. I wrote in reply,

udzumorenu	For what reason
kabane wo nani ni	was she seeking
tadzunekemu	those unburied remains?
koke no shita ni ha	And now her own body
mi koso narikere	dwells beneath the moss.

The person who had been my sister's nurse, breaking into tears again and again, lamented, "Now, what is there to keep me here?" As she was about to leave to return to her former home,[140] I wrote to her:

furusato ni	Oh, to end up
kaku koso hito ha	returning to your old home
kaherikere	in this way!
ahare ikanaru	Alas, how sad a parting
wakare narikemu	this must be for you.

"Without you, what will I have as a keepsake of the past?" and I ended with, "Since the water in my inkstone is frozen solid, all the rest of my feelings must stay locked inside," adding,

kakinagasu	I set the brush
ato ha tsurara ni	to flow, but its traces are
todjitekeri	locked in[141] icicles.
nani wo wasurenu	What will I have now as a keepsake
katami to ka mimu	to remember our beloved?

138. "That period" is the forty-nine-day period of official mourning after someone's death.

139. This tale, *Kabane tazunuru miya*, has not survived, but fragments of it are included as poem prefaces in the *Fūyō wakashū* (1271), an anthology of poetry gleaned from tales.

140. In Heian aristocratic society, the nurse of one's infancy would often stay on as a close servant for one's whole life. Indeed, the relationship between nursemaid and child was often more affectionate than that between birth mother and child. But with the death of the author's elder sister, this nurse has no reason for staying with the household so must now return to the home she left many years ago.

141. The verb *todzu* (locked in) is associated with the image of ice, and the author uses ice as a metaphor to express the numbing quality of grief. Her sister died at the beginning of the previous summer, but the nurse stayed in residence with the Sugawara family until the onset of winter.

She replied:

nagusamuru	There no way for me
kata mo nagisa no	to find comfort at water's edge—
hama chidori	why would the plover
nani ka ukiyo ni	leave its tracks on the shore of this
ato mo todomemu	world awash in suffering?[142]

This nurse went to see the place where my sister had been cremated, returning to her home in tears. I wrote,[143]

noborikemu	On the moor,
nobe ha keburi mo	where she rose to the sky, not even
nakarikemu	smoke must remain.
idzuko wo haka to	Where then could she look
tadzunete ka mishi	to seek the grave?[144]

When she heard about this, the woman who had been our stepmother[145] wrote,

soko ha ka to	Though she did not go
shirite yukanedo	knowing that such and such a place
saki ni tatsu	was the dear one's grave,
namida zo michi no	surely the tears that flowed ahead
shirube narikeru	served as a guide on the path.

And the person who had sent *The Prince Who Sought the Remains of His Beloved*[146] wrote:

sumi narenu	Over the traceless tracks
nobe no sasa hara	of the scrub bamboo moors
ato haka mo	where no one lives—
naku naku ika ni	aimless, crying,[147] how must
tadzunewabikemu	she have suffered on her search.

142. This poem puns on *kata mo naki* (no way or means) and *nagisa* (water's edge), made possible because Heian kana was written without the diacritical marks that distinguished *ki* and *gi*. The plover's footprints were often used as a metaphor for writing, or messages. Here, however, the plover is used as a metaphor for the nurse herself, who now has no reason to stay any longer, just as the plovers must fly away when the beach is taken away by the high tide.

143. The author writes the following poem imagining the nurse's grief at the cremation site. There is no grave to seek, as the sister's remains have vanished in the fire, so the image of the nurse seeking the sister's remains has a special poignancy. This situation also recalls *The Prince Who Sought the Remains of His Beloved*, the story mentioned in the previous entry. In this subtle way, the author pulls together various threads in her narrative, and by evoking the extreme grief of the sister's nurse, the author indirectly expresses her own grief.

144. This poem puns on *haka* (aim, object) and *haka* (grave).

145. This is the stepmother who accompanied the author and her sister to their father's posting in Kazusa Province. The elder sister's nurse presumably lived with the family in Kazusa, too, and therefore would be familiar to the stepmother. The fact that the stepmother sends an answer to Takasue no Musume's poem indicates that the author sent her poem of personal grief to others.

146. It makes sense that she would send her poem also to the friend who sent the copy of *The Prince Who Sought the Remains of His Beloved*, both in return for the kindness of her gesture of sending the tale after her sister's death and because the content of the tale and of the poem reflect each other.

147. This poem picks up the pun on *haka* (aim, object) and *haka* (grave) from the previous poem by the author and alters it slightly into the form of *ato haka mo naku* (aimless, without a trace of a trail / without the trace of a grave), another pun on *naku* (without) and *naku naku* (crying, crying), to pick up the image of tears introduced in the stepmother's poem. Thus it seems to indicate that the author of this poem had seen both previous poems.

Since he had actually accompanied our sister's remains that night, my elder brother wrote:

mishi mama ni	Since as I watched,
moeshi keburi ha	the smoke from the cremation fire
tsukinishi wo	vanished utterly,
ikaga tadzuneshi	how could she find anything
nobe no sasa hara	on the moors of scrub bamboo?[148]

At a time when the snow had been falling for days, I imagined how it must be for the nun living in the Yoshino Mountains:[149]

yuki furite	With the snow falling,
mare no hitome mo	even the rare visits of others
taenuramu	must have ceased—
yoshino no yama no	it is a steep path up to the
mine no kakemichi	peaks of the Yoshino Mountains.

The next year,[150] during the promotion rounds of the First Month, although my father had expected good news, the day dawned fruitlessly.[151] From someone who could be expected to sympathize with our household[152] came this: "All the time thinking, 'This time for sure,' ah, the frustration of waiting until dawn.

akuru matsu	Waiting until dawn,
kane no kowe ni mo	to have all one's dreams dispelled
yume samete	at the tolling of the bell.
aki no momo yo no	Did it not feel as though one had
kokochiseshi kana	waited a hundred autumn
	nights?"[153]

In response to this, I composed,

akatsuki wo	Why, I wonder,
nani ni machikemu	did we wait for daybreak?
omofu koto	Since what

148. Thus ends the cycle of mourning poems for the elder sister. It is clear from the way that the three poems echo one another that the author sent her own poem to these three people and also shared the responses with the group. The ordering suggests that she sent her stepmother's response, along with her own poem, to the person who had sent the tale and then showed all three poems to her elder brother. It is noteworthy, too, that although the stepmother is included in this circle of mourners, there is no mention of her father and mother's grief. Certainly, this could not be because the parents did not feel grief. Rather, it reveals the author's exercise of literary choice. This recorded cycle of poems has a literary unity underpinned by the allusion to *The Prince Who Sought the Remains of His Beloved*. It is fitting that this memorial poem cycle for the elder sister included a subtle nod to the tale literature that both the elder and the younger sister loved. Yet the elder brother's closing poem to the cycle sounds a particularly cold note of reality: "I saw her burn away to nothing with my own eyes; there is no grave, no remains to seek." It is almost as though the author uses his words to begin to rouse herself from her romantic illusions.

149. The Yoshino Mountains, famed for their cherry blossoms and autumn leaves, are southeast of Kyoto. This is the first of the four communications with nuns referenced in the diary. In one case, the referent is "a relative [who] had become a nun," but with no other identification, and it is not even clear that all three cases refer to the same nun. What is clear is that these references seem to occur when the author is feeling particularly bereft and in need of consolation, as they stop the narrative's forward action and provide transitional moments of quiet.

150. The year is 1025, and the author is eighteen years old.

151. Promotions, which included the awarding of provincial governorships, were announced in the first month of the lunar calendar. In the *Pillow Book*, under the heading "Depressing Things," Sei Shōnagon describes a household waiting through the night for news of a posting that does not arrive. See Morris, trans., *Pillow Book*, 1:22–23.

152. This would be a member of the extended family, perhaps an aunt or a cousin, who was privy to the father's hopes.

153. Autumn nights were known for seeming long.

naru tomo kikanu   we hoped for was not told
kane no oto yuwe   in the tolling of the bell.[154]

Toward the end of the Fourth Month,[155] for a certain reason, I moved to a place in Higashiyama.[156] Along the way, the paddies had been flooded and the rice shoots planted. I gazed out at the surrounding scene, somehow charmed by its green hue. The place where I was to stay was deep in the shade of the mountain, and right in front of me was the touching and forlorn sight of the evening twilight. Water rails cried out loudly.[157]

tatakutomo   Knocking at the door—
tare ka kuhina no   "Who comes?"[158] Only water rails
kurenuru ni   in the falling dusk
yamdji wo fukaku   must have come to visit
tadzunete ha komu   this path deep in the mountains.

Since Ryōzen Temple[159] was nearby, I went to worship there. Even though the path was steep, I made it all the way to a spring welling up between the boulders at this mountain temple. There was a person with me[160] who, drinking the water from cupped hands, said, "One feels as though one could drink this water forever without tiring of it."[161] I replied,

okuyama no   Cupping and lifting
ishi ma no midzu wo   to your lips this water from
                                        boulders
musubi agete   deep in the mountains,
akanu mono to ha   did you just realize now
ima nomi ya shiru   you would never tire of it?

When I said this, the person who was drinking answered,

yama no wi no   More even than of
shidzuku ni nigoru   the "water clouded by drops"
                                        falling

154. This poem puns on *naru* (to be fulfilled) and *naru* (to sound), as in "make a bell sound."

155. Since this is the Fourth Month in the lunar calendar, it would be early summer in the same year of 1025, when the author was eighteen years old.

156. Thus begins the author's account of a four-month sojourn in Higashiyama. Up against the eastern hills, this district was slightly cooler than the city in summer and thus a popular place for aristocrats to have a second dwelling. But since the author does not specify the reason for her stay in Higashiyama, we can only speculate. It is likely that the family was still without a proper house of their own since the fire that had destroyed their residence at Sanjō two years earlier. Because the father had not obtained a position as provincial governor the year before, he probably could not have afforded to rebuild. Perhaps the family had to split up and borrow or rent various dwellings from acquaintances. Or since her stay is only over the summer months, perhaps the family wanted her, for her health, to escape the heat. For a discussion of the literary complexity of the Higashiyama record, see chapter 2.

157. Water rails (*kuhina*) are shy, waterside birds whose call was thought to simulate the sound of knocking.

158. This poem puns on the *ku* of the phrase *tare ka ku* (Who comes?) and the first syllable of the Japanese name of the water rail, *kuhina*.

159. Ryōzen is short for the full name, Ryōjusen. The name of the present-day temple on the site is Shōhōji, located in Higashiyama Ward at Seikanji and Ryōzenchō.

160. There is no way to know whether this person is a man or a woman. From the intimate tone of the poems they exchange, it is easy to imagine that it is a man, but poems of friendship between women in the Heian period employ the same vocabulary and tone as those exchanged between lovers.

161. Her companion's remark recalls Ki no Tsurayuki, *Kokinshū*, poem 404: *musubu te no/shidzuku ni nigoru/yama no i no/akademo hito ni/wakarenuru kana* (My thirst still unslaked / droplets from my cupped palms cloud / the pure mountain spring— / still would I tarry with one / from whom I must now take leave) (Laurel Rasplica Rodd, trans., *Kokinshū: A Collection of Ancient and Modern Poems*]Princeton, N.J.: Princeton University Press, 1984], 163). Both poems that follow allude to that poem.

midzu yori mo	into the mountain spring,
ko ha naho akanu	I feel as though I would
kokochi koso sure	never tire of this one.

On the way back, with the evening sun glowing, the capital area lay spread out clearly before us. The person who had spoken of the "water clouded by drops" had to return to the capital but seemed very sorry to leave. The next morning, this came:

yama no ha ni	As the rays
irihi no kage ha	of the setting sun disappeared
iri hatete	on the mountain rim,
kokoro bosoku zo	I could not help gazing out,
nagame yarareshi	lost in forlorn thoughts.

One morning, while I was listening with a sense of awe to the prostrations of a monk chanting the Buddha's name at daybreak, I slid open the door and saw mist drifting across the lush dark tips of the trees as the rim of the mountain grew light little by little.[162] More even than crimson leaves or blossoms at their peak, somehow this scene of the skyline of lush vegetation partly obscured by mist was captivating, and there was even a cuckoo[163] on a tree branch very close by, calling out again and again,

tare ni mise	To whom could I show this?
tare ni kikasemu	Whom could I have listen to this?
yamazato no	The mountain dwelling,
kono akatsuki mo	this moment of daybreak, and
ochikaheru ne mo	this singing back and forth.

On the last day of this month, at the top of a tree in the direction of the ravine, a cuckoo was noisily singing away:[164]

miyako ni ha	Cuckoo! Even though
matsuramu mono wo	you are eagerly awaited
hototogisu	in the capital,

162. The phrasing recalls the famous opening passage of the *Pillow Book*: *yauyau shiroku nari-yuku yamagiha* (The rim of the mountain growing light little by little) (Hagitani Boku, ed., *Makura no sōshi*, 2 vols., Shinchō Nihon koten shūsei [Tokyo: Shinchōsha, 1977], 1:18).

163. The Japanese bird is a *hototogisu*, which belongs to the cuckoo family and has the same habits as the European bird but a much more liquid and complex song. In the capital, the cuckoo was heard only after the Fifth Month, but up in these foothills, the author hears it as early as the Fourth Month, which feels like a special gift.

164. It is about ten days after the first mention of the cuckoo, so what was first so fresh and beautiful to her ears has become familiar and even a bit of a bother.

kefu hinemosu ni	today, the whole day through, you
nakikurasu kana	just spend your time singing here![165]

and all I could do was keep gazing out at this scene. Someone who was with me said,[166] "I wonder if there are people in the capital listening to the cuckoo, too, just at this moment? And I wonder if they are imagining us gazing out like this.

yama fukaku	Deep as we are
tare ka omohi ha	in the mountains, who could possibly
okosubeki	be moved to think of us?
tsuki miru hito ha	Even though there would be many
ohokarame domo	who would gaze at the full moon."[167]

I responded,

fukaki yo ni	I do not know what
tsuki miru wori ha	people feel when they gaze at the
shiranedomo	moon late at night, but
madzu yamazato zo	if it were I, I could not help sending
omohi yararuru	my thoughts to this mountain village.

One night just when I was thinking that dawn must be about to break, there was the sound of many people coming from the mountain. I was startled, and when I looked out, I saw that deer had come right up to the edge of the veranda and were crying to one other. Heard from close up like that, their voices were not charming.[168]

aki no yo no	On autumn nights,
tsuma kohikanuru	the voices of deer longing
shika no ne ha	for their mates

165. The humor of this poem is based on the large number of poems about people in the capital who are eagerly awaiting the cuckoo's call. Meanwhile, the author, living in the countryside, has heard quite enough.

166. Again, we have to keep an open mind as to whether the companion is a man or a woman. If a man, the scene would have a romantic aura.

167. The odd thing about this and the next poem is that they speak of the moon, even though—given that the time for this exchange is already established as the "last day of the month" in the lunar calendar—there would be no moon to see. Instead, it seems that the author and her companion are sitting in the dark, listening to the cuckoo's call. The notion of the moon as a point of contact between people separated by distance is a long-established trope in both Chinese and Japanese literature. Having raised the question of whether there are people in the capital thinking of them as they listen to the cuckoo, the author's companion appears to answer the question negatively and then muse whether it would be different if the moon were visible.

168. The author of the *Kagerō Diary* describes a similar encounter with "talking deer" when she is on a pilgrimage to Ishiyama. See Sonja Arntzen, trans., *The Kagerō Diary: A Woman's Autobiographical Text from Tenth-Century Japan* (Ann Arbor: Center for Japanese Studies, University of Michigan), 1997), 209. She, too, experiences a disjunction between the actual sounds the deer make and her expectation of the sound of their voices based on descriptions in poetry. Takasue no Musume is likely alluding to that passage, which results in a kind of intertextual joke.

tohoyama ni koso	should indeed be heard
kikubekarikere	from mountains far away.

Upon hearing that someone I know had come quite close but had ended up returning without visiting:

mada hito me	Even the pine wind
shiranu yamabe no	on the mountain side, who is not
matsukaze mo	used to other's eyes,
oto shite kaheru	makes some sound before returning,
mono to koso kike	that is indeed what I have heard. . . .

The Eighth Month arrived.[169] The moon of the twentieth day of the month[170] lingering in the dawn sky was terribly touching; the dense dark greenery of the mountainside and the sound of the waterfall were unlike anything I had ever known. I could not help just gazing at them rapt in contemplation:

omohi shiru	How I would love to show
hito ni misebaya	someone who could understand—
yamazato no	this mountain village
aki no yo fukaki	in the depths of an autumn night,
ariake no tsuki	the moon at daybreak.

Upon starting my return to the capital, I noticed that all the rice paddies, which had been full of water when I came, had now been completely harvested.

nahashiro no	Until the paddies,
midzu kage bakari	where I saw only young shoots
mieshi ta no	mirrored in the water,
karihatsuru made	have ended up all harvested,
nagawi shi ni keri	such a long stay have I had.

169. The Eighth Month corresponds to September in the Western calendar and is therefore autumn.
170. That is, the waning quarter moon.

Toward the end of the Tenth Month when I had the occasion to come back and view that place just briefly, every single leaf of that dark lush forest had scattered and lay in disorder on the ground. Looking around feeling terribly moved, I noticed that the stream that had burbled along so cheerfully was now buried in fallen leaves; all one could see was where it had been.

midzu sahe zo	Even the water
sumitaenikeru	has clearly ceased to dwell here[171]
ko no ha chiru	in the desolation
arashi no yama no	of this stormy mountain where
kokorobososa ni	all the tree leaves have fallen.

On my way back home, I said to a nun who lived on that mountain,[172] "If I stay alive until spring, I will certainly come and see you. Please be sure to let me know when the blossoms are at their peak." But when the new year had come and it was past the tenth day of the Third Month, and there still was no word from her:

chigiri okishi	Despite the promise
hana no sakari wo	I begged of you, you send no news
tsugenu kana	of the blossoms' peak.
haru ya mada konu	Has spring not yet come?
hana ya nihohanu	Are the blossoms not aglow?

I had gone on a trip around the time of the full moon and was staying at a place right beside a bamboo grove; awakened by the sound of the wind, I was unable to melt back into sleep.

take no ha no	By the rustle of
soyogu yo goto ni	bamboo leaves night after night,
nezame shite	I am awakened,
nani tomo naki ni	and for no particular reason,
mono zo kanashiki	feelings of sadness engulf me.

171. This poem puns on *sumi* (to be clear) and *sumi* (to dwell).
172. This is the second of the four communications with nuns, which appear to serve as segues between topics and provide moments of quiet reflection and sadness.

Around the time of autumn, leaving that place and moving to another,[173] I addressed this to that former host:

idzuko tomo	It matters not where,
tsuyu no ahare ha	I only want to part from
wakareji wo	the pathos of dew,
asadji ga hara no	yet I will recall fondly this autumn
aki zo kohishiki	on the "plain of short reeds."[174]

Our stepmother continued to be called "Kazusa no Taifu"[175] when she went back to serve at court. When Father heard that she was still being referred to by this name even after she had become involved with another man, he said, "Let's inform her that in the present circumstances, this is not appropriate." So I wrote, in Father's place,[176]

asakura ya	Asakura![177]
ima ha kumowi ni	I hear even though you dwell
kiku mono wo	way up in the clouds.[178]
naho ko no maro ga	How is it you still call yourself
nanori wo ya suru	by the name of this old log?[179]

In this way, life went on,[180] and airy musings continued to be my preoccupation. When on the rare occasion I went on a pilgrimage, even then I could not concentrate my prayers on becoming somebody in the world. Nowadays it seems that people read the sutras and devote themselves to religious practice even from the age of seventeen or eighteen, but I was unable to put my mind to that sort of thing.[181] Instead, I daydreamed about being hidden away in a mountain village like Lady Ukifune, happy to be visited even only once a year by a high-ranking man, handsome of face and form, like the Shining Genji in the tale.[182] There I would gaze out in melancholy languor at the blossoms, the crimson leaves, the moon, and the snow, awaiting his splendid letters, which would come from time to time. This was all I mused about, and it was even what I wished for.[183]

I passed the time aimlessly thinking in the back of my mind that if my father became successful,[184] I might even be settled into a distinguished

173. This recording of moving from place to place seems to indicate that perhaps the family still does not have a permanent residence. It also is hard to tell from her record whether the author is staying by herself at these places or with other members of her family.

174. This may be the name for the garden at the residence of her "former host"—that is, the host at the place where she was wakened in the middle of the night by the rustle of the bamboo leaves.

175. The text says literally that she "was called by the name of the province to which [we] had gone down." As we pointed out in chapter 1, women's names were often derived from the names of their husbands or other male relatives. This was the case here; *taifu* was a general title for men holding at least the fifth rank, a major dividing line among the Heian aristocracy, and *taifu* often was part of the nickname of women serving at court who had a relationship with a man of that rank. Thus Kazusa no Taifu is the equivalent of being called the "Kazusa governor's wife."

176. We might have expected her to express some sadness at having to compose on her father's behalf this poem of remonstrance to her beloved stepmother, but when one sees the very witty and humorous nature of her poem, we can imagine both women smiling over it. Nonetheless, this poem is the last mention of the stepmother in the diary and so marks a decisive break. Since the stepmother's poem in the imperial anthology *Goshūi shū* (1086) was still listed under Kazusa no Taifu, it seems that such appellations were hard to change.

177. *Asakura ya* is a conventional poetic tag to announce *ko no maro* in the fourth line, which is another pronunciation for *ki no maru* (tree in the round)—therefore, "log." The phrase refers to the temporary palace of logs that Empress Saimei had built in Asakura in Kyushu while she was gathering support for a campaign on the Korean Peninsula in the seventh century, but it is not this historical context that is important here. Because *maro* also is a first-person male pronoun in Heian Japanese, the expression contains a pun on "I" or "me." The poem as a whole alludes to a poem in the seventh-century *Manyōshū* (*Collection of Ten Thousand Leaves*): *ya asakura / ko no maru dono ni / wagaworeba / nanori wo shitsutsu / iku ha ta ga ko zo* (Asakura! / when I am here / in the hall of unbarked logs / whose child is that, / who passes by, announcing his name?) (Joshua Mostow, trans., *Pictures of the Heart: The Hyakunin Isshu in Word and Image* [Honolulu: University of Hawai'i Press, 1996], 142). The general import of this poem makes it an appropriate allusion here.

178. Dwelling "way up in the clouds" was a common metaphor for serving at the imperial court.

179. To understand the mention of "log," see note 177.

180. This one phrase covers more than six years of her life because the next datable passage is the following one, in which she recounts her father's long-awaited acquisition of a provincial governor post in 1032. This passage marks an important juncture in her life and summarizes her state of mind in her teens and early twenties. At least in regard to practical concerns like marrying, her life during this period was more or less on hold because of her father's stalled career.

181. The fact that this remark is prefaced by "nowadays" indicates its retrospective nature.

182. Her imagined scene combines two characters in the *Tale of Genji* who are not connected in the tale itself. Genji is the hero of the first forty-one chapters of the work, but Ukifune does not appear until chapter 49. It is Kaoru who hides Ukifune at Uji. For a discussion of this disjunction, see chapter 5.

183. For a discussion of the role played by this "what I wished for" passage in the structure of the work as a whole, see chapter 2.

184. There is a lacuna in the text here: the term "successful" is not in the extant text but has been added to make sense of the passage.

position,[185] but it came about instead that my father was to take up a post far away in the distant East Country.[186] Father explained: "For years now, I have been hoping to receive a posting in the nearby provinces, and then, with a mind free of worry, the first thing I could attend to would be taking care of you in fine style. I could take you with me on tours of duty, show you the seaside and mountain scenery, and then, as a matter of course, see you settled into a higher social position than mine, with all your needs met.[187] This is what I wanted, but since it is our fate, both yours and mine, not to be blessed with good fortune after all this waiting and hoping, now I am to take up a post far away. In your youth, even when I took you with me down to the East Country, at times when I felt even a little ill, I would worry, thinking, 'What will happen if I have to abandon her to wander lost in this wild province? If it were just I alone facing the dangers of this strange land, I could be calm, but having dragged the household with me, I cannot even say what I want to say, nor do what I want to do.' How painful it was; my heart was torn to pieces. Now, this time, it will be even worse. I cannot take you off to the provinces as an adult. If I were to die, you would, as a matter of course, be left without support in the capital . . . still, imagining you abandoned, wandering around as a country rustic in the East Country; that, too, would be terrible. Alas, there is no relative or intimate friend whom I can expect to take responsibility for you here in the capital. Nonetheless, since I am not in a position to refuse this posting, which I have just barely been given, all I can do is have you stay behind in the capital and resign myself even to the possibility of never seeing you again. And it does not appear that I will be able to leave you set up in an appropriate manner even here in the capital."[188] I felt so sad listening to my father lament like this day and night that I even lost my feeling for the blossoms and crimson leaves. Although I bemoaned this situation terribly, what could I do about it?

Father went down to his province on the thirteenth day of the Seventh Month.[189] For five days before his departure, he had been unable to bear seeing me and so had not come into my room. On the day he was to leave, everyone was busy with the departure, so how much worse I felt at the very moment when he raised the bamboo blind of my room and looked at me with tears pouring down his face. He left

185. This is a reference to arranging a good match for her marriage. Heian women relied principally on their fathers for arranging a marriage.

186. The year is 1032, and the author is twenty-five years old. Her father is sixty years old and has been expecting to get a provincial governorship in one of the provinces close to the capital, but instead he is appointed to Hitachi, the province next to his former post in Kazusa. This is the province she mentioned at the opening of her diary as being "the end of the road to the East Country."

187. A posting in a nearby province would allow an easy commute between the provincial office and the capital, and because such a posting would be both prestigious and lucrative, it would allow her father to attract a husband of high rank for his daughter.

188. The father's rambling, repetitive speech reflects the anxiousness of his mind.

189. This would be in August 1032.

just like that. My eyes were blind with tears, and I had just lain down in my room when the household servants who were to remain behind came back from seeing him off and delivered this letter, written on folded paper:[190]

omofu koto	If I were in a
kokoro ni kanafu	position that fulfilled the
mi nariseba	wishes of my heart,
aki no wakare wo	then would I savor deeply
fukaku shiramashi	the feeling of this autumn
	parting.[191]

This was all he had written, yet I could hardly read it through. Even in ordinary times, I can think up only verses with "broken backs,"[192] but somehow I felt I must say something, so in that state of mind I wrote almost unconsciously,

kakete koso	Never at all
omohazari shika	did I ever think that
kono yo nite	in this world,
shibashi mo kimi ni	even for a little while
wakarubeshi to ha	I would be parted from you.

Now more than ever, no visitors came. I gazed constantly into space feeling lonely and bereft, imagining day and night how far he might have gone. Since I knew the path he was taking, as the distance grew between us, there was no limit to my loving thoughts of yearning. From dawn until dusk, I would spend my days staring at the rim of the mountains to the east.

Around the Eighth Month, when I was on my way to a retreat in Uzumasa (figure 6),[193] we came upon two ox carriages carrying men that had stopped by the side of the road (perhaps they were waiting for companions to catch up with them before continuing on to wherever they were going). As our party passed by, they sent over one of their attendants to deliver this message:[194]

FIGURE 6 An Edo-period print of Kōryū Temple in Uzumasa.

190. This scene is very similar to the passage in the *Kagerō Diary* in which Michitsuna's mother describes her father leaving for a provincial posting. See Arntzen, trans., *Kagerō Diary*, 67.

191. Parting in autumn, although sad, is celebrated in poetry. If her father had received the post he hoped for, he would have been able to appreciate the poetic feelings of parting in autumn. In his current situation, though, there is no such pleasure.

192. A "broken back" is a fault in poetry composition in which the third line (thought of as the backbone of a poem) does not connect well with the fourth line.

193. She made an earlier pilgrimage to Uzumasa with her parents shortly after arriving to live in the capital.

194. The message consists of the last two lines of a *waka* and challenges the author and her party to come up with a suitable beginning for the poem.

| *hanami ni yuku to* | We were on our way to see flowers; |
| *kimi wo miru kana* | how wonderful to see you instead. |

My companion said, "In a case like this, it is impolite not to respond." So I had someone deliver this reply:

chigusa naru	With hearts as always
kokoro narahi ni	pulled by myriad attractions,
aki no no no	in the autumn moors.[195]

With just that, we passed by. On the seven days of the retreat, I was finally able to separate my mind from frivolous things; all I could think of was the road to the east. My prayer was, "Please let me see him safe again." I felt as though the Buddha might have listened with compassion.

Winter came. On a night after a day when the rain had been falling all day long, a wind capable of returning all the clouds to their home blew fiercely, the sky cleared, and the moon was strikingly bright. The rushes that reached up close to the eaves had been blown about terribly by the wind and lay broken in disarray. Moved by the touching sight:

aki wo ika ni	In winter's depths,
omohi idzuramu	how much must they recall
fuyu fukami	the fine days of autumn,
arashi ni madofu	withered leaves of rushes
wogi no kareha ha	blown in disarray by the storm.

Someone came from the East Country bearing a letter:

"While I was touring the shrines of this province performing the offical ritual prayers,[196] in an area where there were lovely flowing streams and wide, wide plains, there was one place with a forest grove. 'What a charming place,' I thought to myself, and right away I was reminded of you and sorry that I could not show it to you. 'What is this place called?' I asked, and someone replied, 'Sir, they say it is called "Longing for One's Child Forest."'[197] Since I could not help comparing

195. This suggested beginning for the poem subtly criticizes the men for having fickle hearts.
196. It was the custom for the new provincial governor to make a tour of the province and offer prayers for good fortune at all the shrines.
197. The Japanese place-name that her father gives in his letter is Ko shinobi. There is a place-name, Oshinabe, in present-day Ibaraki Prefecture (part of the Heian-period Hitachi Province) that might be the place to which he is referring. It has been conjectured that her father either misheard the place-name or intentionally altered it to fit his own sentiments.

it to myself and feeling terribly sad, I dismounted and gazed at it deep in thought for a couple of hours or more.

todomeokite	Having left
waga goto mono ya	a child behind, how like me,
omohikemu	it must have felt.
miru ni kanashiki	Looking at it, I feel sad,
ko shinobi no mori	'Longing for One's Child Forest'

That is just how I felt."

One must imagine my feelings when reading this letter. I replied with this:

ko shinobi wo	Just hearing,
kiku ni tsukete mo	"Longing for One's Child," I regret
todomeokishi	being left behind;
chichibu no yama no	"Father Mountain"[198] all alone
tsuraki adzumadji	on the roads of the East Country.

In this way, as I drifted along in life, I wondered why I had not gone on pilgrimages. Of course, my mother was very old-fashioned: "A trip to Hatsuse (figure 7)?[199] How frightening the thought! What would I do if you were abducted on the Nara Slopes?[200] If we went to Ishiyama,[201] it would be terrifying to cross Sekiyama.[202] And Kurama (figure 8);[203] the thought of taking you to that mountain also scares me. Anyway, until your father gets back, it is out of the question." She seemed to think me troublesome and just ignored me. Finally, she took me on a retreat to Kiyomizu Temple (figure 9).[204] But that time, too, as was my habit, I could not concentrate and pray for serious and proper things. As it was around the time of the equinox rites,[205] the temple was crowded to an alarming degree. When I finally fell into a fretful slumber, I dreamed that a monk, apparently a kind of steward, dressed in a blue woven habit and wearing a brocade headpiece and brocade shoes, approached the guard railing on the side of my curtain-of-state and said in a chiding way, "Unaware of the sad future awaiting you, you just waste your time on frivolous concerns." Then he made as though to enter my

FIGURE 7 The gallery walkway of Hase (Hatsuse) Temple.

198. Although Chichibuyama (Father Mountain) was in neighboring Musashi Province, not in Hitachi Province, it was a fitting East Country reference.

199. Hatsuse is the location of Hatsuse Temple (now commonly abbreviated as Hase Temple), which still exists in the mountains east of Nara next to the Hatsuse River. Along with Ishiyama Temple, Hatsuse Temple was a prime center for Kannon worship during the Heian period and a very popular place of pilgrimage, particularly for women. Nearly all the texts by women in the Heian period mention pilgrimages to Hatsuse.

200. These hills north of Nara on the way to Hatsuse had a reputation as a favorite site for robbers.

201. Ishiyama Temple, located on the shore of Lake Biwa, was another center of Kannon worship and also a popular site of pilgrimage for women.

202. Sekiyama (literally, "Barrier Mountain") was the mountain where the Ōsaka Barrier was located, which had to be crossed in order to reach Lake Biwa.

203. Kurama Temple, located in the mountains north of the capital, was dedicated to the deity Bishamonten.

204. Kiyomizu Temple, located in the eastern hills of the capital and therefore an easy destination to reach, was also a center of Kannon worship.

205. Seven days of special rites were held on both the autumn and spring equinoxes.

curtain-of-state. Even having had such a dream and having woken up with a start, I did not tell people, "I have seen such and so," and not even taking it particularly to heart, I returned home.

Then Mother had a mirror cast, one foot in circumference, and declaring that it would take my place, she sent it with a monk on a pilgrimage to Hatsuse.[206] She apparently told him, "Go perform devotions for three days. Please have a dream to divine what future is in store for my daughter." For that same period of time, she also had me perform purifying rituals.[207]

This monk returned and made the following report: "Were I to come back without having had at least one dream, it would be disappointing, and what would I have to say for myself? So I fervently made obeisances, and when I fell asleep, I saw a wonderfully noble and lovely looking woman garbed in lustrous robes emerge from behind a

FIGURE 8 The forest at Kurama Temple.

FIGURE 9 An Edo-period print of Kiyomizu Temple.

206. This is the same Hatsuse Temple mentioned earlier.
207. Although the monk is making the pilgrimage in place of the author, she is to observe a period of seclusion and devote herself to purifying rituals, as though she were making the pilgrimage herself.

curtain-of-state; she was carrying the offering mirror in her hand. 'Was there a letter of vows[208] with this?' she asked. I respectfully replied, 'There was not. This mirror by itself is the offering.' 'How strange,' she said. 'This should be accompanied by a letter of vows.' Then she said, 'Look at what is reflected here in this mirror. What you see will make you very sad!' and she wept and sobbed softly. When I looked in the mirror, there was a reflection of someone collapsed on the floor crying and lamenting. 'When you look at this reflection, it is very sad, is it not? Now, look at this,' and she showed me the reflection on the other part of the mirror.[209] Amid beautiful bamboo blinds and other hangings, various robes poured out from under curtains-of-state; plum and cherry blossoms were in bloom; and from the tips of tree branches, warblers were singing.[210] 'Looking at this makes one very happy, does it not?' she said. That is what I saw in the dream." This, it seems, was his report. But I did not pay attention, not even to the extent of being surprised by how much he had seen and what it might mean.[211]

Even though I was of such a frivolous turn of mind, there was someone who was always telling me, "Pray to the Holy Deity Amaterasu." I had no idea of where Amaterasu might be or even whether this friend was speaking of a god or a buddha.[212] Even so, I gradually became interested and asked about it. I was told, "It is a god; this god dwells in Ise. In Kii Province, the one they call the 'Creator of Ki' is also the same holy god.[213] Moreover, it is also this god who is the guardian deity in the Sacred Mirror Room in the palace."[214] Going to Ise Province to worship did not seem to be anything I could consider, and how could I go to worship in the Sacred Mirror Room of the palace? Since it seemed that all there was to do was to pray to the light of the sky, I felt rather up in the air.

A relative of mine had become a nun[215] and entered Shūgakuin Temple.[216] In wintertime, I wrote to her,

namida sahe	So much that I have
furi hahetsutsu zo	to wipe away tear after tear;
omohiyaru	my thoughts are with you,
arashi fukuramu	at your mountain village in winter
fuyu no yamazato	where storms must be blowing.

208. An offering usually was accompanied by a formal written statement of vows that made a specific request and state promises that the petitioner pledged to keep if the request was granted.
209. Bronze mirrors have only one polished side, and from the description it seems that two scenes are presented on the one mirror.
210. This description evokes life at a high-ranking noble's residence or at the imperial palace.
211. This very record belies her statement here. She listened closely to what was said and recorded it carefully. Much later in the diary, she refers to this dream again at a critical moment in her life. For a discussion of this dream and its significance, see chapter 3.
212. The author claims ignorance of whether Amaterasu, the Sun Goddess and tutelary deity of the imperial family, is a god or the Buddha. Moreover, it is interesting that she appears not to know that this deity is female.
213. This response actually betrays confusion between a pre–Nara period official title, Creator of Ki, and the worship of the Sun Goddess in Kii Province.
214. This information is correct.
215. This is the third of the four communications with nuns, which seem to punctuate the work and be related only obliquely to the narrative context.
216. This was a temple named Shūgakuin in the vicinity of the present-day Shūgakuin District in northeast Kyoto, but it no longer exists.

Her reply,

wakete tofu	The extent of your
kokoro no hodo no	sympathy may be seen in
miyuru kana	your kind inquiry,
kokage woguraki	parting the lush foliage of summer
natsu no shigeri wo	in the dim shadows of the trees.[217]

My father, who had been down in the East Country, finally came back up to the capital,[218] and after he settled down in a residence in the Western Hills,[219] we all went to see him there. Wonderfully happy on a bright moonlit night, we spent the whole night chatting together. I wrote:

kakaru yo mo	That such a night
arikeru mono wo	could also exist in such a world—
kagiri tote	ah, that autumn when
kimi ni wakareshi	we parted, I thought, this is the end;
aki ha ikani zo	I will never see him again.

Father broke into tears and wrote in return:

omofu koto	Why does nothing ever
kanahazu nazo to	go the way I want, I grieved,
itohikoshi	hating to go on;
inochi no hodo mo	now, to have lived as long as this,
ima zo ureshiki	what happiness it is!

Yes indeed, compared with the sadness I felt when he came to tell me of his imminent departure, this joy of having him return safely after the long wait could not be exceeded by anything. Yet Father kept saying, "Judging from what I have observed of other people, when an old man whose abilities have declined mixes in society, he looks foolish. So I intend to close my gate and just retreat from the world." The way

217. This response, with summer imagery, to a poem about winter is one of the conundrums of the text. This disjunction bothered Teika when he was copying the manuscript because he added in the margin above *natsu no shigeri wo* (lush foliage of summer) a note that says *shimo no ku hon* (following phrase in source manuscript). See Akiyama, ed., *Sarashina nikki*, 66; see also Fujiwara no Teika, *Gyobutsubon: Sarashina nikki* [facsimile of manuscript copy] (Tokyo: Musashino shoin, 1984), 9. A section of text may be missing here, or perhaps the nun is simply remembering that the author's last visit was in summer.

218. Takasue returned to the capital in 1036 at the age of sixty-four. The author is twenty-nine years old.

219. The Western Hills refer to the northwest section of the capital in the vicinity of Kinugasa Hill.

he seemed to have given up all hope for the rest of his life made me unbearably forlorn.[220]

To the east of this house,[221] wild moors stretched out into the distance and one could clearly see the eastern mountain ridge right from Mount Hiei down to Mount Inari.[222] To the south, the Narabi Hills[223] were close enough that the one could hear the pine wind blowing from them. In between, almost up to the base of these hills, were what are called "rice paddies," from which came the sound of bird clappers.[224] All in all, it was a place that felt very much like the countryside, very charming, and on nights when the moon was bright, I enjoyed staying up until dawn gazing at the lovely scene. Now that we had moved so far away, I never heard from my friends, so I was surprised when a messenger who had come with other correspondence passed me a note from a friend asking, "How have you been?" I sent back,

omohi idete	There is no one who
hito koso tohane	remembers to call on us,
yama zato no	yet in the miscanthus
magaki no wogi ni	hedge of this mountain village,
akikaze ha fuku	at least an autumn breeze rustles.[225]

In the Tenth Month, we moved to the capital.[226] Mother became a nun; although she stayed in the same house with us, she lived apart in her own quarters.[227] Father just wanted me to assume the position of mistress of the household, but when I saw that this would mean I would be hidden away and never mix with the world, I felt shorn of support. Around this time, from someone to whom we were connected and who was aware of my situation, came an invitation for me to serve at court.[228] She said, "Surely it would be better than having her mope around the house with nothing to do." My old-fashioned parents found the idea of my becoming a lady-in-waiting very distasteful, so they kept me at home. However, several other people said things like "Nowadays, almost every young woman goes into service like this, and there have been cases of women who have done very well for themselves, indeed. Why don't you give it a try?" so grudgingly Father agreed to send me to court.

220. She likely feels bereft for both her father's sake and her own situation. Her father's giving up the world of political activity would mean that he also was giving up on her prospects in the world, for either a good marriage or a career at court.

221. She is now describing the landscape from her father's new residence in the Western Hills.

222. Mount Hiei is at the northeast corner of the capital, and Mount Inari is at the southeast edge of the capital in the Fushimi District.

223. The Narabi are small hills south of the present-day Muro and Ninnaji Districts.

224. Bird clappers were pieces of wood hung from strings so that they would clatter in the wind and scare away birds and other animals. The wording here recalls the description in "Writing Practice" (Tenarai), chapter 53 of the *Tale of Genji*, of Ukifune's retreat in the Ono District: ". . . rice fields nearby. There was something pleasing too about the sound of the bird clappers. It all reminded her of the East she had once known" (Royall Tyler, trans., *The Tale of Genji* [New York: Viking, 2001], 1085). With this allusion, she signals her own nostalgia for the East Country of her youth.

225. This poem was chosen for inclusion in the first "Autumn" section of the imperial anthology *Shinshūishū* (1364), poem 329. In the anthology, however, the last line of the poem was changed to the more emphatic *akikaze zo fuku*, which might be rendered "Ah, it is the autumn breeze that rustles."

226. Thus it seems that the residence in the Western Hills was temporary until the family could find a suitable residence in the capital proper.

227. As the text indicates, her becoming a nun does not mean that she has entered a monastery. But she has cut her hair short, accepted the monastic regulations regarding a nun's behavior, and will devote herself to performing services for the Buddhist image installed in her apartment. Her duties as a wife, however, are over. In the Heian period, becoming a nun within her own household was an aristocratic woman's most common form of taking the tonsure.

228. Serving at court meant taking a position as lady-in-waiting in the entourage of any of the members of the imperial family.

On the first occasion, I went into service for just one night.[229] I wore eight layers of gowns in the chrysanthemum color combination alternating light and dark,[230] with a jacket with a lustrous crimson silk.[231] For me—who had just lost myself in reading tales and knew nothing else and who, not even having visited other relatives, was used only to gazing at the moon and the blossoms living under the protection of my old-fashioned parents—my feelings at this moment of stepping out into court service—I could hardly believe it was I or that this was reality. I returned home at dawn.

When I was housebound, I occasionally used to feel that rather than being stuck forever at home, serving at court would give me the opportunity to experience interesting things and might even brighten my outlook, but now I felt uncertain. It seemed to me that indeed some things about this new life would cause me anguish. But what could I do about it?

In the Twelfth Month, I went again to serve. This time, I was given my own quarters and stayed for several days. Sometimes I would go up to my mistress's chambers and serve night duty. Having to lie down among strangers, I was unable to sleep a wink. I felt so embarrassed and constrained that I could not help weeping in secret. At the first light of dawn while it was still quite dark, I would go back to my own sleeping quarters and spend the whole day distractedly yearning for my father, thinking about how close we had become, living side by side, now that he was old and in decline and seemed to rely on me even more. Then there were my orphaned nieces,[232] who had been with me since they were born and slept on my left and right side at night and got up with me in the morning; how poignantly I now recalled them. So I would end up spending my days lost in homesick reverie. My ears would sense that someone was listening outside and peeking in at me, so uneasy I was.

After ten days of service, when I returned home, I found my father and mother waiting, having kindled a fire in the brazier. At the moment of seeing me get down from the carriage, Father broke into tears and said, "When you are at home, we see people from time to time and the servants are around, but in the last few days, I haven't heard the sound of human voices or seen a soul. How forlorn and lonely I have been!

229. She became a lady-in-waiting to Princess Yūshi (1038–1105), who at the time was an infant of less than two years old. Princess Yūshi was the daughter of the reigning Emperor Go-Suzaku (1009–1045) and the late Princess Genshi, the adopted daughter of Fujiwara no Yorimichi (992–1074). Thus Princess Yūshi was being raised in the Takakura Palace of her adoptive grandfather, Yorimichi, who held the post of regent at this time. Service in that household had the potential of putting the author in touch with members of the innermost circle of Heian aristocracy. It appears from this entry that she started as a part-time lady-in-waiting for a trial period in the winter of 1039, when she was thirty-two years old.

230. The chrysanthemum color combination was white with a lining of dark reddish purple. The edge of the lining would be visible, resulting in the layering of light and dark at the garments' openings and skirt edges.

231. "Lustrous" silk was soft silk that had been "fulled" by pounding with soft mallets to bring out its shine.

232. The nieces were the children of her elder sister. It is now fifteen years since her sister died.

If this goes on, what is going to become of me?" Seeing this made me feel so sad. The next morning, Father exclaimed, "Since you are home today, there is lots of coming and going; how lively the house feels." Face to face with him, I was moved to the verge of tears, wondering what on earth it was about me that made him feel that way.

Even though religious adepts find it very difficult to learn about former lives through dreams, and even though I was someone who felt aimless and confused, I had the following dream: I was sitting in the main hall of Kiyomizu Temple. A monk who was a kind of steward came out and reported, "You actually were once a monk in this very temple. As a monk artisan, you accumulated merit by making many Buddha statues. And so you were born into this life well above that lowly station. You built the one *jō*, six *shaku* Buddha[233] that resides in the east section of this hall (figure 10). As a matter of fact, you passed away while you were applying the gold foil to this image." "My goodness!" I said, "Does this mean that I applied the gold foil to that Buddha over there?" "Because you died while you were doing it, it was a different person who finished applying the gold foil and a different person who performed the offering ceremony when it was done." Now after seeing such a dream, if I had made fervent pilgrimages to Kiyomizu Temple, surely, on the strength of having worshipped the Buddha at that main hall in a former life, something might have come of it, but there is no use talking about that now because in the end I became no more serious about making pilgrimages than before.

On the twenty-fifth of the Twelfth Month,[234] I was invited to attend the rite of "Calling the Buddha's Names"[235] at the princess's palace. I went expecting to stay only that night. There were as many as forty attendants, all in layers of white robes with jackets of lustrous crimson silk. I hid myself behind the lady who was my mentor at court and, after barely showing myself, returned home at dawn. Snow had begun to flutter down. In the very cold and sharp chill of the dawn light, the moon reflected faintly on my lustrous sleeves truly recalled the "face damp with tears" of long ago.[236] On the road back, I wrote:

toshi ha kure　　　　　　The year is ending,
yo ha akegata no　　　　　the night begins to dawn,

FIGURE 10   The veranda off the main hall of Kiyomizu Temple.

233. This measurement corresponds to roughly sixteen feet. From the size and description of its placement, the monk is likely referring to the central image of Amida Buddha in the main hall of Kiyomizu Temple.
234. The intercalary Twelfth Month of 1039.
235. The rite of "Calling the Buddha's Names" was an annual event at the imperial palace that involved reciting all the Buddha's three thousand names in order to expiate the sins of the past year. After the performance of the rite at the imperial palace, the event was repeated in the home palaces of the imperial consorts. The ceremony the author attends is presumably at the Takakura Palace.
236. This is an allusion to poem 756 in the *Kokinshū*: *ahi ni ahite / mono omofu koro no / waga sode ni / yadoru tsuki sae / nururu kao naru* (Matching its feeling to mine, / when I am lost in melancholy, / even the moon / dwelling in these sleeves of mine / has a face damp with tears).

tsuki kage no	this brief moment when
sode ni utsureru	the rays of the moon are reflected
hodo zo hakanaki	on these wet sleeves, how
	ephemeral.[237]

Well, even though my debut had been like this, somehow I began to accustom myself to service at court. Although I was somewhat distracted by other things, it was not to the extent that people regarded me as eccentric, and as a matter of course, it seemed as though I was coming to be accepted and treated as one of the company. But my parents did not understand, and before long, they ended up shutting me away at home.[238] Even so, it was not as though my way of life became suddenly happy and lively; rather, although I was used to feeling very much at odds with life, the situation I found myself in now was quite contrary to all my hopes.

iku chitabi	How many thousand times
midzu no ta zeri wo	have I plucked the field parsley[239]
tsumi shika ha	from the water thus,
omohishi koto no	without a dewdrop falling
tsuyu mo kanahanu	in the direction of my hopes.

With just this private complaint, I let matters go.

Meanwhile, I became distracted by this and that and completely forgot even about the world of the tales. I actually ended up feeling quite down to earth. Over the years and months as I lay down and got up in meaningless activity, why had I not devoted myself to religious practices or pilgrimages? Ah, but the things I had hoped for, the things I had wished for, could they ever really happen in this world? After all, was a man like the Shining Genji ever likely to exist in this world? No, this is a world in which being hidden away at Uji by Captain Kaoru could never happen.[240] Oh, how crazy I was and how foolish I came to feel. Such were the thoughts that had sunk in, and had I then carried on with my feet on the ground, maybe things would have been all right, but that just was not possible.[241]

237. The author's poem is similar to one in the *Murasaki Shikibu Diary*: *toshi kurete / waga yo fuke yuku / kaze no oto ni / kokoro no uchi no / susamajiki kana* (As does the year / So my days draw to an end; / There is a coldness / In the voice / Of the night wind) (Yamamoto Ritatsu, ed., *Murasaki Shikibu nikki, Murasaki Shikibu shū*, Shinchō Nihon koten shūsei [Tokyo: Shinchōsha, 1980], 72; Richard Bowring, trans., *Murasaki Shikibu: Her Diary and Poetic Memoirs* [Princeton, N.J.: Princeton University Press, 1982], 113). The author may have had Murasaki Shikibu's experience in the back of her mind. Just before she composed this poem, Murasaki Shikibu reflected on the first night that she ever served at court. Both Takasue no Musume and Murasaki Shikibu entered court life relatively late in life and found it difficult to fit in. As expressed in the poems, their feelings at the end of the year coincide nicely, although Murasaki Shikibu emphasizes a feeling of chilly loneliness, and Takasue no Musume stresses the ephemeral nature of her experience.

238. This is a veiled reference to her marriage to Tachibana no Toshimichi (1002–1058). From her following comments, it does not appear that at first it was a match to her liking.

239. "Plucking field parsley" was a proverbial expression for putting all one's heart into a project and having it come to nothing.

240. This is a reference back to her youthful dream to be kept in a rural setting by someone as handsome as Genji or Kaoru.

241. In other words, she was not able to give up her romantic dreams or her fascination with the world of tales. Nonetheless, as the beginning of this passage testifies, she had begun to live a more "down-to-earth" life. She had settled into married life, and from later references, we can assume she must have had a child quite soon after marrying.

Some friends had informed the place at which I had first gone into court service that it did not appear staying cooped up at home was really my true wish, so there were endless requests for my attendance. Among them came a particular one, "Send the young lady to court,"[242] an order that could not be ignored, so I found myself drawn back into occasional service in the course of presenting my niece to court. But it was not as though I could entertain the vain and immodest hopes that I had in days gone by; after all, I was just being drawn along by my niece. On the occasions when I went to serve, the situation was like this. The women really familiar with court service are in a class by themselves and greet any occurrence with a knowing face, but even though I could not be regarded as a novice, neither could I be treated as an old hand, so I was kept at a distance like an occasional guest. Although I was in this uncertain position, since I did not have to rely solely on that kind of work,[243] I was not particularly envious of those who were so much better at it than me. In fact, I felt rather at ease, going to court just on suitable occasions, chatting with those women who happened to have time on their hands. On celebratory occasions—and other interesting, pleasant occasions too—in my present situation I thus was able to mix with society. Of course, since I had to maintain a reserve and take care not to push myself forward too much, I was privy only to the general goings-on at court. As I went along in this way, a time came when I accompanied the princess to the imperial palace.[244] One dawn when the moon was very bright, I thought to myself, "The god Amaterasu to whom I have been praying actually resides right here in the palace's Mirror Room;[245] I would like to take this occasion to worship there." So in the brightness of the moonlight of the Fourth Month, ever so secretly I went to pay my respects with the guidance of an acquaintance, Hakase no Myōbu,[246] who served as mistress of the inner chambers. In the very faint light of the lamp stand, she looked amazingly ancient and had a divine quality. As she sat there speaking about things one might expect, she seemed scarely like a human being; one might even think she was the god manifesting itself.

On the next night, too, the moon was very bright, and when I opened the east door of the Fujitsubo Pavilion[247] to gaze at the moon and was chatting with the various ladies whom one would expect to be there,

242. This request was to present the author's niece for service in Princess Yūshi's entourage.
243. This is because she is married. According to Teika's commentary, Toshimichi assumed the post of governor of Shimotsuke Province (roughly corresponding to present-day Tochigi Prefecture in the northeastern end of the Kantō region) on January 25 in Chōkyū 2 (1041), just one year after their marriage. We can assume that she stayed in the capital and that they lived apart for four years. This would have made it easier for her to continue her occasional service at court. The earnings from her husband's post would have provided a solid financial foundation for the family, so she did not have to feel economically dependent on her service at Princess Yūshi's court.
244. This took place in 1042. Teika added a detailed note in the margin of his copy of the manuscript about this event: it occurred in Chōkyū 3 (1042) on the thirteenth day of the Fourth Month, and the party was lodged in the Fujitsubo apartment of the palace until the twentieth. This appears to have been the first opportunity for Takasue no Musume to experience life in the imperial palace.
245. In the midst of her early infatuation with tales, she had a dream in which a monk, who was constructing an artificial stream for the Princess of the First Rank, instructed her to worship Amaterasu. Then, after the dream prophecy by the monk who took a mirror offering to Hatsuse Temple in her place, she records that several people told her to worship Amaterasu. Gradually, it becomes clear that worshipping Amaterasu is associated with achieving success in a court career. Now the author is actually staying at the imperial palace itself and thus has her first chance to worship the deity directly.
246. As noted earlier in regard to middle-ranking ladies in waiting, Hakase is translated literally as "doctor of letters" and implies that a male relative of the lady held a doctorate.
247. Readers of the *Tale of Genji* will recognize the name of this apartment as the sobriquet of Genji's stepmother. It literally means "Wisteria Pavilion" and was one of the apartments reserved for consorts of the emperor. Princess Yūshi's mother had likely resided there.

we heard the rustling sound of the Umetsubo Pavilion Consort[248] going up to serve His Majesty. It was an enchantingly elegant moment, yet the other women could not help remarking, "If our late mistress[249] were still in this world, it would have been her going to serve His Majesty like that." Truly, it was sad.

ama no to wo	Although they all
kumowi nagara mo	dwell in the clouds together,[250]
yoso ni mite	the moon feels estranged[251]
mukashi no ato wo	from heaven's door, perhaps because
kofuru tsuki kana	it longs for traces of the past.

It was winter, and there was no moon nor was snow falling, but on a night when the vast sky was stretched right to its edges clear and cold in the starlight, I spent the whole night talking until dawn with the ladies-in-waiting from the regent's household.[252] When it grew light, we all separated and went back to our various places, but one of the women recalling that night sent this to me:

tsuki mo naku	There was no moon,
hana mo mizarishi	nor were there blossoms to see,
fuyu no yo no	yet that winter's night
kokoro ni shimite	penetrated my heart, and I long
kohishiki ya nazo	for it. I wonder why?

That was how I felt, too, and it was charming that we shared the same feeling.

saeshi yo no	The ice that formed
kohori ha sode ni	on that clear, cold night rests
mada tokede	unmelted on my sleeves.
fuyu no yo nagara	All through the winter's night,
ne wo koso ha nake	I weep aloud remembering it.[253]

248. Umetsubo literally means "Plum Pavilion," where the consort in residence was Seishi (1014–1068), the daughter of Fujiwara no Norimichi (996–1075), who in turn was the younger brother of Fujiwara no Yorimichi, Princess Yūshi's adoptive grandfather.

249. This is Princess Genshi, the mother of Princess Yūshi, who died in the third year of Shoryaku (1039) at the age of twenty-four.

250. "In the clouds" was a conventional epithet for the imperial court.

251. The moon stands for the collective body of the ladies-in-waiting who long for the old days when their mistress was still alive. Heaven's door stands for the emperor's quarters in the palace.

252. Fujiwara no Yorimichi is the current regent and the adoptive grandfather of Princess Yūshi, whom Takasue no Musume is serving. Yorimichi's residence was the Kaya no In, and Princess Yūshi was installed in his Takakura Palace. The two mansions were just across Tsuchimikado Ōji Avenue from each other, and the ladies-in-waiting of both households seem to have known one another well and could visit with one another when there were no pressing duties. This passage records such an occasion.

253. It is the sympathetic resonance between them that brings her tears, not sadness.

On night duty in our mistress's chamber,[254] as I lay there listening, my eyes opened each time I heard the voices of the water birds as they flapped about all night long—

waga goto zo	They are just like me,
midzu no ukine ni	awake until dawn, sleeping
akashitsutsu	fitfully on the water,
uhage no shimo wo	struggling to brush away
harahiwabunaru	the frost on their wings.[255]

—was what I murmured to myself, but the person sleeping next to me heard and said,

mashite omohe	Just try to imagine,
midzu no karine no	even from your own transient sleep
hodo dani zo	on the water,
uhage no shimo wo	how I struggle every night to
harahiwabikeru	brush the frost away.[256]

One day, a good friend of mine in the next apartment slid open the door, and we spent the day chatting. Since another good friend of ours had gone up to serve our mistress, we repeatedly invited her to come and visit us. When she sent back a message, "If you really insist I come, I will try to get away," we sent her this poem attached to a withered stalk of pampas grass:

fuyugare no	Our waving sleeves tired,
shino no wo susuki	like this plumeless stalk of grass
sode tayumi	withered by winter,
maneki mo yoseji	we will invite no more but
kaze ni makasemu	leave our entreaties to the wind.[257]

Since it seemed that the persons designated to wait directly on the high court nobles and the senior courtiers[258] were fixed from before, given that I was an inexperienced homebody, I could not expect anybody to even be aware of my presence. Nonetheless, on a very dark

254. Every night, a group of attendants slept close to the princess's side.

255. This passage and its poem are reminiscent of a passage in the *Murasaki Shikibu Diary*, in which she, too, expresses a feeling of empathy with the water birds: *midzutori wo / midzu no uhe to ya / yoso ni mimu / ware mo ukitaru / yo wo sugushitsutsu* (Birds on the water; / Can I look at them / Dispassionately? / I too am floating through / A sad uncertain world) (Yamamoto, ed., *Murasaki Shikibu nikki*, 39; Bowring, trans., *Murasaki Shikibu*, 75).

256. Her companion attendant changes the *ukine* (fitful sleep) in Takasue no Musume's poem to *karine* (transient sleep), referring to the part-time nature of the nighttime duties performed by Takasue no Musume. She asks her to sympathize on the basis of her own brief experience with the hardship of someone like herself on permanent night duty. Although the circumstances and tenor of the exchange are somewhat different, this pair of poems resembles an exchange between Murasaki Shikibu and Lady Dainagon in the *Murasaki Shikibu Diary*. Murasaki Shikibu is back home for a rest and writes to a colleague at court whom she finds herself missing, even though she found service at court itself rather trying. She sends this poem: *ukine seshi / midzu no uhe nomi / kohishikute / kamo no uhage ni / sae zo otoranu* (My longing for / Those waters at the court / On which we lay / Is keener than the frost / On duck feathers) (Yamamoto, ed., *Murasaki Shikibu nikki*, 58; Bowring, trans., *Murasaki Shikibu*, 97). Lady Dainagon's reply is *uchiharafu / tomo naki koro no / nezame ni ha / tsugahishi woshi zo / yoha ni kohishiki* (Awakening / In the dead of night / To find no friend / To brush away the frost, / She longs for her) (Yamamoto, ed., *Murasaki Shikibu nikki*, 58; Bowring, trans., *Murasaki Shikibu*, 97).

257. Plumes of pampas grass bending in the wind were thought to resemble beckoning hands.

258. The two terms designate the highest two levels of court society. Although these designations were not tied precisely to court rank, in general, high court nobles (*kandachime*) held the first three ranks in the court hierarchy, and senior courtiers (*tenjōbito*) held the fourth or fifth rank. For a discussion of these designations, see McCullough and McCullough, trans., *Tale of Flowering Fortunes*, 2:791.

night in the early part of the Tenth Month, there was a service of unin-
terrupted readings of the sutras.[259] When someone said, "Monks with
particularly lovely voices are reciting at this time," a companion and I
went up to a doorway close to the reading, and while we were stretched
out on the veranda listening and chatting away, a man came up to us
(figure 11). My companion whispered, "It would look awkward if we
were just to escape inside and call other, more experienced women
in the ladies-in-waiting apartment. So be it. Let us just stay here and
do our best in the circumstances." So I stayed with her listening to the
conversation and found that the man spoke with a mature and quiet
demeanor, not unpleasant at all. He asked, "Who is your companion?"
without a hint of the usual insinuating tone men use, and he spoke so
sensitively of various touching things in life that in spite of my natural inclinations, there were several points in the conversation when I
found it difficult just to withdraw in silence, and so both of us ended
up conversing with him. He said things like "Well now, there still are
some people here that I have not met before," which seemed to indicate
that he found us interesting, and he did stay for a while making no
move to leave quickly. It was dark without even the light of stars; from
time to time, drizzle fell, and the sound of it falling on the leaves of
the trees was charming. He said, "It is an enchantingly lovely evening,
is it not? If it were bright with the moon shining into every corner, I
expect we would find it embarrassingly dazzling."[260] He spoke of the
seasons: "Spring mist is lovely; with the sky gently overcast, even the
moon's face is dimmed, and it seems the light flows to us from afar. On
such a night, how thrilling it is to hear someone plucking a *biwa* tuned
to the 'Fragrant Breeze' mode.[261] Or again, when it is autumn and the
moon is very bright: although haze may be stretched across the sky,
the moon shines through so clearly that you feel as though you could
reach out and take it in your hand, and with the sound of the wind and
the voices of the insects making one feel that all the delights of autumn
have been brought together, to hear someone casually strumming the
strings of the *sō no koto*[262] accompanied by sharp, clear notes blown
on a flute—well then, one wonders why one was ever enthralled with
spring. But then again, when you think about it, on a winter's night
when the sky is perfectly clear and light from the sky meets the light

FIGURE 11 The veranda off the Isonokami Shrine.

259. Services involving continuous readings of sutras for a fixed period of time were commissioned with the object of either gaining some benefit in this world or ensuring salvation for someone who had passed away. The monks here shared the chanting duties in two-hour shifts, in which they melodiously chanted sutras like the *Lotus Sutra* and the *Prajna Paramita Sutra*. Because the voices of the monks differed in quality, word would get around, as we infer from this passage, as to which groups of monks were good singers. This particular reading, which likely took place in 1042, may have been commissioned for Princess Yūshi's mother, the late Princess Genshi, who had died roughly three years earlier. The reading takes place in the Takakura Palace, and if we assume that it was being held for the late empress, it would explain why high-ranking courtiers were in attendance. The wide verandas of Heian-period dwellings made good meeting places.

260. His implication is that the women would feel uncomfortable and shy if they were exposed in the light of the moon.

261. The name of one of the tuning modes for the *biwa*, a kind of lute.

262. The thirteen-string koto, a stringed instrument plucked from above by the seated player.

from the fallen, piled-up snow and the wavering notes of the *hichi-riki*[263] sound forth—then we forget all about spring and autumn." He continued, "If I may ask, ladies, with which season would your hearts be lodged?"[264] In response, my companion answered that her heart was drawn to the autumn night, and since I did not want to say the same thing, I replied with this poem:

asa midori	Lucent green—
hana mo hitotsu ni	misting over, becoming one
kasumitsutsu	with the blossoms too;
oboro ni miyuru	dimly it may be seen,
haru no yo no tsuki	the moon on a night in spring.[265]

Repeating this over and over softly to himself, he said, "Well, well, this consigns the autumn night to oblivion, doesn't it?"

koyohi yori	From this night on,
nochi no inochi no	if it should be that my life
moshimo araba	continues on,
sa ha haru no yo wo	I shall always consider the spring night
katami to omohamu	a souvenir of you and this occasion.

Then the person whose heart was drawn to autumn said,

hito ha mina	It would seem that
haru ni kokoro wo	all people's hearts are drawn
yosetsumeri	to spring.
ware nomi ya mimu	Shall I be left to gaze alone
aki no yo no tsuki	at the moon on an autumn night?[266]

It seems that his interest was piqued by this, and yet having the air of finding himself in a difficult situation, he said, "I have heard that even in far Cathay, from ancient times when it came to choosing between

263. A small reed instrument that makes a strident, piercing sound.
264. The seasons are compared in other classical literature texts but are found particularly often in the *Tale of Genji*.
265. The author's use of *asa midori*, rendered here as "lucent green," is both evocative and original. It is very difficult to define the precise quality of the color to which this phrase refers, as there was no clear demarcation between the colors green and blue in classical Japan and China. Accordingly, the grass could be described as blue and the sky as green. That said, however, the word *midori* in Japanese has a close connection with the fresh new green of spring, so at least part of the connotation of this term is the atmosphere of "green" in spring. It is a night scene, and the term *asa midori* can be used to refer to the radiant quality of the sky on a starry night when one might be inclined to call the sky "pale indigo," a sensation of color that is both dark and radiant. The author seems to be seeking a combination of both the green atmosphere of spring and the radiant darkness of a clear night sky. This is the first poem by Takasue no Musume to be included in an imperial poetry anthology, the *Shinkokinshū* (1205), poem 56 in the first "Spring" section. The *Shinkokinshū* signaled an important new direction in classical Japanese poetry. For a detailed discussion of the color issue and the originality of this poem, see Itō Moriyuki, "*Sarashina nikki* no 'asamidori . . .' ei ni kansuru kōsatsu," in *Genji monogatari kara, Genji monogatari e*, ed. Nagai Kazuko (Tokyo: Kasama shoin, 2007), 346–66.
266. The companion's poem alludes to a poem in "Bamboo River" (Takegawa), chapter 44 of the *Tale of Genji*: *hito ha mina / hana ni kokoro wo / utsusuramu / hitori zo madofu / haru no yo no yami* (It would seem that / people's hearts have all gone over / to the blossoms; / all alone I wander / through the spring night's darkness) (Abe Aiko et al., eds., *Genji monogatari*, Shinpen Nihon koten bungaku zenshū 24 [Tokyo: Shōgakukan, 1997], 73; see also Tyler, trans., *Tale of Genji*, 810). The companion has deftly adapted the *Genji* poem to suit her own situation by shifting the poem reference from spring to autumn. Her alluding to the *Tale of Genji* at this point also signals that she is aware that their conversation is like something out of *Genji*. This mutual savoring of elegant conversation supported by a shared literary connection creates an intimate bond among the three of them.

spring and autumn, people were unable to decide.[267] And you, my esteemed ladies, must have your own reasons for choosing the way you have. As for where one's own heart is pulled, when one feels touched or delighted on a specific occasion, it seems that just naturally the look of the sky at that moment, the appearance of the moon or the flowers, becomes engraved on one's heart. I would love to hear the details of what it is that led both of you to feel the way you do about spring and autumn. From long ago, the look of the moon on a winter's night has been held up as the epitome of a dreary, uninteresting phenomenon,[268] and at any rate, it is so cold at that time that one is not particularly inclined to spend much time looking at it. However, once when I was assigned the duty of imperial envoy to go down to Ise on the occasion of the priestess's 'Assumption of the Train' ceremony[269] and I was to return to the capital at dawn, the light of the moon was shining on the snow that had been falling and piling up for days. I was feeling somewhat forlorn, given that I was to travel that day, but when I went to take my leave, I was struck by the sense of awe that this place inspires more than any other. I was beckoned to sit in the appropriate place by a serving woman from the august era of Retired Emperor Enyū[270] who, with her old-fashioned air and deep sense of refinement, seemed almost divine herself. She talked to me about memories of the old days, weeping from time to time, and she did me the honor of bringing out a well-tuned lute for me to play.[271] I could scarcely believe I was in this world, and I regretted even that the night was going to break into day. Thoughts of the capital were quite extinguished, and since that time when I was so moved, I have come to deeply appreciate nights in winter when snow has fallen. Even if I have to hold a small brazier in my arms, I cannot help going out onto the veranda and contemplating the scene. Surely you ladies must have similar reasons of your own for how you feel about the seasons. And now from this night on, nights when the winter drizzle falls into the deep darkness, my heart will be steeped in this same feeling. I certainly feel that tonight is not inferior to the snowy night at Ise." And when he had finally parted from us after saying such things, I thought, "I would prefer that he not find out who I am."[272]

267. This is a direct allusion to the most famous comparison of the four seasons in the *Tale of Genji*, which takes place in chapter 19, "Wisps of Cloud." See Tyler, trans., *Tale of Genji*, 359. The male visitor signals his recognition of the allusion in the companion's poem and follows it up with a *Genji* allusion of his own. We can only imagine how much this must have charmed Takasue no Musume.

268. This is another allusion to the *Tale of Genji*, chapter 20, "The Bluebell" (Asagao), in which Genji disparages the conventional opinion that the night sky in winter is dreary. See Tyler, trans., *Tale of Genji*, 373. In fact, this section in the *Tale of Genji* is the first time in the history of the aesthetic appreciation of the seasons in Japan that someone argues for the beauty of winter scenery. In the medieval period, aesthetic taste shifted toward an appreciation of the beauty of cold and wintry things, summed up in the term *hie* (chill), and this early reference in the *Genji* seems to presage that.

269. The "Assumption of the Train" ceremony was a coming-of-age ceremony for girls, usually held when they were about twelve. The long trailing garment was worn as part of the formal costume for women. A princess was chosen at the beginning of each new era to serve as the priestess of the Ise Shrine, where Amaterasu, the tutelary deity of the imperial family, was enshrined. The ceremony itself would have taken place at the Saikū residence of the Ise priestess and not at the Ise Shrine itself. The man's recital of this episode in his court service allowed Teika to identify the male visitor as Minamoto no Sukemichi (d. 1060). At the end of the manuscript, Teika appends a substantial synopsis of Sukemichi's successful official career. At the time of his death, he had managed to achieve the very high rank of junior second. Sukemichi's surname, Minamoto, which was given to surplus imperial male progeny, marks him as someone of royal blood, if not status. In addition, this surname is often referred to by an alternative reading for the first character, *gen*, with the addition of *ji* (clan; that is, "member of the Minamoto clan"), which is the same Genji as in the name of the hero of the famous tale. Teika also appends a note about the "Assumption of the Train" ceremony for which Sukemichi was the imperial envoy. According to Teika, the ceremony took place in Manju 2 on the third day of the Twelfth Month, or January 2, 1026. Teika gives Sukemichi's age at the time of his death as fifty-six; therefore, he would have been in his early twenties at the time of his service as imperial envoy. This would make him thirty-eight years old at the time of this winter's night conversation, only about three years older than the author.

270. Emperor Enyū reigned from 969 to 984. This lady-in-waiting has served at the shrine through the reigns of five emperors—in other words, for more than forty years—which would put her in her late sixties or early seventies.

271. Sukemichi's fame as a singer and player of the *biwa* (lute), *wagon* (zither), and flute is noted in official court histories.

272. Given her evident excitement and joy at this encounter with Sukemichi, this final remark may seem difficult to understand. Her reaction might have had many reasons. She might feel that the brief encounter was precious just for what it was, not as a prelude to a serious relationship. She was of much lower status than Sukemichi, and as already a mature married woman, she might be embarrassed to have him learn these facts about her.

The next year in the Eighth Month when our mistress was visiting the imperial palace,[273] there was an all-night performance being held in the emperor's presence; I had no idea that that person was in attendance. I was spending that night in the lower apartments, and when I pushed open the sliding doors of the narrow hall and looked out, just as I was confused at the soft light, wondering whether or not it was the dawn moon, there was the sound of footsteps and a man reciting a sutra. The man reciting the sutra stopped in front of the opening, and when I replied to his words, he suddenly remembered me and said, "Indeed, I have never forgotten my fond memories of that short time we shared on the night of winter drizzle." It was not an occasion for answering at length or making a great deal out of answering, so I said,

nani sa made	Why, I wonder, should
omohi idekemu	you remember that so well,
nahozari no	since it was only
ko no ha ni kakeshi	the winter drizzle falling as
shigure bakari wo	it does on the leaves of trees.

But I had barely got this out when some other people came up, so I just slipped away inside, and since that night our party withdrew from the palace, I heard only later from the other woman who had been my companion on the first occasion that he had passed on a reply for me. Apparently he had said, "On another occasion like the night of the winter drizzle, I would like to play for you on the *biwa* all the pieces I know." When I heard that, I eagerly awaited such a chance, but it never came.

Around spring on a gentle, quiet evening, I heard that he had come to our mistress's residence for a visit, and my companion of that other night and I crept out quietly hoping to meet him, but other people had come visiting too, and since all the usual ladies-in-waiting were there, after getting that far, we went back in. Perhaps he, too, had been hoping to see us again and so had come purposefully on this quiet evening, but since it turned out to be noisy, it seems that he withdrew.

273. Teika's marginal note confirms that Princess Yūshi and her sister Baishi visited the imperial palace on the twenty-third day of the Seventh Month of Chōkyū 4 (1043) and stayed in the Ichijō In (because of a fire in the palace the year before). They apparently stayed until the tenth day of the Eighth Month. Teika does not note the reason for the special visit.

kashima mite	The heart of one,
naruto no ura ni	who, seeing a chance at Kashima
kogare idzuru	rowed out yearning
kokoro ha eki ya	for Naruto Sound—did you
	understand,
iso no amabito	fisherman on the rocky shore?[274]

It all ended with my just writing this poem. Since he was a person of very upright character, he was not one to make prying inquiries as a more worldly man might, and so time passed and that was it.

Now I had come to the point that I was deeply aware of regretting my absurd fancies of the past, and I also could not help recalling with vexation that I had not been taken along on my parents' pilgrimages and such. So now, resolving to concentrate single-mindedly on achieving a state of wealth that would allow me to raise my "little sprout"[275] with all the plentiful care I wished and to accumulate a status for myself that would exceed that of Mikura Mountain,[276] and with aspirations extending to the world to come as well, just past the twentieth of the Eleventh Month,[277] I set off on a pilgimage to Ishiyama Temple.[278]

Snow was falling; the scenery along the way was beautiful. Upon seeing the Ōsaka Barrier, I suddenly recalled that when we crossed this barrier station long ago,[279] it also was winter and, that time too, how wildly the wind blew.

afusaka no	The voice of the Ōsaka
seki no seki kaze	Barrier wind blowing now
fuku kowe ha	through the station,
mukashi kikishi ni	is no different at all
kaharazarikeri	from the one I heard long ago.

Seeing how splendidly the Barrier Temple[280] had been built up, I recalled that time before when one could see only the roughly hewn face of the Buddha; realizing how many months and years had passed was very moving.

The area around Uchiide Beach and so forth looked no different from before. We arrived at the goal of our pilgrimage just as it was

274. This poem is a complex of double entendres on place-names. Kashima is a place in the Inland Sea close to Naruto. Kashima can also mean *kashi ma* (an interval when no one is looking) and also evokes the adjective *kashimashi* (noisy). Thus the single place-name calls up the chance of a meeting and the reason why the meeting was forestalled. Naruto no ura (Naruto Bay) is a body of water close to the famous Naruto Whirlpool, whence the name *naru + to* (sounding gate). The translation here takes advantage of the double meaning of "sound" in English for both the sound one hears and the term for a body of water. Thus the place-name Naruto evokes both the noisy party that sent Sukemichi away and the promised sound of his *biwa* that the author had ventured out hoping to hear. In addition to these double meanings, the verb *kogare* (rowed) also puns on the verb *kogaru* (to burn with yearning).

275. This is a reference to a son she had with Toshimichi. Later in the diary, she mentions children in the plural, and it is recorded that she had another son and one daughter with Toshimichi, but the diary gives no precise information about the births. From other sources, we also know that Toshimichi was the governor of Shimotsuke Province beginning in 1041 and would have returned to the capital around the time of this entry.

276. Mikura Mountain (located in present-day Tottori Prefecture) was an *utamakura* whose literal meaning, "Great Treasure House" Mountain, is linked to the idea of accumulating wealth.

277. The year 1045, and the author is thirty-eight years old.

278. Ishiyama Temple on Lake Biwa in Shiga Prefecture is still a popular place of pilgrimage and, as mentioned earlier, an important site of Kannon worship.

279. The author crossed the Ōsaka Barrier, in the hills between the capital and Lake Biwa, when she was thirteen years old and on her way to the capital from the east.

280. She refers to the temple as Sekidera (literally, "Barrier Temple"), which was its common name.

getting dark, and getting down at the Purification Pavilion, we went up to the Sacred Hall. No one spoke; I found the sound of the mountain wind frightening. I dozed off while I was praying, and in a dream a person told me, "Some musk deer incense has been bestowed on us by the Chūdō.[281] Quickly announce this over there." I woke up with a start, and when I realized that it had been a dream, I felt that it must be auspicious, so I spent the whole night in religious devotions.

The next day, too, snow fell wildly. I tried to soothe my feelings of uneasiness by chatting with the friend I had got to know at court who had accompanied me on the pilgrimage. We stayed in retreat for three days and then returned.

That following year, there was a great buzz about the procession for the Great Purification preceding the Great Festival of Thanksgiving that was to be held on the twenty-fifth day of the Tenth Month.[282] I had started fasting in preparation for a pilgrimage to Hatsuse Temple,[283] and I was to leave the capital on that very day. People whom one might expect to take an interest in my affairs said things like, "One gets to see something like this only once in a reign; even people from the countryside and all over the place are coming in to see it. After all, with so many days and months in a year, for you to go off and desert the capital on that very day, why, it's crazy!" Although my brother[284] fumed about it, the father of my children said, "No matter what, do what you think best."[285] I was moved by his willingness to send me off in accordance with the vow I had made. It seems that those who were to accompany me wanted very much to view the procession. Although it was sad for them, I thought to myself, "After all, what does sightseeing amount to? The zeal of the intention to make a pilgrimage on this kind of occasion will surely be recognized as such. I shall certainly see a sacred sign from the Buddha." I strengthened my will and left at the first light of that day. Just as we were passing along the grand avenue of Nijō itself[286] (I had had my attendants wear pilgrim's white garments and those in front carry holy lanterns), there were a lot of people going to and fro, some on horseback, some in ox carriages, some on foot, on their way to take their places in the viewing stands. Surprised and disconcerted at seeing us, people in the crowd murmured, "What on earth is this?" and some even laughed derisively and jeered.

281. The *chūdō* (central hall) is the center of a temple complex in which the main object of worship is enshrined. The most famous *chūdō* in the capital region was that of Enryakuji on Mount Hiei, and the reference here may be to that specific hall.

282. The Great Festival of Thanksgiving is the grander version of the annual Festival of First Fruits. The Grand Festival was held during those years when a new emperor was officially enthroned. Emperor Go-Reizei (1025–1068) had assumed the throne the previous year, and it was the custom to hold the official enthronement rites the year after the succession. In the Great Purification preceding the festival, the new emperor performed a ritual ablution on the banks of the Kamo River. The pomp and pageantry made it a popular event for sightseeing.

283. More than a decade earlier, the author's mother had sent a mirror with a monk to Hatsuse Temple on the author's behalf. This, then, is the author's first personal pilgrimage to this center of Kannon worship.

284. This is likely the same brother, Sadayoshi, who was mentioned much earlier in her account of the journey from Kazusa to the capital as the one who carried her on horseback to say farewell to her nurse.

285. This is the first direct mention in the diary of the author's husband, and it casts a surprisingly positive light on their relationship. He appears to be the only one in the household to support her decision.

286. Nijō Avenue is the avenue down which the procession would pass.

When we passed in front of the house of the guard commander Yoshiyori,[287] it seemed that he was just about to move to his viewing stand. The gates were pushed open wide, and people were standing around. Someone said, "That seems to be somebody going on a pilgrimage. And to think of all the other days she could have chosen." Amid those laughing over this, there was one (I wonder what was in his heart) who said, "What is so important about delighting one's eyes for a moment? With such fervent zeal, someone like that is sure to receive the Buddha's grace. Maybe we are the ones without sense. Giving up the sightseeing and making up our minds to do something like that; that is what we ought to be doing." So there was one person who could speak with some sense of seriousness.

So as not to be exposed to the eyes of others on the road, we had left while it was still dark. Now, in order to wait for those who had left later to catch up and hoping that the alarmingly deep fog would lift a little, we stopped at the main gate of Hōshō Temple.[288] There, we could really see the crowds of people coming in from the countryside to sightsee; they flowed on and on like a river. Everywhere, it was hard to get through. Even some rather strange-looking urchins, who seemed hardly old enough to understand things, looked askance at our carriage as we forced our way against the stream. There was no end to it. Seeing all these people, I even began to wonder why on earth I had set out on this trip, but concentrating my thoughts single-mindedly on the Buddha, I finally arrived at Uji.[289]

There, too, was a crowd of people wanting to cross over to this side. The boat helmsmen were in no hurry to make the crossings; they stood around, sleeves rolled up, leaning on their oars, looking quite arrogant as though they were not even aware of all the people waiting to cross. Looking around, singing songs, they appeared very smug. We were unable to cross for an interminable amount of time. When I looked carefully around me, I recalled the daughters of the Uji prince in Murasaki's tale.[290] I had always been curious about what kind of place she had had them live in; so this must be it, and indeed, it is a lovely place. Thinking these thoughts, I finally was ferried across. Also, when I went in to look at the Uji villa belonging to His Lordship,[291] the first thing

287. Yoshiyori was the eldest son of Fujiwara no Takaie (979–1044) and brother of the late Empress Teishi.

288. Hōshō Temple was located at the southeast edge of the capital, directly on the road to Uji, where now the Zen temple Tōfukuji occupies approximately the same location. It was a popular place to break one's journey on the way to Uji.

289. Travelers had to be ferried across the Uji River. The place-name Uji was an *utamakura* for poems about sorrow because Uji was regarded as homophonous with *ushi* (sorrow, suffering).

290. These are the daughters of the Eighth Prince in the *Tale of Genji* who moved to Uji after his residence in the capital burned down. The courtship of these sisters, the untimely death of the elder sister, and, finally, the installation of their half sister Ukifune at Uji by Kaoru make up the content of the so-called Uji chapters of the *Tale of Genji*. The author's reference here to the *Tale of Genji* as "Murasaki's tale" seems to indicate that Heian readers had already started to refer to the author of the *Tale of Genji* by the nickname Murasaki.

291. This is the villa of Fujiwara no Yorimichi, who, as the adoptive grandfather of Princess Yūshi, was the author's employer, which is likely why she was able to tour the villa. Seven years after this date, Yorimichi rebuilt the villa magnificently and eventually had it consecrated as a temple, the Byōdōin, which survives.

that sprang to mind was, "Would not the Lady Ukifune have lived in just such a place as this?" (figure 12).²⁹²

Since we had left before light, my people were very tired, so we stopped at a place called Yahirouchi.²⁹³ While we were having something to eat, my attendants talked among themselves, "Say, isn't this the infamous Mount Kurikoma?²⁹⁴ It is getting toward dusk. We had better get everyone ready to go." I listened to this with apprehension.

We made it over that mountain, and just as we arrived in the area of Nieno Pond,²⁹⁵ the sun was setting over the rim of the mountain. "Now let us stop for the night," my attendants said, and they spread out to seek lodging. It was not a suitable area. They reported back, "There is only this rather poor and shabby little house." "What else can we do?" I replied, and so we ended up lodging there. There were only two, rather seedy-looking men servants in charge, who said, "Everyone else has gone up to the capital." That night, too, we did not get a wink of sleep. The men servants kept wandering into and out of the house. I heard the maidservants in the rear of the house ask, "What on earth are you doing roaming around like that?" "Oh nothing much, but here we are putting up strangers. We got to thinking, suppose they were to make off with the cauldron, what would we do? We can't sleep for worrying, so we are wandering around keeping an eye on things." They spoke like this thinking we were asleep; hearing their words was both strange and amusing.

Early the next morning, we left and went to pray at Tōdai Temple.²⁹⁶ The Isonokami Shrine truly looked as old as its name makes one imagine;²⁹⁷ it was all wild and overgrown (figure 13).

That night we stayed at a place called Yamanobe. Although I was very tired, I tried to read the sutras a little. I dozed off, and in a dream, I saw myself visiting an amazingly beautiful and noble lady. The wind was blowing hard. She looked at me and smiled, "What brings you here?" she asked. "How could I not pay my respects?" I replied. "It is expected that you will live at the imperial palace. It would be good for you to discuss this with Hakase no Myōbu"²⁹⁸ is what I thought she said. I felt very happy and put much store by this dream. My faith strengthening more and more, I continued along the Hatsuse River and that night arrived at the holy temple. After performing ablutions, I

FIGURE 12 The Byōdōin, originally the Uji villa.

292. This is another reference to the Uji chapters of the *Tale of Genji*.
293. This place-name does not correspond exactly to any present-day place-name. In Teika's copy of the manuscript, it was marked with red dots as a possible copyist's error.
294. Mount Kurikoma was noted for bandits.
295. Nieno Pond was in the area of Ide Street in the Tsuzuki District of present-day Kyoto Prefecture. The pond is mentioned in other diary texts of the period; apparently, it was one of the major landmarks on the pilgrimage path to Hatsuse Temple.
296. The temple is Tōdaiji in present-day Nara City, which houses the huge statue of the Buddha.
297. The Isonokami Shrine was in the village of Furu, a place-name homophonous with the words "to age" and the "passing of time." Hence, the Isonokami Shrine became an *uta-makura* for poems about the passing of time and growing old.
298. Hakase no Myōbu was mistress of the inner chambers at the imperial palace who had acted as her guide to the Sacred Mirror Room when she visited the palace for the first time.

FIGURE 13 The pond at the Isonokami Shrine.

went up to worship. I stayed in retreat for three days. I was to start the return journey at dawn; night came, and I dozed off. From the direction of the main hall came a voice, "You there, here is a cedar of good omen bestowed from the Inari Shrine,"[299] and as the person appeared to reach out and throw me something, I woke up with a start and realized it was a dream (figure 14).

At dawn while it was still dark, we departed. We found it difficult to get lodgings that night but finally asked to stay at a house on this side of the Nara Slopes.[300] My attendants talked among themselves: "This place has a suspicious air. Don't even think of sleeping. If something odd happens, no matter what, don't look afraid or alarmed. Please lie down and hold your breath." Just hearing this, I was miserable and afraid. I felt as though it took a thousand years for dawn to break. Finally, just as it began to get light, one of my attendants said, "This is the home of thieves. The woman who is our host was acting suspiciously, you know."

FIGURE 14 The main hall of Hase (Hatsuse) Temple.

299. The Inari Shrine at Fushimi, south of the capital. The custom was to obtain cedar seed-lings from the Inari Shrine and take them home to plant. If the tree grew, one's wishes would be fulfilled.
300. The Nara Slopes are hills north of Nara. Earlier, the author's mother mentioned this area's reputation as being dangerous.

On a day when the wind was blowing hard, we crossed the Uji River and rowed very close by the fish weirs.

oto ni nomi	Having only heard
kikiwatari koshi	of the sound of the waves
udjikaha no	lapping against
ajiro no nami mo	the fish weirs of Uji River,
kefu zo kazofuru	today, I can even count them.[301]

Since I have been writing consecutively in no particular order of events that were two, three, four, or five years apart, it makes me look like a devout practioner who was continually going on pilgrimages, but it was not like that; years and months separated these events.

Around springtime, I went on retreat at Kurama (figure 15).[302] The rims of the mountains were covered in mist; it was warm and gentle. From the direction of the mountainside, some people came with mountain yams they had just dug up. This, too, was fascinating. When I set out on that trip, all the blossoms had fallen from the trees and there was nothing really to see, but when I made the same trip again around the Tenth Month, the mountain scenery at that time along the way was much better. The mountainsides looked as though they had been spread with brocade, and the water seemed to be scattering crystals[303] as it flowed and burbled. It was more splendid than anywhere else. When we reached the monks' quarters, the crimson leaves moistened thus with the winter rains were beyond compare.

oku yama no	In the mountain recesses,
momidji no nishiki	brocades of crimson leaves,
hoka yori mo	more than anywhere else,
ika ni shigurete	how did the winter rains manage
fukaku somekemu	to dye them so deeply?

About two years later, when I went again on retreat at Ishiyama, the rain fell hard the whole night through. Listening to it and thinking how unpleasant rain is when one is traveling, I opened the shutters and looked out to find that the moon at dawn was shining right down to

FIGURE 15 The gate at Kurama Temple.

301. The fish weirs at Uji were a favorite subject for poetry.
302. Kurama is a temple halfway up Mount Kurama, north of the Heian-period capital.
303. The expression here, *suishō wo chirasu yau ni* (as though scattering crystals), is unusual. A similar expression, *suishō nado no waretaru yau ni midzu no chiritaru* (water scattering as though it were broken crystals), can be found in the *Pillow Book*. See Hagitani, ed., *Makura no sōshi*, 2:125; and Morris, trans., *Pillow Book*, 1:195.

the bottom of the ravine, and what I had taken for the rain falling was actually the sound of water flowing from the base of the trees.

tanigaha no	Although I took
nagare ha ame to	the rush of the ravine's stream
kikoyuredo	for rain, now I behold
hoka yori ke naru	the light of the dawn moon,
ariake no tsuki	unlike anything anywhere else.[304]

When I went again on a pilgrimage to Hatsuse Temple, unlike the first time, I felt somehow secure. Here and there, we were entertained along the route; it was hard to make much progress.[305] It was a time when the Hahaso Forest[306] of the Yamashiro District was very charming with crimson leaves. When we crossed the Hatsuse River,

hatsusegaha	Like rapids repeating
tachikaeritsutsu	in Hatsuse River, back again
tadzunureba	have I come questing.
sugi no shirushi mo	I wonder, this time too, will I see
kono tabi ya mimu	the cedar of good omen?[307]

With such thoughts, I was filled with hopeful expectations.

After performing devotions for three days, on the way back we stopped at the same place this side of the Nara Slopes. Since, given the size of our party this time, it was not possible to lodge in a small house, a temporary shelter was erected for some of us in the midst of an open field. The others spent the night just sitting up in the field. On the grass, they spread their saddle chaps and then laid straw matting on top, such a wretched way to spend the night. Their heads were drenched with falling dew. The moon at daybreak spread clear light over the scene; it was something out of this world.

yukuhe naki	In the sky
tabi no sora ni mo	of this aimless journey,
okurenu ha	a companion who
miyako nite mishi	has not failed to keep up with us,

304. This poem was chosen for the "Miscellaneous" section of the imperial anthology, *Shinshūishū* (1364), poem 1634. The fourth line was slightly altered to *hoka yori haruru*, which would result in a translation of the last two lines as "the light of this dawn moon / clearer than anywhere else."

305. Her description implies that her husband accompanied her on this pilgrimage. Accordingly, they would have traveled with a larger entourage and received invitations from dignitaries along the route.

306. This forest was located at the site of the present-day Hōzono Shrine on Seika Street in the Sōraku District of Kyoto Prefecture. The place-name Hahaso was an *utamakura* associated with crimson leaves.

307. This refers to the dream she had on her previous pilgrimage to Hatsuse, in which a figure offered her a cedar seedling from the Inari Shrine at Fushimi.

ariake no tsuki   the dawn moon we saw in the
                                     capital.[308]

In this way, then, I was able to go on pilgrimages far afield, follow-ing my own inclinations, with nothing getting in the way.[309] On these trips, the various interesting, and even the trying, experiences natu-rally lightened my spirits and also made me hopeful for the future. At that time, because I found nothing particularly troubling in my life, I just concentrated my hopes on seeing my young ones[310] grow up as I desired, and so the years and months passed by with that goal seem-ing still far in the future, and of course, my mind was full of earnest thoughts for the one on whom I depended, praying that he should achieve happiness in his career as others had.[311]

There was a friend with whom in the past I had conversed avidly, exchanging poems day and night over a long period of time, and although our communication was not quite what it had been in the old days, we still kept in constant touch. However, after she married the governor of Echizen Province[312] and accompanied him to his post-ing, I heard not a word from her. Finally, there was an opportunity that I barely seized to send a message to inquire after her:

taezarishi   Alas, even the
omohi mo ima ha   constant fire of our love has been
taenikeri   extinguished, it seems,
koshi no watari no   in the deep snows of the
yuki no fukasa ni   environs of Koshi.[313]

The reply she sent back:

shirayama no   Buried beneath the
yuki no shita naru   snows of Shirayama,
sazare ishi no   how could the sparks of
naka no omohi ha   loving thoughts in this flint
kiemu mono ka ha   ever be extinguished?[314]

308. This poem was included in the "Travel" section of the imperial anthology *Shoku gosenshū* (1235), poem 1306. The fourth line was revised to *miyako wo ideshi*, which would result in the translation of the last line as "the dawn moon that came out from the capital."

309. This entry is likely from the period after 1045 when we know from official records that her husband, Toshimichi, had just completed a tour of duty as provincial governor in Shimotsuke Province. This governorship would have resulted in substantial economic benefit for the family.

310. The reference here, *osanaki hitobito* (young people), is clearly plural. She is recorded to have had three children with Toshimichi.

311. This is another direct reference to her husband.

312. In the Heian period, Echizen Province occupied the eastern part of present-day Fukui Prefecture on the Japan Sea side. It is an area of heavy snowfalls.

313. Koshi is the general name for the area that contained Echizen Province. This poem puns on *omohi* (thoughts of longing) and *hi* (fire).

314. Shirayama, known today as Mount Hakusan, is a volcano in Heian-period Echizen Province. Therefore, the response picks up on the notion of "fire" introduced by the preceding poem, and it extends this train of thought by using the metaphor of sparks in a flint for the loving thoughts in the friend's heart.

Around the first of the Third Month, I went to a place deep in the Western Hills.[315] There, unseen by sightseers in the gentle mist, touchingly forlorn cherry blossoms were blooming in wild abandon:

sato tohomi	To this mountain path,
amari oku naru	too deep in the hills, far away
yamadji ni ha	from people's dwelling,
hanami ni tote mo	no one will even think
hito kozarikeri	to come blossom viewing.[316]

At a time when I found my relationship troubling,[317] I went on retreat to Uzumasa,[318] and while I was there, a colleague with whom I had been on intimate terms at court kindly sent me a letter. Just as I was about to reply to her, I heard the sound of the temple bell:

shigekarishi	Even the tangled, petty,
ukiyo no koto mo	troubles of this world,
wasurarezu	I am unable to forget,
iriahi no kane no	as the evening bell tolls for
kokorobosasa ni	my heart's desolation.

This I wrote and sent to her.

On one warm and gentle day at court, three of us, who were kindred spirits, spoke together heart to heart. The following day, I returned home, and with time on my hands, I recalled fondly our conversation and addressed this to my two friends:

sode nururu	While I know
araiso nami to	it was a rough shore with waves
shirinagara	that drenched one's sleeves,
tomo ni kadzuki wo	our diving in together
seshi zo kohishiki	I remember with longing.[319]

After I sent it, from one of my friends came this:

araiso ha	On this rough shore,
asaredo nani no	although one seeks shellfish,

315. This was likely the family country house in the western part of Kyoto, whose rural environs she described earlier in the diary.
316. This poem was included in the "Spring" section of the imperial anthology *Gyokuyōshū* (1313), poem 185.
317. The phrase used here, *yo no naka* (literally "relations in the world"), is used more often than not in Heian-period writing to refer to conjugal relationships between men and women, but it can also mean one's relations in general with society. Another possible meaning here is that the author was having troubles with her social relationships at court.
318. See notes 103 and 193.
319. With associative language of the sea and fishing, the author creates a metaphoric evocation of working at court: "Yes, the work was hard and our sleeves were drenched with tears of disappointment, but the fact that we worked side by side makes me remember it with longing."

kahi nakute	no good comes of it.[320]
ushiho ni nururu	Ah, drenched indeed with brine,
ama no sode kana	are the sleeves of this fisher.

And from the other friend:

mirume ofuru	If this were not a bay
ura ni arazu ha	where the see-you weed[321] grows,
araiso no	then I would not want
namima kazofuru	to be a fisher gauging the space
ama mo araji wo	between this rough shore's waves.

There was another kindred spirit with whom I corresponded in the same way, someone with whom I could share the sad and fascinating things in life. After she had gone down to Chikuzen,[322] on a night when the moon was very bright, I fell asleep longing for her, thinking again and again that on a night like this, serving together at court, we would not have slept a wink but would have stayed up the whole night gazing at the moon. I was startled to awaken from a dream in which I saw her just as she had been in reality when we had served together at court. The moon was just nearing the rim of the mountains. Feeling as though "had I known it was a dream, I would have not awakened,"[323] I sank into reverie.

yume samete	Awakened from a dream,
nezame no toko no	this bed of fitful slumber
uku bakari	still afloat on tears,
kohiki to tsuge yo	please tell her that I miss her,
nishi he yuku tsuki	moon on your way to the west.[324]

For various reasons, I went down to Izumi Province around autumn.[325] We started by boat from Yodo,[326] and the beautiful and touching sights along the way were beyond description. That night we anchored off a place called Takahama;[327] it was very dark, and late at night, we heard the sound of boat oars. When someone asked what it was, it turned out to be the sound of women entertainers approaching.

320. This poem puns on *kahi* (shellfish) and the expression *kahi naku* (without good result).

321. This poem puns on *mirume* (seeing eye), which is also the name of a type of seaweed, to say, "If I could not see you from time to time, I would not want to work here."

322. Chikuzen is the name for the northwest part of present-day Fukuoka Prefecture. It is likely that her friend accompanied her husband on a tour of duty.

323. Ono no Komachi, *Kokinshū*, poem 552: *omohitsutsu / nureba ya hito no / mietsuramu / yume to shiriseba / samezaremashi wo* (When I fell asleep / longing so for him / he seemed to appear— / had I known it was a dream, / I would not have awakened).

324. Poems very similar to this one, based on the image of the moon journeying west, were exchanged between Murasaki Shikibu and a friend who was going off to the western provinces. See Bowring, trans., *Murasaki Shikibu*, 219, poems 6 and 7.

325. In 1049, the author's elder brother, Sugawara no Sadayoshi, took the post of governor of Izumi Province, roughly the southwest part of present-day Osaka Prefecture. Thus the author may have gone to Izumi to visit her brother.

326. Yodo is in the Fushimi District of present-day Kyoto Prefecture. This voyage was down the Yodo River.

327. Takahama was a port on the Yodo River at a place now within the Osaka city limits.

We all were interested and tossed a line to attach their boat to ours. In the light of lamps set at a distance, we could see these women wearing singlets[328] with long sleeves, hiding their faces with fans and singing songs; it was very moving.[329]

On the day after, just as the sun was setting over the rim of the mountains, we rowed by Sumiyoshi Bay.[330] The sky was completely misted over, and the scene of the branch tips of the pine trees, the surface of the sea, and the shore on which the waves lapped was so beautiful that it could not be captured in a painting.

ika ni ihi	How to tell of it;
nani ni tatohete	to describe it, with what
kataramashi	could I compare it—
aki no yufube no	this evening in autumn
sumiyoshi no ura	on Sumiyoshi Bay.

I gazed fixedly on the scene and as we were drawn past it, I could not help looking back again; I felt I could never tire of it.

At the onset of winter,[331] we had just boarded a boat at a place called Ōtsu[332] to return to the capital when, that night, rain fell and the wind blew violently enough to move even boulders. What's more, thunder crashed and roared, and with the sound of the surging waves and the way the wind blew everything around wildly, it was terrifying. I lost control of my thoughts and was sure I was going to die. They pulled the boat up onto a hillock, and we stayed up all night. The next day, the rain let up but the wind still blew; they did not launch the boat. Unable to go anywhere, stranded on top of the hillock, we remained for five or six days. Finally, when the wind abated a little and I raised the blinds and looked out, the way the evening tide had, in a breathless moment, flooded in to the peak, with cranes along the inlet crying in full voice, it all seemed lovely.[333] People from the province gathered around and observed, "If my lady had managed to set out that night for Ishizu,[334] there is no doubt that your boat would have been lost without a trace." I listened uneasily to their words.

aruru umi ni	On that rough, tossed sea,
kaze yori saki ni	what if we had launched our boat

328. A singlet was an unlined kimono; in other words, the entertainers were dressed casually.
329. This is the diary's third reference to female entertainers, and once again, the moving quality of the women's performance is the focal point of the author's perception.
330. Sumiyoshi is a district in the present-day city of Osaka and the site of the ancient Sumiyoshi Shrine. The shrine was right on Sumiyoshi Bay in the Heian period, but now the spread of reclaimed land has separated the shrine some distance from the sea. From ancient times, since so many poems were written about the shrine, the god of Sumiyoshi came to be regarded as the god of poetry. As an *utamakura*, Sumiyoshi had several connotations. Because the name literally means "Good for Living," it figures in auspicious poems. Poems about Sumiyoshi usually include references to the sea, waves, and pines—elements also in screen paintings of this place. Finally, Sumiyoshi is an important setting in some chapters of the *Tale of Genji*.
331. The author appears to have visited Izumi from early autumn to the beginning of winter, quite a long stay of about three months.
332. Ōtsu was a large port in Izumi Province.
333. This phrasing is almost an exact quotation from "The Pilgrimage to Sumiyoshi" (or Channel Buoys; Miotsukushi), chapter 14 of the *Tale of Genji*: "The scene's stirring mood, with the evening tide flooding in and the cranes along the inlet crying in full voice . . ." (Tyler, trans., *Tale of Genji*, 292). Chapter 14 describes Genji's pilgrimage to Sumiyoshi to give thanks to the god of Sumiyoshi for his good fortune after his deliverance from the trials of his exile in Suma, which included the survival of a great storm. In the same general geographical area, the author happens to see a similar scene after having survived a terrible storm herself.
334. Ishizu was the next large port along the coast to the capital located at the mouth of the Ishizu River. It corresponds to the Sakai municipality of present-day Osaka Prefecture.

funade shite	ahead of the storm
ishizu no nami to	and vanished utterly
kienamashikaba	in the billows of Ishizu . . .

During my life in one way or another, I had expended my heart worrying. How might my court service have turned out if I had only been able to devote myself to it single-mindedly? But since I went to serve only occasionally, it seems that I could not really have expected it to have amounted to anything. I had gradually passed my prime and could not help feeling that it was unseemly for me to carry on as though I were still young. My body had become weak through illness, so I could no longer go on pilgrimages according to my wishes. I had even stopped going out on rare occasions. While I hardly felt that I should live much longer, nonetheless lying down and getting up everyday, I was plagued with the thought, "How much I wish to live long enough in this world to see the young ones properly settled."[335] Meanwhile, I worried anxiously to hear news of a fortunate appointment for the one I relied on.[336] Autumn arrived, and it seemed that what we were waiting for had come, but the appointment was not what we expected.[337] It was a pity to be so disappointed. It did seem as though my husband's post was a little closer than the East Country, the going to and returning from which we knew from my father's time.[338] Anyway, what could we do about it? We hurried with preparations for his imminent departure. He was to make the preliminary start a little after the tenth day of the Eighth Month from the residence to which his daughter had just moved.[339] Unaware of what was to come, he took his leave in lively fashion, with lots of people bustling around.

Our son accompanied him when he left for the provinces on the twenty-seventh day.[340] Our son, with a sword at his side, wore purple trousers of a twill weave, with a hunting cloak of the bush clover color combination[341] over a crimson robe that had been fulled to a glossy sheen. He walked behind his father, who wore dark blue trousers and a hunting cloak.[342] At the central gallery, they mounted their horses. After the lively procession had departed, I felt somehow at loose ends with nothing to do. Since I had heard that their destination was not so very far,[343] I did not feel quite as bereft as I had on previous occasions.[344]

335. This is a reference to the author's children with Toshimichi.
336. This is a reference to her husband, Toshimichi.
337. In 1057, Toshimichi received a post as the governor of Shinano Province (present-day Nagano Prefecture) in the Japan Alps. It had a harsh climate and was far away.
338. Her father had served in Kazusa and Hitachi Provinces, and her husband already had served in Shimotsuke Province—all of which were in the East Country.
339. This is apparently Toshimichi's older daughter from an earlier marriage. He received the appointment on the thirtieth day of the Seventh Month (September 1) in Tengi 5 (1057) and was already preparing to leave a mere ten days later.
340. Their eldest son is about seventeen years old, and the author is fifty years old.
341. The bush clover color combination was maroon with a lining of green.
342. Women's diaries from the Heian period frequently describe clothing, no doubt because a substantial part of a wife's work was overseeing and actively participating in its manufacture.
343. Shinano Province was a little more than half the distance to the East Country.
344. The previous occasion extensively described in the diary is her father's departure for Hitachi Province in 1032.

Those who had gone along to see the party off came back the next day and said, "They departed in great splendor." And when they said, "This morning at dawn, a very large soul fire appeared and came toward the capital,"[345] I thought surely it must be from one of his attendants. Did even an inkling of this being a bad omen come to me?

At the time, all I could think about was how to raise the young children into adults. My husband came back to the capital in the Fourth Month of the following year;[346] summer and autumn passed. On the twenty-fifth day of the Ninth Month, my husband fell ill; on the fifth day of the Tenth Month, he died.[347] I felt as though it were a bad dream; I could not imagine something like this happening. The image seen in the mirror offered to Hatsuse Temple[348] of a figure collapsed on the ground weeping; this now was me. The image of the joyous figure had not come to pass. Now it seemed hardly likely that it could ever be in the future. On the twenty-third day, the night when the evanescent clouds of smoke were to be kindled, the one whom I had watched go off with his father last autumn in such a magnificent costume now wore mourning white over a black robe and accompanied the funeral carriage crying and sobbing as he walked away. Seeing him off and remembering the other time—I had never felt like this before. I grieved as though lost in a dream, and I wondered whether my departed one could see me.

Long ago, rather than being infatuated with all those frivolous tales and poems, if I had only devoted myself to religious practice day and night, I wonder, would I have been spared this nightmarish fate? The time that I went to Hatsuse Temple when someone in a dream threw me something, saying, "This is a cedar of good omen bestowed by the Inari Shrine," if I had just gone right then and there on a pilgrimage to Inari, maybe this would not have happened. The dreams that I had had over the years in which I had been told to "worship the god Amaterasu" had been divined[349] as meaning that I should become a nurse to an imperial child, serving in the palace and receiving the protection of the imperial consort.[350] But nothing like that had ever come to pass. Only the sad image in the mirror had been fulfilled. Pitifully, I grieved. Since I had ended up as one without one thing going as I had wished, I had drifted along without doing anything to accumulate merit.

345. "Soul fire" is the translation of *hitodama*, a bluish ball of light that was thought to depart from a person who was soon to die.

346. In the Fourth Month of the following year, 1058, her husband was given permission to leave his post, possibly for health reasons, although the author says explicitly only that he had fallen ill in the autumn.

347. The text itself does not state explicitly that he died; instead, it merely speaks of feeling as though one were having a bad dream.

348. This is another reference to the mirror that her mother had cast and sent as an offering to Hatsuse Temple in order to try to foretell the author's future as a young woman.

349. In the entries for these earlier dreams, the author remarks that she told no one about them. It is clear from this entry, however, that she sometimes had her dreams interpreted.

350. Here readers are finally given the precise content of her hopes for a successful career at court.

Yet somehow it seemed that even though life was sad, it would continue. I worried that perhaps even my hopes for the afterlife might not
be granted. There was only one thing I could put my faith in. It was a
dream that I had had on the thirteenth day of the Tenth Month in the
third year of Tengi.[351] Amida Buddha[352] appeared in the front garden
of the house where I lived. He was not clearly visible but appeared
through what seemed like a curtain of mist. When I strained to look
through gaps in the mist, I could see a lotus dais about three to four
feet above the ground; the holy Buddha was about six feet in height.
He glowed with a golden light, and one of his hands was spread open;
with the other he was forming a *mudra*.[353] Other people could not see
him; only I could. Inexplicably, I experienced a great sense of fear and
was unable to move closer to the bamboo blinds to see. The Buddha
deigned to speak: "If this is how it is, I will go back this time, but later
I will return to welcome you." Only my ears could hear his voice; the
others could not. This was the dream I had, and when I woke up with a
start, it was the fourteenth. My only hope for my afterlife is this dream.

My nephews, whom I had seen day and night when we lived in the
same place, had gone off to different places after this regrettably sad
event, so I seldom saw anyone. On a very dark night, the sixth youngest nephew[354] came for a visit; I felt this was unusual. This poem came
spontaneously:

tsuki mo idede	Not even the moon has
yami ni kuretaru	emerged in the darkness deepening over
wobasute ni	Old Forsaken Woman Peak.
nani tote koyohi	How is it, then, that you
tadzune kitsuramu	have come visiting this night?[355]

And to a friend with whom I had corresponded warmly before but
from whom I had not heard since I had come to this pass:

ima ha yo ni	Is it that you think
araji mono to ya	I am one no longer living
omofuramu	in this world of ours?

351. The year was 1055, three years before her husband's death. This is the only time in the diary that the author gives such a specific date. For a detailed discussion of this dream, see chapter 3.

352. This is the Buddha whose vow was to save—by bringing them to dwell in the Pure Land of the West—all those with a believing heart who, when they were dying, called out his name.

353. The *mudra* is a sacred hand gesture.

354. This reference has puzzled commentators because the author never before has mentioned having as many as six nephews. Her elder sister could not have had more than three children. Although there is no record of how many children her elder brother had, he may have had a large family.

355. Old Forsaken Woman (Obatsuteyama) is the name of a mountain in the Sarashina District of Shinano Province. Its literal meaning is "the mountain where old women are abandoned." It is an *utamakura* with complex associations. The place-name is connected with both a folk belief about an ancient custom of abandoning old women and a reputation for being a beautiful place to view the moon. The association with the moon arose from an anonymous poem in the *Kokinshū*, poem 878: *waga kokoro / nagasamekanetsu / sarashina ya / obasuteyama ni / teru tsuki wo mite* (My heart / is inconsolable, / Ah! Sarashina / where over Old Forsaken Woman Peak / I see the moon shining). This poem was given a narrative context in a collection of tales about poems, the *Tales of Yamato*. The place-name Sarashina has a further personal association for the author because Sarashina and Obasuteyama are in Shinano Province, the place of her husband's last posting. The author derived the title for her diary from this allusion to the Sarashina of the *Kokinshū* poem and the *Tales of Yamato* story. For a full discussion of this, see chapter 6.

ahare naku naku	Sadly I cry and cry,
naho koso ha fure	yet I do indeed live on.

At the time of the Tenth Month, crying as I gazed out at the exceeding brightness of the full moon:

hima mo naki	Even to a heart
namida ni kumoru	clouded by tears that fall
kokoro ni mo	with no respite,
akashi to miyuru	the light pouring from the moon
tsuki no kage kana	can appear so radiant.[356]

The months and years change and pass by, but when I recall that dreamlike time, my mind wanders, and it is as though my eyes grow so dark that I cannot recall clearly the events of that time.

Everyone has moved to live elsewhere; only I am left in the old house. One time when I stayed up all night in gloomy contemplation, feeling bereft and sad, I sent this to someone from whom I had not heard for a long time:

shigeri yuku	Mugwort growing
yomogi ga tsuyu ni	ever thicker, sodden
sobochitsutsu	with dew;
hito ni toharenu	a voice sought by no one
ne wo nomi zo naku	cries out all alone.[357]

She was a nun.[358]

yo no tsune no	In the mugwort of a
yado no yomogi wo	dwelling in the everyday world,
omohiyare	please imagine
somuki hatetaru	the dense grasses in the garden
niha no kusa mura	of final renouncement.

356. The moon has served almost as a leitmotif for the entire text, so it is fitting that close to the end, she invokes the moon at its most radiant one more time.

357. The images in this poem evoke descriptions of the circumstances and dwelling of Suetsu-muhana (Princess Safflower) in the *Tale of Genji*.

358. This is the last of the four communications with nuns that have punctuated the text, occurring at points of sadness and reflection. For an explication of the ambiguity of meaning in the last poem, see chapter 6.

AFTERWORD

ITŌ MORIYUKI

*M*ore than forty years have passed since the existence of the *Sarashina Diary* became widely known in the English-speaking world. Ivan Morris's translation, *As I Crossed a Bridge of Dreams*, was published in 1971 and was so swiftly circulated that the very next year, I, a student at the time, was able to buy a copy at a bookstore in Sendai (a city in Japan's central northeast region).

Even now, I vividly remember my surprise at the title when I first picked up the volume. Because the words "a Bridge of Dreams" in the English title harked back to the title of the last chapter of the *Tale of Genji*, I opened the book thinking that it must be a new study or a group of essays on the *Tale of Genji*, but the main body of the work was a translation of the *Sarashina Diary*. There must be some mistake, I thought as I repeatedly went back and scanned the book jacket, but the subtitle indicated only that it was a diary by a woman of the Heian period; the word "Sarashina" was nowhere to be seen.

When I read Morris's introduction, it became clear that the source of his decision to change the title in this way was his dismissive attitude toward the original title. Morris was of the opinion that the title of the diary had nothing to do with the author herself. In contrast, Sonja Arntzen and I take exactly the opposite position on this point and have stressed in this volume the fact that the title the *Sarashina Diary* is imbued with a deep literary symbolism. Furthermore, beyond the issue of the title, we find it impossible to trivialize Sugawara no Takasue no Musume's qualities as an author. We see both the *Sarashina Diary* and its author, Takasue no Musume, as encompassing a shape-shifting complexity. Although at first glance the *Sarashina Diary* seems to be written in an easy-to-understand style, at every turn the work displays extremely elaborate literary techniques, which any reader who has read this far in our volume will understand by now.

Although the opening passage in our translation may seem slightly diffuse, for example, this rambling quality is in the original Japanese, and we have simply reflected it. Since this rambling quality disappears from the entries covering the latter half of the author's life, we suggest that the immaturity of the writing style in the opening passage was constructed to create a childlike quality. Moreover, a special feature of the record of the author's journey to the capital, which follows the opening passage, is that it contains several wordplays on place-names along the way that are similar to the wordplays in the *Tosa Diary*'s record of the poet Ki no Tsurayuki's journey up to the capital about a century earlier. It is as though Takasue no Musume were acknowledging that famous text and its author while borrowing a technique that dovetails perfectly with the child persona. Then, in the later entries, recording her days of court service, she pays her respects to the influence she received from the *Murasaki Shikibu Diary* in a similar way.

The author writes that in her youth, she read the *Tale of Genji* so thoroughly that she came to know it by heart. But the *Tale of Genji* was not the only work that Takasue no Musume read so well and often. She sought out many kinds of literary works, not only fiction like the *Tale of the Bamboo Cutter* and the *Tales of Ise*, but also many poetry collections and diaries like the *Tosa Diary*, and she must have read them over and over. For Takasue no Musume, who happened to be born in the golden age of *kana* literature, just after such masterworks as the *Pillow Book* and the *Tale of Genji* had been completed, life and literature were inseparable. In the *Sarashina Diary*, the nature of a life lived with and through literature is expressed in both the content of the work and the way it is written.

To characterize the literary quality of the *Sarashina Diary*, I have used the metaphor of a finely polished crystal. Surely this work is rare in the way that the impression of the text and its form shifts so dramatically depending on the angle of the reader's viewpoint. Owing to this particular quality, it had been an unfulfilled dream of mine to have a translation published in English that reflected as much as possible the insights into the text gleaned from the research by many scholars, primarily Japanese scholars. For someone like me, who could not bring a superb command of the English language to the task, this desire was essentially an impossible dream. Then, however, thanks to encountering Sonja Arntzen, the English translator of the *Kagerō Diary*, at the Pacific Ancient and Modern Language Association Conference in 1998, my dream began to be realized. If I had been Takasue no Musume, I certainly would have recorded in my diary the three days I spent in Claremont, California, the site of the conference that year, because it was a special time of literary exaltation. During the three days of our first meeting, it was as though we had been transported back to our student days. From morning to night, we discussed Japanese literature and culture, particularly the Zen monk Ikkyū's *Crazy Cloud Anthology* (*Kyōunshū*), the *Kagerō Diary*, the *Sarashina Diary*, and the *Tale of Genji*. When the time came for us to leave—perhaps out of a sense of appreciation for this strange encounter—we bowed to each other, just like a couple of Zen monks. We realized that even in such a short time, we had been able to gain a deep understanding of each other's views of literature and humanity. Indeed, I believe that the project to produce a new English translation of the *Sarashina Diary* actually began with that moment of mutual recognition. I therefore would like to conclude by pointing out the marvelous nature of person-to-person encounters, something I can only call wonderful, as well as expressing my gratitude to Lynne Miyake for organizing the PAMLA panel that brought Sonja Arntzen and me together.

Appendix 1

FAMILY AND SOCIAL CONNECTIONS

*T*he following two charts summarize the family relationships and connections diagrammed in Akiyama Ken, ed., *Sarashina nikki*, Shinchō Nihon koten shūsei (Tokyo: Shinchōsha, 1980), 191–93. For example, not all siblings and not all marriage relationships are included in the Sugawara family tree (figure A1.1). Rather, our intention was to show only those people cited in the diary or those needed to illustrate the web of personal, political, and literary connections in which the author lived. Lighter lines connect those related by blood, and darker lines with solid circles indicate marriages. Adoption is shown by a dashed line. The names by which people are referred to in the diary are in quotation marks. Information that either clarifies relationships or, especially in figure A1.2, shows literary connections is in italics. The number in parentheses after the names of emperors indicates their order of ascension to the throne.

The connections between the Fujiwara family and the imperial family are shown together because the relationships between the Fujiwara clan, particularly the family's most powerful northern line (beginning with Fujiwara no Kaneie in figure A1.2), and the imperial family were so closely intertwined. This figure reveals the rivalry among the male siblings of the northern line, which was played out in each successive generation. Michinaga and Michitaka competed fiercely over which of their daughters would be the "winning" consort to provide the closest family connection to the succeeding emperor. Michinaga won, first by marrying daughters to two successive emperors, Ichijō and Sanjō, and then by becoming the grandfather of Emperors Go-Ichijō and Go-Suzaku. In the next generation, Yorimichi and Norimichi competed in the same way with their offspring. Because Yorimichi did not have any daughters to marry to Emperor Go-Suzaku, he strategically adopted Genshi, the great-granddaughter of Michitaka (a loser in his own generation), and her two daughters, in order to stay in the all-important game of marriage politics. Quite by chance, he thus provided an opportunity for Takasue no Musume to serve in the infant Princess Yūshi's household. Note that the author's Fujiwara mother and the author herself are positioned in the opposite far corners of figure A1.2, which graphically represents their distant and tenuous connection to the centers of power.

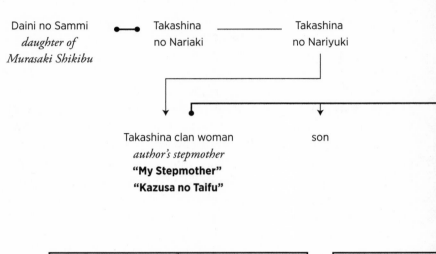

Daini no Sammi
daughter of
Murasaki Shikibu

Takashina
no Nariaki

Takashina
no Nariyuki

Takashina clan woman
author's stepmother
"My Stepmother"
"Kazusa no Taifu"

son

first wife

Tachibana no Toshimichi
"Father of My Children"
"The One I Rely On"

daughter
"His Daughter"

FIGURE A1.1 The Sugawara family tree.

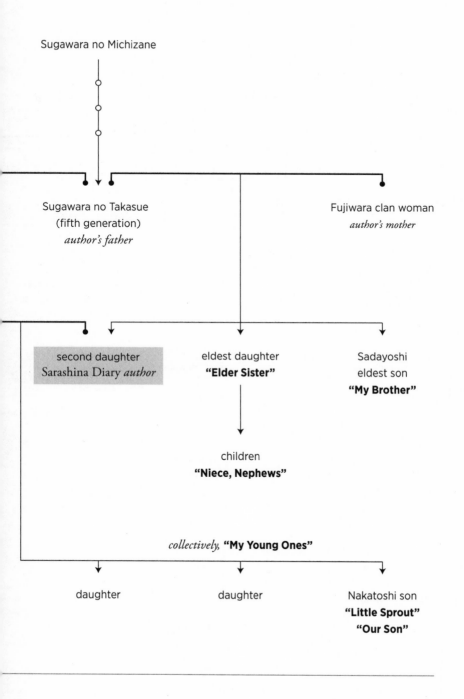

Sugawara no Michizane

Sugawara no Takasue
(fifth generation)
author's father

Fujiwara clan woman
author's mother

second daughter
Sarashina Diary *author*

eldest daughter
"Elder Sister"

Sadayoshi
eldest son
"My Brother"

children
"Niece, Nephews"

collectively, **"My Young Ones"**

daughter

daughter

Nakatoshi son
"Little Sprout"
"Our Son"

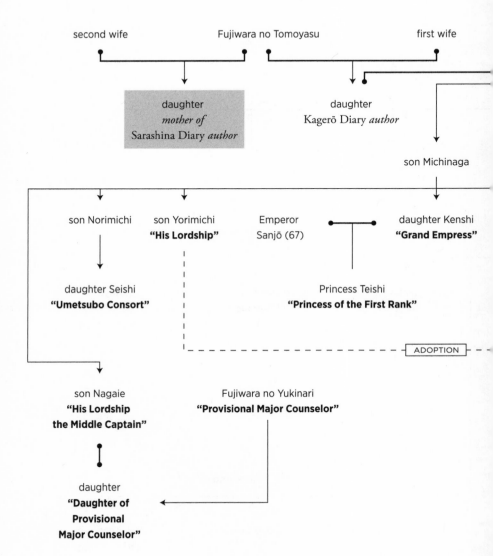

FIGURE A1.2 Connections between the Fujiwara clan and the imperial family.

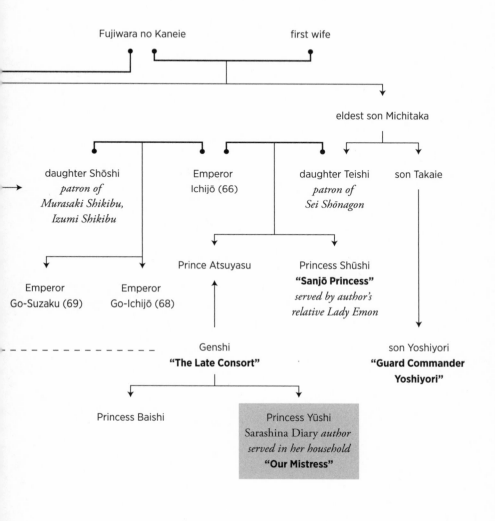

Fujiwara no Kaneie — first wife

eldest son Michitaka

daughter Shōshi
*patron of
Murasaki Shikibu,
Izumi Shikibu*

Emperor
Ichijō (66)

daughter Teishi
*patron of
Sei Shōnagon*

son Takaie

Emperor
Go-Suzaku (69)

Emperor
Go-Ichijō (68)

Prince Atsuyasu

Princess Shūshi
"Sanjō Princess"
*served by author's
relative Lady Emon*

Genshi
"The Late Consort"

son Yoshiyori
**"Guard Commander
Yoshiyori"**

Princess Baishi

Princess Yūshi
Sarashina Diary *author
served in her household*
"Our Mistress"

Appendix 2

MAPS

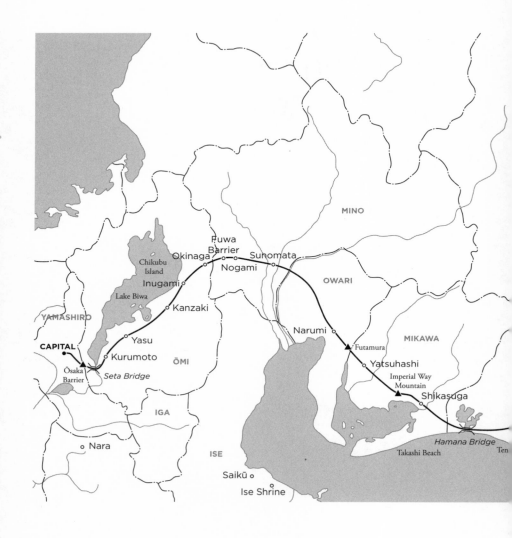

FIGURE A2.1 The trip from Kazusa to the capital.

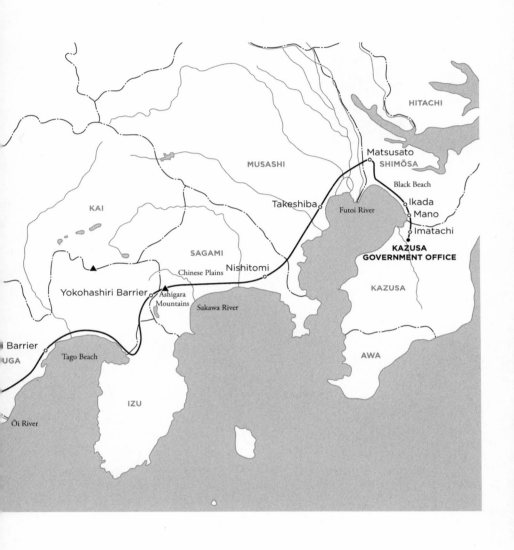

HITACHI

MUSASHI

Matsusato
SHIMŌSA

Black Beach

KAI

Takeshiba
Futoi River
Ikada
Mano
Imatachi

SAGAMI

Nishitomi
Chinese Plains

KAZUSA
GOVERNMENT OFFICE

Yokohashiri Barrier
Ashigara
Mountains
Sakawa River

KAZUSA

Barrier
UGA
Tago Beach

AWA

IZU

Ōi River

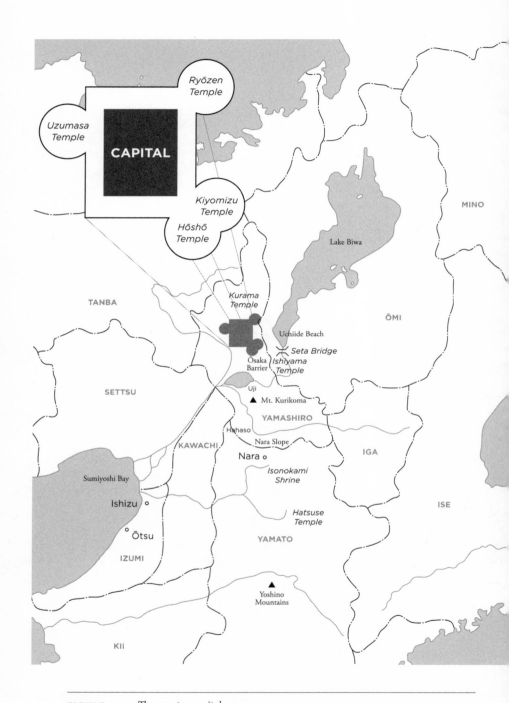

FIGURE A2.2 The greater capital area.

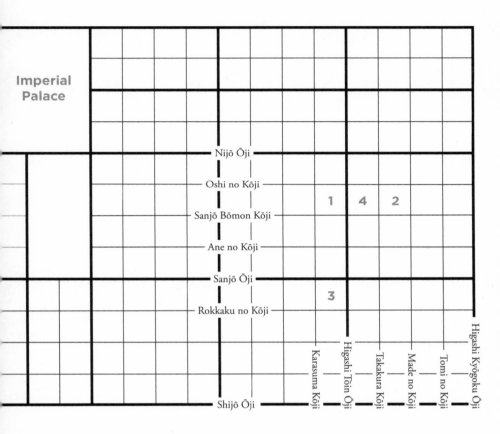

1 Sanjō In (Princess of the First Rank)   **2** Sanjō Palace (Sanjō Princess)
3 Hexagonal Hall (Rokkakudō)   **4** Sugawara Residence

FIGURE A2.3 Detail of the capital, showing the location of the Sugawara residence in 1020.

BIBLIOGRAPHY

Abe Akio et al., eds. *Genji monogatari.* Shinpen Nihon koten bungaku zenshū 24. Tokyo: Shōgakukan, 1997.

Akiyama Ken, ed. *Sarashina nikki.* Shinchō Nihon koten shūsei. Tokyo: Shinchōsha, 1980.

Arntzen, Sonja, trans. *The Kagerō Diary: A Woman's Autobiographical Text from Tenth-Century Japan.* Ann Arbor: Center for Japanese Studies, University of Michigan, 1997.

Bowring, Richard, trans. *Murasaki Shikibu: Her Diary and Poetic Memoirs.* Princeton, N.J.: Princeton University Press, 1982.

Cranston, Edwin A., trans. *The Izumi Shikibu Diary: A Romance of the Heian Court.* Cambridge, Mass.: Harvard University Press, 1969.

Davies, Robertson. *Reading and Writing.* Salt Lake City: University of Utah Press, 1992.

Fujiwara no Teika. *Gyobutsubon: Sarashina nikki.* Facsimile of manuscript copy. Tokyo: Musashino shoin, 1984.

Fukuya Toshiyuki. "*Sarashina nikki* bōtō hyōgen to jōraku no ki no seiritsu-saburaina to dokusha no mondai." *Waseda daigaku kyōiku sōgōkagaku gakujutsu kenkyū,* no. 60 (2012): 37–50.

Hagitani Boku, ed. *Makura no sōshi.* 2 vols. Shinchō Nihon koten shūsei. Tokyo: Shinchōsha, 1977.

Haraoka Fumiko, ed. and trans. *Sarashina nikki.* Tokyo: Kadokawa sofia bunko, 2003.

Heldt, Gustav. *The Pursuit of Harmony: Poetry and Power in Early Heian Japan.* Ithaca, N.Y.: East Asia Program, Cornell University, 2008.

——, trans. "Tosa Diary." In *Traditional Japanese Literature: An Anthology, Beginnings to 1600,* edited by Haruo Shirane, 204–13. New York: Columbia University Press, 2007.

Hochstedler, Carol, trans. *The Tale of Nezame: Part Three of Yowa no Nezame Monogatari.* Ithaca, N.Y.: China-Japan Program, Cornell University, 1979.

Hurvitz, Leon, trans. *Scripture of the Lotus Blossom of the Fine Dharma*. New York: Columbia University Press, 1976.

Ienaga Saburō. *Jōdai bukkyō shisōshi kenkyū*. Tokyo: Unebi shobō, 1942.

Ikeda Kikan. "Seikatsu maka no geijutsu toshite no *Sarashina nikki*." In *Kyūtei joryū nikki bungaku*, edited by Tokyo teikoku daigaku kokubungaku kenkyūshitsu, 133–50. Tokyo: Shibundō, 1927.

Inaga Keiji. "Takasue no Musume no hatsukoi no hito wa 'shizuku ni nigoru hito' ka." *Kokugo to kokubungaku*, December 1968, 9–19.

Itō Moriyuki. "*Hamamatsu Chūnagon monogatari* to *Sarashina nikki* no kōsaku suru tabiji." In *Heian kōki monogatari*, edited by Inoue Mayumi et al., 76–92. Tokyo: Kanrin shobō, 2012.

——. *Sarashina nikki kenkyū*. Tokyo: Shintensha, 1995.

——. "*Sarashina nikki* no 'asamidori . . .' ei ni kansuru kōsatsu." In *Genji monogatari kara, Genji monogatari e*, edited by Nagai Kazuko, 346–66. Tokyo: Kasama shoin, 2007.

——. *Sarashina nikki no enkinhō*. Tokyo: Shintensha, 2014.

——. "*Sarashina nikki* to *Genji monogatari* no sennenki." *Gakushūin joshi daigaku kiyō*, no. 11 (2009): 1–8.

Kamens, Edward. *The Buddhist Poetry of the Great Kamo Priestess: Daisaiin Senshi and Hosshin Wakashū*. Ann Arbor: Center for Japanese Studies, University of Michigan, 1990.

——. *The Three Jewels: A Study and Translation of Minamoto Tamenori's Sanbōe*. Ann Arbor: Center for Japanese Studies, University of Michigan, 1988.

——. *Utamakura, Allusion, and Intertextuality in Traditional Japanese Poetry*. New Haven, Conn.: Yale University Press, 1997.

Katagiri Yōichi. *Utamakura, utakotoba jiten*. Tokyo: Kasama shoin, 1999.

Keene, Donald, trans. "The Tale of the Bamboo Cutter." *Monumenta Nipponica* 11, no. 4 (1956): 1–127.

Kodama Rie. "*Sarashina nikki*—Sakusha Sugawara no Takasue no Musume no shūkyō ishiki: Butsuzō no byōsha o megutte." *Kokubun*, no. 61 (1984): 55–65.

Kroll, Paul W., trans. "The Song of Lasting Regret." In *The Columbia Anthology of Traditional Chinese Literature*, edited by Victor Mair, 478–85. New York: Columbia University Press, 1994.

Mair, Victor, ed. *The Columbia Anthology of Traditional Chinese Literature*. New York: Columbia University Press, 1994.

McCullough, Helen Craig, ed. and trans. *Classical Japanese Prose: An Anthology*. Stanford, Calif.: Stanford University Press, 1990.

——, trans. *Ōkagami, The Great Mirror: Fujiwara Michinaga (966–1027) and His Times*. Princeton, N.J.: Princeton University Press, 1980.

McCullough, William H., and Helen C. McCullough, trans. *A Tale of Flowering Fortunes: Annals of Japanese Aristocratic Life in the Heian Period*. 2 vols. Stanford, Calif.: Stanford University Press, 1980.

McKinney, Meredith, trans. *Sei Shōnagon: The Pillow Book.* London: Penguin, 2006.

Miner, Earl R., trans. *Japanese Poetic Diaries.* Berkeley: University of California Press, 1969.

Miner, Earl R., Hiroko Odagiri, and Robert E. Morrell, eds. *The Princeton Companion to Classical Japanese Literature.* Princeton, N.J.: Princeton University Press, 1985.

Miyake, Lynne K. "*The Tosa Diary*: In the Interstices of Gender and Criticism." In *Women's Hand: Gender and Theory in Japanese Women's Writing*, edited by Paul Schalow and Janet Walker, 41–73. Stanford, Calif.: Stanford University Press, 1996.

Morris, Dana. "Land and Society." In *The Cambridge History of Japan*, vol. 2, *Heian Japan*, edited by Donald H. Shively and William H. McCullough, 224–26. New York: Cambridge University Press, 1999.

Morris, Ivan, trans. *As I Crossed a Bridge of Dreams: Recollections of a Woman in Eleventh-Century Japan.* New York: Dial Press, 1971.

——, trans. *The Pillow Book of Sei Shōnagon.* 2 vols. New York: Columbia University Press, 1967.

Mostow, Joshua, trans. *At the House of Gathered Leaves: Shorter Biographical and Autobiographical Narratives from Japanese Court Literature.* Honolulu: University of Hawai'i Press, 2004.

——, trans. *Pictures of the Heart: The Hyakunin Isshu in Word and Image.* Honolulu: University of Hawai'i Press, 1996.

Mostow, Joshua, and Royall Tyler, trans. *The Ise Stories: Ise Monogatari.* Honolulu: University of Hawai'i Press, 2010.

Nishida Tomomi. "*Sarashina nikki* no hyōgen to hōhō—*Genji monogatari* o megutte." *Kokugo to kokubungaku*, October 1994, 34–46.

Noguchi Motohiro. "*Sarashina nikki* to *Genji monogatari*—Sugawara no Takasue no Musume no sakkateki shishitsu." *Jōchi daigaku kokubun gakka kiyō*, January 1985, 1–17.

Nomura Seiichi. "*Genji monogatari* to *Sarashina nikki*—Monogatari riarizumu no kaitai." *Kokugo to kokubungaku*, August 1956, 18–28.

Okumura Tsuneya, ed. *Kokin waka shū.* Shinchō Nihon koten shūsei. Tokyo: Shinchōsha, 1978.

Omori, Annie Shepley, and Kochi Doi, trans. *Diaries of Court Ladies of Old Japan.* Boston: Houghton Mifflin, 1920. Available at http://digital.library.upenn.edu/women/omori/court/court.html#1.

Richard, Kenneth L. "Developments in Late Heian Prose Fiction: 'The Tale of Nezame.'" Ph.D. diss., University of Washington, 1979.

Rodd, Laurel Rasplica, trans. *Kokinshū: A Collection of Ancient and Modern Poems.* Princeton, N.J.: Princeton University Press, 1984.

Rohlich, Thomas H., trans. *A Tale of Eleventh-Century Japan: Hamamatsu Chūnagon Monogatari.* Princeton, N.J.: Princeton University Press, 1983.

Ruch, Barbara, ed. *Engendering Faith: Women and Buddhism in Premodern Japan.* Ann Arbor: Center for Japanese Studies, University of Michigan, 2002.

Saigō Nobutsuna. *Kodaijin to yume.* Tokyo: Heibonsha, 1974.

Sargent, G. W., trans. "Tosa Diary." In *Anthology of Japanese Literature: From the Earliest Era to the Mid-Nineteenth Century,* edited by Donald Keene, 82–91. New York: Grove Press, 1955.

Sarra, Edith. *Fictions of Femininity: Literary Inventions of Gender in Japanese Court Women's Memoirs.* Stanford, Calif.: University of California Press, 1999.

Satō Kazuyoshi. "*Sarashina nikki* saishūka wa 'tasha' no uta ka." *Nihon bungaku,* December 1993, 60–64.

——. "*Sarashina nikki* uta no saikentō." *Kokugo to kokubungaku,* June 1994, 14–30.

Seidensticker, Edward, trans. *The Gossamer Years: The Diary of a Noblewoman of Heian Japan.* Rutland, Vt.: Tuttle, 1964.

Shinpen kokka taikan. Tokyo: Kadokawa shoten, 1983–1992, CD-ROM version.

Shirane, Haruo, ed. *Traditional Japanese Literature: An Anthology, Beginnings to 1600.* New York: Columbia University Press, 2007.

Shirane, Haruo, and Tomi Suzuki, eds. *Inventing the Classics: Modernity, National Identity, and Japanese Literature.* Stanford, Calif.: Stanford University Press, 2000.

Shively, Donald H., and William H. McCullough, eds. *The Cambridge History of Japan.* Vol. 2, *Heian Japan.* New York: Cambridge University Press, 1999.

Suzuki, Tomi. "Gender and Genre: Modern Literary Histories and Women's Diary Literature." In *Inventing the Classics: Modernity, National Identity, and Japanese Literature,* edited by Haruo Shirane and Tomi Suzuki, 71–95. Stanford, Calif.: Stanford University Press, 2000.

Tamai Kōsuke. *Sarashina nikki.* Nihon koten zensho. Tokyo: Asahi shinbunsha, 1950.

——. *Sarashina nikki sakkan kō.* Tokyo: Ikuei shoin, 1925.

Tsukahara Tetsuo. "*Sarashina nikki* sakuhin kōsei—Nigen shiten no kasetsu kenshō." *Kaishaku,* April 1978, 32–37.

Tyler, Royall, trans. *The Tale of Genji.* New York: Viking, 2001.

Wada Ritsuko and Kuge Hirotoshi. *Sarashina nikki no shinkenkyū—Takasue no Musume no sekai o kangaeru.* Tokyo: Shintensha, 2004.

Yamamoto Ritatsu, ed. *Murasaki Shikibu nikki, Murasaki Shikibu shū.* Shinchō Nihon koten shūsei. Tokyo: Shinchōsha, 1980.

Yasuda Yojūrō. "*Sarashina nikki.*" *Kokugo to kokubungaku,* no. 8 (1935): 61–82.

Yoshida Kazuhiko. "The Enlightenment of the Dragon King's Daughter in *The Lotus Sutra.*" In *Engendering Faith: Women and Buddhism in Premodern Japan,* edited by Barbara Ruch, 297–324. Ann Arbor: Center for Japanese Studies, University of Michigan, 2002.

INDEX

Major Plays of Chikamatsu, tr. Donald Keene 1961

Four Major Plays of Chikamatsu, tr. Donald Keene. Paperback ed. only. 1961; rev. ed. 1997

Records of the Grand Historian of China, translated from the Shih chi of Ssu-ma Ch'ien, tr. Burton Watson, 2 vols. 1961

Instructions for Practical Living and Other Neo-Confucian Writings by Wang Yang-ming, tr. Wing-tsit Chan 1963

Hsün Tzu: Basic Writings, tr. Burton Watson, paperback ed. only. 1963; rev. ed. 1996

Chuang Tzu: Basic Writings, tr. Burton Watson, paperback ed. only. 1964; rev. ed. 1996

The Mahābhārata, tr. Chakravarthi V. Narasimhan. Also in paperback ed. 1965; rev. ed. 1997

The Manyōshū, Nippon Gakujutsu Shinkōkai edition 1965

Su Tung-p'o: Selections from a Sung Dynasty Poet, tr. Burton Watson. Also in paperback ed. 1965

Bhartrihari: Poems, tr. Barbara Stoler Miller. Also in paperback ed. 1967

Basic Writings of Mo Tzu, Hsün Tzu, and Han Fei Tzu, tr. Burton Watson. Also in separate paperback eds. 1967

The Awakening of Faith, Attributed to Aśvaghosha, tr. Yoshito S. Hakeda. Also in paperback ed. 1967

Reflections on Things at Hand: The Neo-Confucian Anthology, comp. Chu Hsi and Lü Tsu-ch'ien, tr. Wing-tsit Chan 1967

The Platform Sutra of the Sixth Patriarch, tr. Philip B. Yampolsky. Also in paperback ed. 1967

Essays in Idleness: The Tsurezuregusa of Kenkō, tr. Donald Keene. Also in paperback ed. 1967

The Pillow Book of Sei Shōnagon, tr. Ivan Morris, 2 vols. 1967

Two Plays of Ancient India: The Little Clay Cart and the Minister's Seal, tr. J. A. B. van Buitenen 1968

The Complete Works of Chuang Tzu, tr. Burton Watson 1968

The Romance of the Western Chamber (Hsi Hsiang chi), tr. S. I. Hsiung. Also in paperback ed. 1968

The Manyōshū, Nippon Gakujutsu Shinkōkai edition. Paperback ed. only. 1969

Records of the Historian: Chapters from the Shih chi of Ssu-ma Ch'ien, tr. Burton Watson. Paperback ed. only. 1969

Cold Mountain: 100 Poems by the T'ang Poet Han-shan, tr. Burton Watson. Also in paperback ed. 1970

Twenty Plays of the Nō Theatre, ed. Donald Keene. Also in paperback ed. 1970

Chūshingura: The Treasury of Loyal Retainers, tr. Donald Keene. Also in paperback ed. 1971; rev. ed. 1997

The Zen Master Hakuin: Selected Writings, tr. Philip B. Yampolsky 1971

Chinese Rhyme-Prose: Poems in the Fu Form from the Han and Six Dynasties Periods, tr. Burton Watson. Also in paperback ed. 1971

Kūkai: Major Works, tr. Yoshito S. Hakeda. Also in paperback ed. 1972

The Old Man Who Does as He Pleases: Selections from the Poetry and Prose of Lu Yu, tr. Burton Watson 1973

The Lion's Roar of Queen Śrīmālā, tr. Alex and Hideko Wayman 1974

Courtier and Commoner in Ancient China: Selections from the History of the Former Han by Pan Ku, tr. Burton Watson. Also in paperback ed. 1974

Japanese Literature in Chinese, vol. 1: Poetry and Prose in Chinese by Japanese Writers of the Early Period, tr. Burton Watson 1975

Japanese Literature in Chinese, vol. 2: Poetry and Prose in Chinese by Japanese Writers of the Later Period, tr. Burton Watson 1976

Love Song of the Dark Lord: Jayadeva's Gītagovinda, tr. Barbara Stoler Miller. Also in paperback ed. Cloth ed. includes critical text of the Sanskrit. 1977; rev. ed. 1997

Ryōkan: Zen Monk-Poet of Japan, tr. Burton Watson 1977

Calming the Mind and Discerning the Real: From the Lam rim chen mo of Tsoṇ-kha-pa, tr. Alex Wayman 1978

The Hermit and the Love-Thief: Sanskrit Poems of Bhartrihari and Bilhaṇa, tr. Barbara Stoler Miller 1978

The Lute: Kao Ming's P'i-p'a chi, tr. Jean Mulligan. Also in paperback ed. 1980

A Chronicle of Gods and Sovereigns: Jinnō Shōtōki of Kitabatake Chikafusa, tr. H. Paul Varley 1980

Among the Flowers: The Hua-chien chi, tr. Lois Fusek 1982

Grass Hill: Poems and Prose by the Japanese Monk Gensei, tr. Burton Watson 1983

Doctors, Diviners, and Magicians of Ancient China: Biographies of Fang-shih, tr. Kenneth J. DeWoskin. Also in paperback ed. 1983

Theater of Memory: The Plays of Kālidāsa, ed. Barbara Stoler Miller. Also in paperback ed. 1984

The Columbia Book of Chinese Poetry: From Early Times to the Thirteenth Century, ed. and tr. Burton Watson. Also in paperback ed. 1984

Poems of Love and War: From the Eight Anthologies and the Ten Long Poems of Classical Tamil, tr. A. K. Ramanujan. Also in paperback ed. 1985

The Bhagavad Gita: Krishna's Counsel in Time of War, tr. Barbara Stoler Miller 1986

The Columbia Book of Later Chinese Poetry, ed. and tr. Jonathan Chaves. Also in paperback ed. 1986

The Tso Chuan: Selections from China's Oldest Narrative History, tr. Burton Watson 1989

Waiting for the Wind: Thirty-six Poets of Japan's Late Medieval Age, tr. Steven Carter 1989

Selected Writings of Nichiren, ed. Philip B. Yampolsky 1990

Saigyō, Poems of a Mountain Home, tr. Burton Watson 1990

The Book of Lieh Tzu: A Classic of the Tao, tr. A. C. Graham. Morningside ed. 1990

The Tale of an Anklet: An Epic of South India—The Cilappatikāram of Iḷaṅkō Aṭikaḷ, tr. R. Parthasarathy 1993

Waiting for the Dawn: A Plan for the Prince, tr. with introduction by Wm. Theodore de Bary 1993

Yoshitsune and the Thousand Cherry Trees: A Masterpiece of the Eighteenth-Century Japanese Puppet Theater, tr., annotated, and with introduction by Stanleigh H. Jones, Jr. 1993

The Lotus Sutra, tr. Burton Watson. Also in paperback ed. 1993

The Classic of Changes: A New Translation of the I Ching as Interpreted by Wang Bi, tr. Richard John Lynn 1994

Beyond Spring: Tz'u Poems of the Sung Dynasty, tr. Julie Landau 1994

The Columbia Anthology of Traditional Chinese Literature, ed. Victor H. Mair 1994

Scenes for Mandarins: The Elite Theater of the Ming, tr. Cyril Birch 1995

Letters of Nichiren, ed. Philip B. Yampolsky; tr. Burton Watson et al. 1996

Unforgotten Dreams: Poems by the Zen Monk Shōtetsu, tr. Steven D. Carter 1997

The Vimalakirti Sutra, tr. Burton Watson 1997

Japanese and Chinese Poems to Sing: The Wakan rōei shū, tr. J. Thomas Rimer and Jonathan Chaves 1997

Breeze Through Bamboo: Kanshi of Ema Saikō, tr. Hiroaki Sato 1998

A Tower for the Summer Heat, by Li Yu, tr. Patrick Hanan 1998

Traditional Japanese Theater: An Anthology of Plays, by Karen Brazell 1998

The Original Analects: Sayings of Confucius and His Successors (0479–0249), by E. Bruce Brooks and A. Taeko Brooks 1998

The Classic of the Way and Virtue: A New Translation of the Tao-te ching of Laozi as Interpreted by Wang Bi, tr. Richard John Lynn 1999

The Four Hundred Songs of War and Wisdom: An Anthology of Poems from Classical Tamil, The Puṟanāṉūṟu, ed. and tr. George L. Hart and Hank Heifetz 1999

Original Tao: Inward Training (Nei-yeh) and the Foundations of Taoist Mysticism, by Harold D. Roth 1999

Po Chü-i: Selected Poems, tr. Burton Watson 2000

Lao Tzu's Tao Te Ching: A Translation of the Startling New Documents Found at Guodian, by Robert G. Henricks 2000

The Shorter Columbia Anthology of Traditional Chinese Literature, ed. Victor H. Mair 2000

Mistress and Maid (Jiaohongji), by Meng Chengshun, tr. Cyril Birch 2001

Chikamatsu: Five Late Plays, tr. and ed. C. Andrew Gerstle 2001

The Essential Lotus: Selections from the Lotus Sutra, tr. Burton Watson 2002

Early Modern Japanese Literature: An Anthology, 1600–1900, ed. Haruo Shirane 2002; abridged 2008

The Columbia Anthology of Traditional Korean Poetry, ed. Peter H. Lee 2002

The Sound of the Kiss, or The Story That Must Never Be Told: Pingali Suranna's Kalapurnodayamu, tr. Vecheru Narayana Rao and David Shulman 2003

The Selected Poems of Du Fu, tr. Burton Watson 2003

Far Beyond the Field: Haiku by Japanese Women, tr. Makoto Ueda 2003

Just Living: Poems and Prose by the Japanese Monk Tonna, ed. and tr. Steven D. Carter 2003

Han Feizi: Basic Writings, tr. Burton Watson 2003

Mozi: Basic Writings, tr. Burton Watson 2003

Xunzi: Basic Writings, tr. Burton Watson 2003

Zhuangzi: Basic Writings, tr. Burton Watson 2003

The Awakening of Faith, Attributed to Aśvaghosha, tr. Yoshito S. Hakeda, introduction by Ryuichi Abe 2005

The Tales of the Heike, tr. Burton Watson, ed. Haruo Shirane 2006

Tales of Moonlight and Rain, by Ueda Akinari, tr. with introduction by Anthony H. Chambers 2007

Traditional Japanese Literature: An Anthology, Beginnings to 1600, ed. Haruo Shirane 2007

The Philosophy of Qi, by Kaibara Ekken, tr. Mary Evelyn Tucker 2007

The Analects of Confucius, tr. Burton Watson 2007

The Art of War: Sun Zi's Military Methods, tr. Victor Mair 2007

One Hundred Poets, One Poem Each: A Translation of the Ogura Hyakunin Isshu, tr. Peter McMillan 2008

Zeami: Performance Notes, tr. Tom Hare 2008

Zongmi on Chan, tr. Jeffrey Lyle Broughton 2009

Scripture of the Lotus Blossom of the Fine Dharma, rev. ed., tr. Leon Hurvitz, preface and introduction by Stephen R. Teiser 2009

Mencius, tr. Irene Bloom, ed. with an introduction by Philip J. Ivanhoe 2009

Clouds Thick, Whereabouts Unknown: Poems by Zen Monks of China, Charles Egan 2010

The Mozi: A Complete Translation, tr. Ian Johnston 2010

The Huainanzi: A Guide to the Theory and Practice of Government in Early Han China, by Liu An, tr. John S. Major, Sarah A. Queen, Andrew Seth Meyer, and Harold D. Roth, with Michael Puett and Judson Murray 2010

The Demon at Agi Bridge and Other Japanese Tales, tr. Burton Watson, ed. with introduction by Haruo Shirane 2011

Haiku Before Haiku: From the Renga Masters to Bashō, tr. with introduction by Steven D. Carter 2011

The Columbia Anthology of Chinese Folk and Popular Literature, ed. Victor H. Mair and Mark Bender 2011

Tamil Love Poetry: The Five Hundred Short Poems of the Aiṅkurunūru, tr. and ed. Martha Ann Selby 2011

The Teachings of Master Wuzhu: Zen and Religion of No-Religion, by Wendi L. Adamek 2011

The Essential Huainanzi, by Liu An, tr. John S. Major, Sarah A. Queen, Andrew Seth Meyer, and Harold D. Roth 2012

The Dao of the Military: Liu An's Art of War, tr. Andrew Seth Meyer 2012

Unearthing the Changes: Recently Discovered Manuscripts of the Yi Jing (I Ching) and Related Texts, Edward L. Shaughnessy 2013

Record of Miraculous Events in Japan: The Nihon ryōiki, tr. Burton Watson 2013

The Complete Works of Zhuangzi, tr. Burton Watson 2013

Lust, Commerce, and Corruption: An Account of What I Have Seen and Heard, by an Edo Samurai, tr. and ed. Mark Teeuwen and Kate Wildman Nakai with Miyazaki Fumiko, Anne Walthall, and John Breen 2014

Exemplary Women of Early China: The Lienü zhuan of Liu Xiang, tr. Anne Behnke Kinney 2014

The Columbia Anthology of Yuan Drama, ed. C. T. Hsia, Wai-yee Li, and George Kao 2014

The Resurrected Skeleton: From Zhuangzi to Lu Xun, by Wilt L. Idema 2014